THE PRINCIPAL USES OF THE SIXTEEN MOST IMPORTANT HOMŒOPATHIC MEDICINES

Published @ 2017 Trieste Publishing Pty Ltd

ISBN 9780649679638

The Principal Uses of the Sixteen Most Important Homœopathic Medicines by Edmund Capper

Except for use in any review, the reproduction or utilisation of this work in whole or in part in any form by any electronic, mechanical or other means, now known or hereafter invented, including xerography, photocopying and recording, or in any information storage or retrieval system, is forbidden without the permission of the publisher, Trieste Publishing Pty Ltd, PO Box 1576 Collingwood, Victoria 3066 Australia.

All rights reserved.

Edited by Trieste Publishing Pty Ltd.
Cover @ 2017

This book is sold subject to the condition that it shall not, by way of trade or otherwise, be lent, re-sold, hired out, or otherwise circulated without the publisher's prior consent in any form or binding or cover other than that in which it is published and without a similar condition including this condition being imposed on the subsequent purchaser.

www.triestepublishing.com

EDMUND CAPPER

THE PRINCIPAL USES OF THE SIXTEEN MOST IMPORTANT HOMŒOPATHIC MEDICINES

EDMUND CAPPER

THE PRINCIPAL USES OF THE SIXTEEN MOST IMPORTANT HOMŒOPATHIC MEDICINES

Trieste

THE
PRINCIPAL USES

OF THE

SIXTEEN MOST IMPORTANT

Homœopathic Medicines;

ARRANGED ACCORDING TO THE PLAN ADOPTED IN
PHYSICIANS' MANUALS,

AND DESIGNED FOR THOSE WHO REQUIRE A FULL
AND COMPREHENSIVE GUIDE, IN A
CONDENSED AND EASY FORM.

Compiled from the Standard Medical Works of
Jahr, Hull, Hempel, Bryant, &c.

THIRD THOUSAND.

BATH:
EDMUND CAPPER, 33, GAY STREET.
LONDON: TURNER & Co., 77, Fleet Street;
LIVERPOOL: THOMPSON & CAPPER, 43, Bold St., and 4, Lord St.;
MANCHESTER: TURNER & Co.;
And all Homœopathic Chemists.

1862.

THIRD EDITION.—EIGHTH THOUSAND.

Just Published, 32mo., p.p. 200. 1s.

The Text Book for Domestic Practice;

Being plain and concise directions for the administration of Homœopathic Medicines in simple Ailments.

By Samuel Morgan, M.D.

Cases of Medicines to accompany the above and present Work, forming together valuable and compact Pocket Medicine Chests.

BATH : EDMUND CAPPER, 33, GAY STREET ;
AND ALL HOMŒOPATHIC CHEMISTS.

THOMAS B. TABB, PRINTER, BATH.

PREFACE.

It is often remarked that the Domestic Works on Homœopathy seem to contain every phase and symptom of disease, except the particular one which it is required to treat, and from the plan upon which most of the Domestic Treatises are written, it is necessarily difficult to embrace many of those features of disease which commonly arise, without being very lengthy and therefore perplexing in the directions given. With a view of obviating this difficulty, and of rendering this Work comprehensive and clear, it has been formed upon the plan adopted in Physicians' Manuals; and as this plan differs essentially from the ordinary Domestic Works, the following explanation as to the proper application of Homœopathic medicines should be clearly understood :—

Under Homœopathy, the use of every medicine is *definite;* each remedy is adapted to remove certain symptoms *only,* of disease;—that is, a medicine will cure some symptoms of disease of the head, but not others; some symptoms of disease of the eyes, but not others; and so on with each part of the body, removing and curing certain symptoms for which it alone is adapted; and these symptoms being ascertained, indicate when it as a remedy is required, and form the basis of all Homœopathic practice.

Having therefore this knowledge of all or most of

the symptoms of disease which a medicine will cure, its use as a remedy in any disease is *only limited by its entire range of operation;* as for instance, Nux Vomica is adapted to cure certain bilious symptoms, but it is likewise useful in curing certain symptoms of disease of the head, eyes, mouth, throat, &c., so that in any case where any such symptoms exist with derangement of the stomach or bilious symptoms, the application of Nux Vomica as a remedial agent is only limited as well as defined by a knowledge of its entire range of operation throughout the whole body.

It will thus be seen, that wherever any medicine is useful, as for example, Nux Vomica in derangement of the stomach or headache, &c., the only way to meet every case of derangement of the stomach or headache, &c., which may occur, and for which Nux Vomica may be applicable, is to refer to *one* full statement of all the states of disease and symptoms which Nux Vomica will cure, or to insert them *all* at length *every time* Nux Vomica is recommended, otherwise much that the medicine may be useful for, and which may occur, will be omitted.

The *first* of these plans, that of referring for a knowledge of the uses of a medicine to *one* full account of what it will cure and of what it is useful for, is the most comprehensive, and is devoid of much of the perplexity attendant upon the second. It is the plan upon which Physicians' Manuals are formed; and a statement of what each medicine is useful for, will be found in Part II. of the present Work.

PREFACE. 5

The *second* plan, of course, entails a constant repetition wherever the same remedy is prescribed, and as it is impossible to insert *all* that a medicine is applicable for, *every time* it is recommended, much that it may be suitable for in a disease is frequently omitted. This is the plan adopted in most of the Domestic Works on Homœopathy; those symptoms *only* are inserted under each medicine which the author thinks beforehand most likely to occur, and which he thinks most suitable for the guidance of the patient in the selection of the remedy. Hence the frequent expression referred to at the commencement of this preface.

The symptoms even when thus selected are frequently so numerous as to render the Domestic Works perplexing and confusing. Where the reader turns to the article "Indigestion," and finds detailed under Nux Vomica twenty or thirty lines of symptoms (most of which he never had) as appertaining to that complaint, and for which that medicine is useful, it becomes much more difficult for him to make the proper selection of a remedy, than it would be if he had a short statement of what Nux Vomica was *prominently useful* for in the complaint, and was referred to a general article of all that Nux Vomica will cure for any detail he may require to ascertain. All that is necessary is to have a correct knowledge of the character of the disease we have to treat, its symptoms and phases, and a correspondingly correct knowledge of the symptoms of disease which a medicine will cure. A study and comparison of the whole symptoms for which a medicine is applicable and the whole of the symptoms of disease existing in the patient, is then alone necessary to make a right choice.

An endeavour has been made in the present Work to overcome much of this difficulty, by inserting under each medicine in each disease those symptoms only which are *most important*, and by giving a copious Medical Index and statement of what each medicine will cure, by means of which all other details may be easily and speedily learnt.

This Manual is a compilation from the best Authors on the subject, whose names are here inserted; and whose known character as standard references is a sufficient guarantee for the soundness of the work.

The following Standard Works have been made use of in this compilation :—

JAHR'S New Manual of Homœopathic Practice, by A. GERALD HULL, M.D.

JAHR'S and POSSART'S New Manual of the Homœopathic Materia Medica; also concise Repertory to the same, by CHARLES J. HEMPEL, M.D.

Pocket Manual or Repertory of Homœopathic Medicine by J. BRYANT, M.D.

BATH, 1862.

CONTENTS.

INTRODUCTION.

	PAGE.
I.—On the Medicines prescribed in this Book	9
II.—On the plan of this Book and how to use it	11
III.—On the strength and form of the Dose	15
IV.—On the administration and repetition of the Dose	16
V.—On the Diet	18

PART I.

Medical Index, or Alphabetical List of all the most important diseases, conditions or symptoms of disease, with the principal and most suitable Medicines for each 19

PART II.

SECTION 1.—*The Characteristic properties and uses of the Sixteen principal Homœopathic Medicines;* being the most important symptoms for which each is curative.

1.—Aconitum Napellus	147
2.—Arnica Montana	152
3.—Arsenicum Album	156
4.—Belladonna	161
5.—Bryonia Alba	171
6.—Calcarea Carbonica	175
7.—Chamomilla	180

CONTENTS.

PAGE.
8.—China Officinalis 185
9.—Ipecacuanha 189
10.—Mercurius Solubilis 191
11.—Nux Vomica...................................... 197
12.—Phosphorus 204
13.—Pulsatilla 208
14.—Rhus Toxicodendron 215
15.—Sulphur... 220
16.—Veratrum Album 227

SECTION 2.—*The Supplementary Medicines* of special use in a few ailments only.

1.—Cantharis 231
2.—Carbo Vegetabilis 232
3.—Cina 235
4.—Coffea Cruda..................................... 235
5.—Drosera Rotundifolia 235
6.—Hepar Sulphuris Calcareum 236
7.—Lachesis 237
8.—Spongia Tosta 240

SECTION 3.—*The Remedies for external application;* their uses and the forms in which they are applied.

1.—Arnica Montana 241
2.—Calendula Officinalis 241
3.—Rhus Toxicodendron 241

INTRODUCTION.

I.—ON THE MEDICINES PRESCRIBED IN THIS BOOK.

Homœopathy possesses such a large number of medicines adapted for the treatment of disease, that a work professing to treat only of the uses and properties of Sixteen of the principal of them, may appear so limited in its application as to render its usefulness of a very restricted character. But although there are so many remedies to which the practitioner may have recourse, the uses and importance of a few are such as to be far greater than all the remainder put together.

Indeed so extensive and universal is their application, so great are their curative powers, and so well have their virtues been tested and investigated, that it has been remarked by an eminent Physician,—without them, it would be an impossibility to practice, whilst with them the use of the remainder might be dispensed with. A proper knowledge of their uses is alone necessary to show the inexhaustible nature of their application in disease.

Besides the Sixteen principal medicines to which reference is here made, there are eight other remedies mentioned in this Work, of limited use, but which are required for some peculiar ailments, in which they are specially specific. These are termed in this Work *supplementary medicines.*

A few directions are also given for the use of the three most important Tinctures for external application.

INTRODUCTION.

LIST OF MEDICINES

Prescribed in this Book, with the abbreviations which are commonly used for their names, and their English names.

	Name of Medicine.	Abbreviation used.	English name.
1.	Aconitum Napellus	Acon.	*Monkshood.*
2.	Arnica Montana	Arn.	*Leopard's-bane.*
3.	Arsenicum Album	Ars.	*Arsenic.*
4.	Belladonna	Bell.	*Deadly Nightshade.*
5.	Bryonia Alba	Bry.	*White Bryony.*
6.	Calcarea Carbonica	Calc.	*Carbonate of Lime.*
7.	Chamomilla	Cham.	*Chamomile.*
8.	China Officinalis	Chin.	*Peruvian Bark.*
9.	Ipecacuanha	Ipec.	*Ipecaouanha.*
10.	Mercurius Solubilis	Merc.	*Mercury.*
11.	Nux Vomica	Nux.	*Nux Vomica.*
12.	Phosphorus	Phos.	*Phosphorus.*
13.	Pulsatilla	Puls.	*Meadow Anemone.*
14.	Rhus Toxicodendron	Rhus.	*Poison Oak.*
15.	Sulphur	Sulph.	*Sulphur.*
16.	Veratrum Album	Verat.	*White Hellebore.*

SUPPLEMENTARY MEDICINES.

1.	Cantharis	Canth.	*Spanish Fly.*
2.	Carbo Vegetabilis	Carb.	*Vegetable Charcoal.*
3.	Cina	Cin.	*Worm Seed.*
4.	Coffea Cruda	Coff.	*Raw Coffee.*
5.	Drosera Rotundifolia	Dros.	*Sundew.*
6.	Hepar Sulphuris Calcareum	Hep.	*Sulphuret of Lime.*
7.	Lachesis	Lach.	*Poison of the Lance-headed Viper.*
8.	Spongia tosta	Spong.	*Burnt Sponge.*

INTRODUCTION. 11

TINCTURES FOR EXTERNAL APPLICATION.

1. Arnica Montana   *Leopard's-bane.*
2. Calendula Officinalis   *Common Marygold.*
3. Rhus Toxicodendron   *Poison Oak.*

These are in the form of strong tinctures, which should be kept apart from the medicines for internal use.

(For directions and uses see Part II., Section 3.)

II.—ON THE PLAN OF THIS BOOK, AND HOW TO USE IT.

This manual is simply designed to be a condensed and comprehensive Guide for the use of Homœopathic medicines in the treatment of disease, and to contain as much information as possible relative to the choice of an appropriate remedy in any complaint, but it is not intended to give advice as to any accessory treatment. It is therefore divided into two parts; the *first* being a copious Index of all the most important diseases and symptoms of disease alphabetically arranged, with the remedies for each, which the highest authorities have thought most suitable; and the *second* consisting of a list of symptoms under each medicine for which that remedy is esteemed pre-eminently curative.

[Part I. is not to be considered as simply an Index to Part II., but as containing the names of several medicines adapted for certain symptoms, which if they were inserted again under the symptoms for which the medicine is curative in Part II., would render the work too bulky, and moreover, would in most cases be a needless repetition. Each part may be said to be complete of itself, and to make together one harmonious whole.]

INTRODUCTION.

Under Part I. every medicine recommended for any complaint or symptom is of very high curative value, but those which are esteemed most important, or are most frequently indicated, are printed in capital letters. Although this distinction in the value of the remedies in any given disease will be of great service in the choice of the appropriate medicine, it must not be too blindly followed, but each case of disease must be viewed and prescribed for according to its own character, and according to the symptoms existing at the time. (See Preface).

In order to render Part I. as clear and as easily understood as possible, there are appended, in the form of notes at the bottom of each page, explanatory references, or, as they are called, "principal uses," showing in a concise form, the leading features of most of the medicines in each different disease. These are intended to assist the reader, by showing him at a glance the *prominent differences* in the uses of the medicines, the names of which he finds recorded after the different headings in the Index; but as they are only those symptoms which are most likely to occur, and which are *most characteristic* of the use of each medicine in each complaint, he must refer to Part II. for fuller information as to the use of each medicine and to see how far it is suitable. The little "&c." after most of the "principal uses" is intended to show, that, although they may be prominent indications for the use of the remedy, fuller details may be learnt by reference to the medicine in Part II.

To avoid repetition, no references are made at the bottom of the page to that of which the Index itself is

INTRODUCTION. 13

already sufficiently explanatory, or, in other words, what can readily be understood from and found in the Index, is not generally repeated again in the "principal uses."

Part II. SECTIONS 1 and 2 consist of the principal or most important symptoms under each medicine which that medicine will cure, and arranged according to the portion of the body, &c., to which they belong.

Of some of these paragraphs it may be requisite to say a few words. Under *Characteristic Peculiarities* are placed those symptoms which when observed with others in a Patient are an additional proof that the remedy (of which they are characteristic) is well adapted for the ailment. Under *General Symptoms* are included all predominant sensations, states of strength, peculiar circumstances under which the symptoms are aggravated, ameliorated, &c., which could not be included under the other headings. The other sections or paragraphs contain the symptoms which belong to each, and are headed accordingly—Head, Eyes, Ears, Nose, &c.

In using this Manual, all that is necessary is to refer to Part I. for the disease which it is required to treat, then supposing, for example, it is "Dyspepsia," the reader will find certain medicines recommended as excellent in the treatment of it, and some few (distinguished by being printed in capital letters) more especially adapted to meet the general character of Dyspepsia which ordinarily occurs. Glancing his eye over the "principal uses" appended at the bottom of the page, he will be able to see in a concise form, the principal and prominent symptoms for which each remedy is usually chosen in the disease. Having

14   INTRODUCTION.

carefully considered these, if Loss of Appetite, Bitter Taste, Bitter Eructations, &c., be prominent features of his ailment, by turning to these headings in the Index, he will see how far any of the medicines indicated for these symptoms agree with those he has referred to under "Dyspepsia," after which he can refer to the several medicines, or to the medicine fixed upon, in Part II. to see whether in detail it or any of them are adapted to meet the case of Dyspepsia under consideration. When referring to Part II., it must be distinctly understood, that it is not expected for a patient to have all the symptoms under any medicine or section of a medicine, *but that all, or the greater part of the Patient's symptoms must be found under a medicine, if it is the appropriate one in that case.*

* NOTE.—From the above directions it will be seen that in the present Work there exist three distinct ways of obtaining any information that may be required. *First,* by means of the Medical Index, which alone is capable of affording a very great amount of information, as may be seen by turning to any disease and the symptoms of that disease, and by comparing the remedies under each together, as, for instance, in Colic, comparing the medicines under the different varieties of Colic with those under the different Pains in the Abdomen, and these again with the medicines under the heads of Vomiting, Constipation, &c. By simply doing this a very good idea may be formed as to which medicine is best suited to any particular kind of Colic, having pains of a certain character, and accompanied by vomiting or constipation, &c. The employment of different sized type in the Index, will also throw much additional light upon the choice of a remedy, by pointing out at all times, the relative value of a medicine in any particular symptom or disease, and thereby showing at a glance those remedies which are most likely to prove curative in any important feature of the complaint.

INTRODUCTION. 15

The remedy selected should then be administered (see IV.) but if, in an acute case, no abatement in the symptoms is observable after three or four doses, another medicine should be carefully selected and given in the same way. It should likewise be remembered that should the symptoms during treatment completely change their character, they will most likely require a different medicine, which must be selected with the same care according to the Patient's symptoms existing at the time.

III.—ON THE STRENGTH AND FORM OF THE DOSE.

Homœopathic medicines are prepared in the forms of

Secondly, by the "principal uses" of the medicines in each disease, appended at the bottom of the page. These will give a good idea of the particular phase of the disease, in which each will be found useful, and will generally prove a key to the character of the symptoms for which each is adapted in the complaint. *Thirdly*, by an examination of the symptoms and states of disease which each medicine will cure, as stated in Part II., in which a more extended view is obtained of the symptoms of disease for which a medicine is useful, as will be seen by referring to "Throat," under Belladonna, where all the principal symptoms for which that medicine is useful in Sore-throat and other affections of that organ will be found together. Although these three ways of obtaining any desired information can be used separately and distinctly from each other, they should, properly speaking, be considered as *one complete method* for ascertaining the appropriate remedy in any case. They may be used indiscriminately;—what cannot be found out in one part of the Work may be in another, and the reader will thus be enabled, with comparative ease, (and without having the subject placed before him in such a quantity in one form as to be perplexing to him) to ascertain any small amount of special information he may require, or to extend the limits of that information to any considerable length, as may seem desirable.

Tinctures, Pilules, Globules, and Triturations. They are also made of various strengths denoted by the figures 1, 2, 3, 4, up to 30, &c.; No. 1 being the strongest, and decreasing in regular gradation up to 30. The first three strengths, Nos. 1, 2, 3, of the Metals, Minerals, and other insoluble substances, are always prepared in powder by rubbing, and are called *Triturations;* all the remainder 4, 5, up to 30, are prepared in liquid, and are called *Tinctures.* All the strengths Nos. 1 to 30 of the Plants and preparations which are soluble, are made in liquid, and are also called *Tinctures.* The *Pilules* and *Globules* are small pellets or pills of different sizes; they are prepared from the Tinctures, and are perhaps the most convenient form of the medicine for domestic use. These last of course can be made from No. 4 to 30 of the Metals, &c., and from No. 1 to 30 of the Plants, &c. As regards the strength of the medicines for Domestic Practice, if only one potency is kept, it had better be the third; if two, the third and sixth. Two strengths are frequently advisable, as in chronic diseases where one remedy is adhered to for some time, a change of potency is frequently beneficial.

IV.—On the Administration and Repetition of the Dose.

From the condensed and comprehensive plan on which the present Work is formed, no special directions for the administration and repetition of the dose can in every instance be stated; general directions on the subject therefore can alone be given, and will be found all that is needful.

INTRODUCTION. 17

The dose for an Adult should consist of three Globules or one Pilule, or one drop of the Tincture, or one grain of the Trituration;

For a Child—two Globules, or half a Pilule, or half a drop of the Tincture, or half a grain of the Trituration;

For an Infant—one Globule, or one fourth of a Pilule, or one fourth of a drop of the Tincture, or one fourth of a grain of the Trituration.

The above may be easily divided by mixing one Pilule, or one drop of the Tincture, or one grain of the Trituration with two or four spoonsful of cold boiled water, and giving the Child or Infant one spoonful for a dose. As Homœopathic medicines are thought to act more forcibly when given in solution, it is advisable, whenever practicable, to dissolve the remedy in a small quantity of cold boiled water, using a tablespoonful for the medicine for an Adult, a teaspoonful for an Infant, and as it is very necessary that the water in which the remedy is mixed should be very pure—distilled being the best—it is advisable to use such as has been previously boiled and allowed to get cold. This will answer every purpose. Should any cups or glasses be used, great care must be observed as to their cleanliness, and to avoid touching or mixing one medicine with another (bottles for mixing different medicines in are on this account almost inadmissible); and as regards a spoon, nothing but porcelain or silver should be allowed for taking the medicine. The *necessary repetition of the dose* must of course depend on the nature and character of the disease, and the circumstances of the case, and must therefore be left in a great measure to the judgment of the party to administer the medicine. If the disease is *very urgent* and severe, as in Croup, it is frequently necessary to repeat the doses at fifteen minutes to half an hour's interval. If it should be *acute* or painful, but not so urgent, an interval of from one to four or six hours might be allowed; whilst if the ailment should be *chronic* or long standing, the medicine should not be administered more than once or twice daily. If no amendment is observable in acute diseases, after three or four doses, another medicine should be chosen and given, and in all cases, as soon as the symptoms under which the Patient is suffering begin to abate the remedy should be given at longer intervals. The medicine should also be taken if possible upon an empty stomach.

V.—On the Diet.

So much has been written relative to the Diet requisite to be observed whilst under Homœopathic treatment, that it has at last come to be considered almost a portion of that treatment. All that is requisite whilst taking the medicines is to refrain from all *medicinal* or *stimulating* articles of food, such as coffee, spices, green tea, &c., and to let the Diet be plain, simple, nutritious, and easy of digestion.

The proper application of hot and cold water; cold water bandages, poultices, &c., &c., will be found valuable auxiliaries in the treatment of disease, but are not (as has been said before) within the scope of this Manual.

PART I.

Medical Index ;

Or, an Alphabetical list of all the most important Diseases, Conditions, or Symptoms of Disease, with the principal and most suitable Medicines for each. The abbreviations only of the names of the medicines are inserted.

Every medicine mentioned after a symptom or disease is of very high value in the treatment of it; but those medicines of which the names are printed in capital letters, are the most important—that is, they have proved most frequently curative in the treatment of the symptom, or are most adapted to meet the disease in its usual form. See Preface and Introduction; also for Dose, &c.

Abdomen, Burning in the.—ARS.-LACH.-Nux.-PHOS.-Verat.
——— **Coldness in the.**—Ars.-Phos.
——— **Distension of the.**—ACON.-Arn.-ARS.-BELL.-Calc.-CARB.-CHAM.-CHIN.-MERC.-Nux.-Puls.-Rhus.-Sulph.-Verat.
——— ———**Painful.**—Ars.-CHAM.-Rhus.
——— **Excoriation** (Sensation of), in the.—BELL.-NUX.
——— **Fulness in the.**—Chin.-Nux.-Sulph.
——— **Hardness of the.**—Ars.-Calc.-Chin.-MERC.-Phos.
——— **Heat in the.**—Bell.-Nux.
——— **Heaviness** (Sensation of).—NUX.-Sulph.
——— **Pains as from a Bruise.**—NUX.

Abdomen, Pains, Cramplike, in the.—BELL.-Calc.-Cham.-Chin.-HEP.-NUX.-Sulph.
———— ————Cutting.—Acon.-ARS.-Bell.-Calc.-Cham.-Merc.-Nux.-Puls.-Verat.
———— ————Griping.—BELL.-Calc.-Chin.-Ipec.-Sulph.
———— ————Pinching.—Bell.-CHIN.-Ipec.-Merc.-NUX.
———— ————Shooting.—Arn.-Bry.-Merc.-SULPH.
———— ————Spasmodic.—ARS.-Bry.-Calc.-Cham.-Nux.-PULS.-SULPH.
———— ————Stabbing.—Cham.-Merc.
———— ————Tearing.—Ars.-LACH.
———— ————Violent.—ARS.-Chin.-Merc.
———— ————Pressure (as from a Stone).—Bell.-Calc.-Merc.-Nux.-SULPH.
———————— Rumbling in the.—Acon.-Arn.-Calc.-Nux.-Puls.-Sulph.
———————— Soreness of the.—Acon.-Ars.-BELL.-Cham.-MERC.-NUX.-Puls.-SULPH.
———— ———— Soreness (when touched).—Bell.-Cham.-Merc.-NUX.-Puls.-SULPH.-Verat.
———————— Swelling of the.—ARS.-Merc.-Nux.-Verat.
———————— Swelling, Dropsical.—Acon.-ARS.-BRY.-Chin.-Merc.
———————— Weight in the.—NUX.
*Abscess, Acute, inflamed.—BELL.-MERC.-Puls.-SULPH.

The principal uses in the treatment of—
*Abscess.
Bell.—Inflammatory redness of the surrounding skin. Painfulness to the touch. Skin red, hot, and shining. &c.

Abscess, Chronic.—CALC.-HEP.-Merc.-PHOS.-Sulph.
———— **Resolve (to).**—Bell.-BRY.-HEP.-MERC.-Phos.-PULS.
———— **Suppuration (to promote).**—HEP.-LACH.-MERC.
***Afterpains,** (Pains after delivery).—ARN.-Bell.-CHAM.-NUX.-PULS.-Rhus.
Ague.—*See Intermittent Fever.*
Air (Relieved in the open air), In general.—PULS.
——— (Worse in the open air), In general.—Ars.-Calc.-Cham.-Merc.-Nux.-Phos.
Anger, (Sufferings from).—ACON.-Ars.-Bell.-Bry.-CHAM.-NUX.-Phos.-Puls.
Ankles, Swelling of the.—Bry.-Puls.
———— **Weakness of the.**—Chin.

The principal uses in the treatment of—
Abscess, continued.
Bry.—Heat, but not much inflammation. Shooting pains on movement, &c.
Hep.—When suppuration is fully established. To bring to a head. Painful to the touch, &c.
Merc.—Abscess shining and red, or if in the vicinity of glands. Violent itching. Tendency to ulceration, &c.
Sulph.—When suppuration is forming. To heal after discharge. Indolent abscess. Swelling and induration, &c.
See Tumors and Suppuration.
***Afterpains.**
Arn.—In case of injury arising from difficult labour.
Cham.—If very severe.
Nux.—If the pains bear upon the rectum or bladder, with frequent desire to evacuate the bowels or bladder.
Puls.—If fragments of the afterbirth remain.
See Labour Pains.

MEDICAL INDEX.

†**Apoplexy** (In general).—ACON.-ARN.-BELL.-Ipec.-LACH.-NUX.-Puls.

────── **Nervous.**—Bell.-Bry.-CHIN.-Phos.

────── (arising from Congestion).—ACON.-BELL.-LACH.-Nux.

────── (arising from Effusion).—ARN.-MERC.

Appetite, Gluttonous.—CHIN.-CIN.-Merc.

────── **Hunger Extreme.**—Bry.-CALC.-CHIN.-CIN.-MERC.-Nux.-Phos.-Puls.-Rhus.-VERAT.

────── ────── **Unnatural.**—Bry.-CALC.-CIN.-Nux.-PULS.-Rhus.

────── ────── **Loss of.**—Ars.-Bell.-BRY.-CALC.-CHIN.-Ipec.-Merc.-NUX.-PULS.-RHUS.-Sulph.-Verat.

Arms, Cramps in the.—Calc.-Sulph.

────── **Pains, Burning, in the.**—Bry.-Phos.-Puls.

────── ────── **Drawing.**—Bell.-Bry.-Nux.-Puls.

The principal uses in the treatment of—
†**Apoplexy.**

Acon.—Redness and fulness of the face. Distension of the veins of the forehead, &c.

Arn.—Paralysis of the limbs, especially of the left side. Muttering. Involuntary evacuations. If caused by an injury, &c.

Bell.—Stupefaction. Loss of consciousness. Mouth drawn on one side. Difficulty or impossibility of swallowing. Dilated pupils. Face red and bloated, &c.

Ipec.—If from overloaded stomach, &c.

Lach.—Blue face. Trembling of the limbs, especially of the left side. From spirituous liquors, &c.

Nux.—Paralysis of the lower extremities. Giddiness, with headache and ringing in the ears. If arising from an overloaded stomach or spirituous liquors, &c.

Puls.—Violent palpitation of the heart. Almost entire suppression of the pulse, &c.

Arms, Pains, Jerking, in the.—Bell.-Chin.-PULS.
——— ——— **Rheumatic.**—Bry.-Merc.-Phos.-Puls.
——— ——— **Shooting.**—Puls.-Sulph.
——— ——— **Tearing.**—Bry.-Calc.-Chin.-Phos.-Puls.
——— **Rigidity of the.**—Puls.
——— **Swelling of the.**—BELL.-BRY.-SULPH.
——— **Trembling of the.**—Ars.-PHOS.
——— **Weakness of the** (paralytic).—Calc.-Sulph.
***Asthma,** (In general).—Acon.-ARS.-Bry.-Cham.-Chin.-IPEC.-NUX.-Phos.-Puls.-SULPH.

The principal uses in the treatment of—
***Asthma.**

Acon.—Suffocative cough at night. Anxious, short, and difficult respiration. Pressure of blood to the head with giddiness. Useful in young plethoric people who lead a sedentary life, and in general if the paroxysms set in after the least mental emotion, &c.

Ars.—Difficult respiration. Shortness of breath. Oppression and want of breath when walking fast; ascending a height, or at every motion. Suffocative attacks. Great distress as though the patient was going to die, and cold sweats. Great weakness with the attacks, &c.

Bell.—Distressing sighing, and sometimes deep, sometimes short and rapid respiration. Constriction of the larynx, with danger of suffocation on touching the windpipe. Beating in the chest, &c.

Bry.—Frequent cough with pains in the region under the ribs. Frequent stitches in the chest, &c.

Cham.—Swelling of the pit of the stomach. Restlessness. Especially in the case of children, &c.

Chin.—Wheezing in the chest during inspiration. Spasmodic cough and suffocative paroxysms at night. Pressure in the chest as from a pressure of blood, and violent palpitation of the heart, &c.

24   MEDICAL INDEX.

Asthma, Acute.—Acon.-ARS.-Cham.-IPEC.-LACH.
——— Children, in.—Acon.-Bell.-CHAM.-IPEC.-PULS.
——— Chill or Cold, from a.—Acon.-ARS.-Bell.-BRY.-Cham.-IPEC.-Nux.-Sulph.
——— Congestion of blood to the Chest (from).—ACON.-BELL.-Merc.-NUX.-PHOS.-Sulph.
——— Flatulent.—CHAM.-Chin.-NUX.-Sulph.
——— Hysterical.—Acon.-BELL.-Cham.-Ipec.-NUX.-Puls.

The principal uses in the treatment of—
Asthma, continued.

Ipec.—Nightly suffocative fits. Spasmodic constriction of the larynx. Rattling in the chest from an accumulation of mucus. The face is alternately red and hot, or pale, cold, and fallen in. Breathing anxious, quick, and sighing, &c.

Lach.—Shortness of breath after meals; aggravation after eating. Suffocative paroxysms on lying down. Slow and wheezing respiration, &c.

Nux.—Distressing oppression. Spasmodic constriction of the lower part of the chest. The clothes feel tight over the chest and region under the ribs. Pressure of blood towards the chest. Short cough. Worse after a meal, &c.

Phos.—Great anxiety in the chest. Spasmodic constriction of the chest. Shooting, weight, fulness, and tension in the chest. Palpitation of the heart, &c.

Puls.—Hurried, short respiration. Choking as from vapour of sulphur. Expectoration of much mucus. Spasmodic tension, feeling of fulness and pressure in the chest. Deadly anguish, palpitation of the heart; spasmodic contraction of the larynx and chest, &c.

Sulph.—Chiefly in chronic cases. Burning in the chest. Fulness and a feeling of fatigue in the chest. Spasms in the chest, &c.

See *Breathing, Anxious, Obstructed, &c.*

Asthma, Mental Emotions, from.—Acon.-CHAM.-NUX.-PULS.
—— **Nervous.**—Ars.-Cham.-Nux.-Puls.
—— **Old Persons, in.**—LACH.
—— **Spasmodic.**—BELL.-NUX.
—— **Suppressed Eruptions, from.**—Ars.-BRY.-IPEC.-Phos.-Sulph.
***Asthma of Millar.**—Acon.-Ars.-Ipec.
†**Atrophy of Children.**—Ars.-Bell.-CALC.-Chin.-NUX.-Phos.-SULPH.

The principal uses in the treatment of—
***Asthma of Millar.**
Acon.—When the attack is sudden at night with a suffocating cough. Short and anxious respiration with fever, &c.
Ars.—Great oppression. Prostration of strength, &c.
Ipec.—Oppression of the chest with accumulation of mucus. Rattling in the windpipe. Suffocation. Bluish face, &c.
†**Atrophy of Children.**
Ars.—Desire to drink frequently, but little at a time. Excessive agitation and tossing. Greenish or brownish stools. Great emaciation, &c.
Bell.—Swelling of the glands of the neck. Cough at night with mucous rattling. &c.
Calc.—Great appetite. Hollow and wrinkled countenance. Clayey evacuations. Enlargement and induration of the mesenteric glands, &c.
Chin.—Voracity. Discharge of undigested food, or frequent whitish and pap-like stools, &c.
Nux.—Obstinate constipation, &c.
Phos.—Cough with diarrhœa, and frequent exhausting sweats, &c.
Sulph.—Often at the commencement of treatment. Great hunger. Frequent mucous diarrhœa, or obstinate constipation, &c.

C

Back, Pains, as from a Bruise in the.—Acon.-Arn.-NUX.-RHUS.-Verat.
—— —— **Rheumatic.**—Puls.
—— —— **Shooting.**—Puls.-Sulph.
—— —— **Spasmodic.**—Bry.
—— —— **Tearing.**—Nux.
—— **Rigidity of the.**—LACH.-SULPH.
—— **Spasms in the.**—Cham.-Ipec.-Nux.-Rhus.
Baldness.—Calc.-Merc.-PHOS.-SULPH.
*****Bilious Derangement.**—Bry.-CHAM.-Chin.-MERC.-NUX.-Puls.
†**Bilious Fever.**—Acon.-BRY.-Cham.-Chin.-Ipec.-NUX.-PULS.

The principal uses in the treatment of—
*****Bilious Derangement.**
Bry. —Bilious vomiting, especially after drinking. Tension and fulness in the region of the stomach, &c.
Cham.—Greenish, bitter, or sour vomitings. Greenish diarrhœic stools, or like stirred up eggs. Pressure in the pit of the stomach, &c.
Chin.—Evacuations of undigested food. Frequent discharge of fetid flatulence, &c.
Merc.—Bilious mucous vomiting. Painful sensitiveness of the abdomen. Drowsiness in the day-time, sleeplessness at night. Bilious diarrhœa, &c.
Nux.—Constipation, or frequent ineffectual urging to stool. Dulness of the head with giddiness. Pressive spasms in the stomach, &c.
Puls.—Slimy diarrhœa. Vomiting of food. Chilliness. If after pork, fat meats, or rich food, &c.
See Gastric Derangement, Bilious Diarrhœa, Vomiting, &c.
†**Bilious Fever.**
Acon.—At the commencement. Bilious symptoms. Bitter eructations. Burning thirst. Dry heat, &c.
Bry.—When of a very decidedly inflammatory character. Stitches in the head. Constipation. Great debility, &c.

MEDICAL INDEX. 27

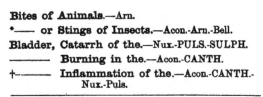

The principal uses in the treatment of—
Bilious Fever, continued.
Cham.—Diarrhœic greenish stools, or like stirred up eggs. Bitter and sour eructations and vomiting. Heat, especially of the face and eyes. Bitter taste. Fetid smell from the mouth, &c.
Chin.—Loathing of food and drink. Diarrhœa of undigested food. Chilliness and shuddering after drinking, &c.
Ipec.—Loathing of all food with desire to vomit. Regurgitation and vomiting of undigested food. Diarrhœic yellowish stools. Headache, especially in the forehead, &c.
Nux.—Pressive headache in the forehead with giddiness. Constipation, with frequent, but ineffectual urging to stool. Painful pressure and tension in the whole region of the stomach. Vomiting of undigested food. Feeling in the limbs as if they had been beaten, &c.
Puls.—Nausea, irresistible desire to vomit. Diarrhœic, white, slimy, or bilious and greenish stools. Frequent chills with absence of thirst. Regurgitation and vomiting of food, or bitter and greenish substances, &c.
***Bites or Stings of Insects.**
Acon.—Fever. Inflammation.
Arn.—When there is no violent inflammation.
Bell.—Great swelling. Throbbing of the arteries, &c.
†**Bladder, Inflammation of the.**
Acon.—Fever. Thirst. Frequent desire to urinate, with discharge of a few drops of bloody urine, &c.
Canth.—Great difficulty and pain in passing the urine. Bloody urine. Violent desire to urinate, &c.
Nux.—If after abuse of spirituous liquors, or if combined with piles, &c.
Puls.—Slimy urine, or bloody urine with purulent sediment. Pressive and burning pains in the bladder, &c.

Bladder, Painful Sensibility of the.—Canth.
Bleeding.—*See Hæmorrhage*, also from the particular organs.
*****Blindness, Attacks of.**— BELL.-Calc.-Merc.-PHOS.-PULS.-Sulph.-Verat.
—————— **Diurnal.**—Acon.-Phos.
—————— **Momentary.**—BELL.-Calc.-MERC.-PHOS.-PULS.
—————— **Nocturnal.**—Bell.-Verat.
—————— **Periodical.**—Chin.-Phos.-Puls.-Sulph.
Blisters (Vesicles).—ARS.-Bell.-Bry.-Chin.-LACH.-MERC.-PHOS.-Puls.-RHUS.-Sulph.
Blood, Congestion of.—*See Congestion.*
—————— **Plethora** (fulness).—Acon.-BELL.-Bry.-Calc.-Chin.-Nux.-Phos.-Puls.

The principal uses in the treatment of—
*****Blindness, Attacks of.**
Bell.—Dilated and insensible pupils. Pressive and expansive pains even to the orbits. If from congestion of blood, or doing fine work. Great dread of light, &c.
Calc.—Especially in reading. Great intolerance of light. Pupils very much dilated, &c.
Merc.—Extreme sensibility of the eyes, especially for the glare of fire or the daylight, &c.
Phos.—Everything seems covered with a grey veil. Great sensibility of the eyes to the light of day, &c.
Puls.—Frequent and copious lachrymation, especially in the open air. Feeling as though there was something before the eyes which might be removed by wiping. Contraction of the pupils, &c.
Sulph.—As if a mist or black veil were before the eyes. Copious lachrymation, or great dryness of the eyes. Great dread of light especially in sunshine, &c.
Verat.—Black spots or sparks before the eyes. Copious lachrymation, &c.
See Dimness of Sight.

*Blood, Spitting of.—Acon.-ARN.-Bell.-Bry.-CHIN.-
IPEC.-Phos.-Puls.-Rhus.
——— Want of.—ARS.-Calc.-CHIN.-Merc.-Puls.-
Rhus.
†Boils (In general).—ARN.-BELL.-Calc.-HEP.-MERC.-
PHOS.-Sulph.
——— Against a disposition.—Phos.-Sulph.
‡Bowels, Inflammation of the.—ACON.-ARS.-
Bell.-Bry.-Cham.-Chin.-MERC.-Nux.-
Puls.

The principal uses in the treatment of—
*Blood, Spitting of.
Acon.—If the blood comes in gushes and much at a time. Burning pain in the chest. Excited by a slight dry cough, &c.
Arn.—If caused by a fall or a blow.
Bell.—Tickling in the throat with desire to cough which aggravates the hæmorrhage. Sensation as if there was too much blood in the chest, &c.
Chin.—Great weakness and feeling of faintness, &c.
Ipec.—Short cough with expectoration of blood-streaked mucus. When there remains a taste of blood in the mouth, &c.
Puls.—If from suppression of the menses. Black and coagulated blood, &c.
Rhus.—Blood bright red. Great agitation and irritability, &c.
See Hæmorrhage.
†Boils.
Arn.—If the boils are very small.
Bell.—Great inflammation and pain.
Hep.—If slow in coming to a head.
Merc.—If *Bell.* is insufficient.
Sulph.—Useful if *Arn.* is not sufficient, and where there is a constitutional susceptibility.
See Abscess, Suppuration, &c.
‡Bowels, Inflammation of the.
Acon.—Violent fever. Tension and pressure in the abdomen. Painful sensibility to the touch, &c.

Brain, Concussion of the.—Acon.-ARN.-Bell.-Bry.-Merc.

*——— **Dropsy of the.**—ACON.-Arn.-BELL.-Bry.-Merc.

The principal uses in the treatment of—
Bowels, Inflammation of the, continued.
Ars.—If involuntary discharges of fetid liquid stools set in. Sunken countenance. Coldness of the extremities. Great prostration, &c.
Bell.—Delirium. Bowels hard and distended, sore, hot, with crampy pains. Pressure in the abdomen as from a stone, &c.
Bry.—If caused by drinking cold water when overheated. Griping and cutting pains in the abdomen. Serous diarrhœa, &c.
Cham.—Stools watery or slimy, whitish or greenish with violent colic, especially at night. Starting during sleep, &c.
Merc.—Abdomen tender to the touch, hard and distended. Bilious stools. Urging to stool, followed by straining and the passage of blood. Violent cuttings and shootings as if caused by knives, &c.
See Inflammation of the Stomach, Inflammatory Fever, &c.

*Brain, Dropsy of the.
Acon.—In the first stage of fever. Violent burning pains through the entire brain, &c.
Arn.—In the second stage, when effusion seems to have set in, &c.
Bell.—Heat in the head. Delirium. Throbbing of the arteries of the neck. Dilated pupils. The patient buries his head in the pillow. The least noise, light, or motion aggravates, &c.
Bry.—Confusion of the head. Giddiness. Difficult respiration. General languor, &c.
Merc.—Looseness of the bowels. Dull and stupid feeling, with weakness of memory, &c.

MEDICAL INDEX. 31

*Brain, Inflammation of the.—ACON.-BELL.-Bry.-Merc.
Breasts, (Female), Abscess in the.—HEP.-Phos.
——— Erysipelas of the.—Bell.-Phos.-Sulph.
——— Excoriation of the.—ARN.-Calc.-Cham.-Puls.-SULPH.
†——— Inflammation of the.—BELL.-BRY.-Merc.-Phos.
——— Suppuration of the.—Merc.-Phos.
——— Swelling (Inflammatory).—BELL.-BRY.-Merc.-Phos.-Puls.
Breath, Offensive.—Arn.-ARS.-Bry.-CARB.-Cham.-Chin.-MERC.-NUX.-Puls.
Breathing, Anxious.—ACON.-Arn.-ARS.-Bell.-Bry.-Cham.-IPEC.-PHOS.-Puls.

The principal uses in the treatment of—
*Brain, Inflammation of the.
Acon.—At the commencement. Violent inflammatory fever. Burning pains throughout the whole head, &c.
Bell.—The patient buries his head in the pillow. The least noise or light aggravates. Violent delirium. Difficulty of swallowing. Lethargic sleep. Throbbing of the arteries of the neck, &c.
Bry.—Chills of long continuance, red face, heat and great thirst. Constant stupor with delirium. Burning and pressing pains in the head, &c.
Merc.—If inflammation threatens to run into dropsy of the brain, &c.
†Breasts, Inflammation of the.
Bell.—Breasts swollen and hard, with shooting pains and erysipelatous redness, &c.
Bry.—Tensive or shooting pains in the swelling, and burning heat on the outside, &c.
Merc.—When neither *Bell.* nor *Bry.* are able to remove the inflammation, and the parts continue hard and painful, &c.
Phos.—Perfect ulceration of the breasts, &c.

32 MEDICAL INDEX.

Breathing, Deep.—BRY.-IPEC.
———— **Irregular.**—Bell.-Cham.
———— **Loud.**—Arn.-Cham.-Chin.-Phos.-Spong.
———— **Obstructed.**—Acon.-ARS.-Bry.-Cham.-Ipec.-PHOS.-Sulph.-Verat.
———— **Oppressed.**—Acon.-ARN.-ARS.-BELL.-BRY.-Calc.-Cham.-Chin.-IPEC.-LACH.-Merc.-NUX.-PHOS.-PULS.-Rhus.-SULPH.-VERAT.
———— **Panting.**—Acon.-Arn.-Ipec.-Phos.
———— **Quick (Short).**—ACON.-Arn.-Ars.-BELL.-Bry.-CARB.-Chin.-IPEC.-Nux.-PHOS.-Puls.-Rhus.-Sulph.
———— **Rattling.**—Acon.-BELL.-Bry.-Calc.-Cham.-Chin.-HEP.-IPEC.-Phos.-Puls.-Sulph.
———— **Sighing.**—Bell.-BRY.-IPEC.-Puls.
———— **Slow.**—BELL.-Bry.-Chin.-Ipec.-Nux.
———— **Suffocative Fits.**—Acon.-ARS.-Cham.-Chin.-HEP.-IPEC.-Nux.-Phos.-Puls.-Sulph.-Verat.
———— **Want of.**—ARS.-MERC.-Puls.
———— **Wheezing.**—Ars.-Bell.-Nux.
*****Bronchitis.**—ACON.-Bell.-BRY.-Cham.-PHOS.

The principal uses in the treatment of—
*****Bronchitis.**
Acon.—Short dry cough with constant irritation. Stitches in the chest. Burning febrile heat, &c.
Bell.—Spasmodic cough which allows no time for breathing. Worse at night or in the evening in bed, &c.
Bry.—Spasmodic or suffocative cough. Vomiting of food. Stitches in side, or pains in the head on coughing, &c.
Cham.—Dry cough occasioned by constant irritation in the larynx and chest. Worse at night in bed, &c.
Phos.—Stitches in the throat, or pains in the chest. Dry cough from tickling in the throat, &c.
See Cough.

Bronchitis, Chronic.—Calc.-Nux.-PHOS.-Sulph.
Bruises.—ARN.-Rhus.
Bunions.—Arn.-Rhus.
Burns.—Arn.

---

*Carbuncle.—Arn.-ARS.-BELL.-Nux.
Catalepsy.—BELL.-Bry.-Cham.-Ipec.
Cataract, (Film on the Eye),—CALC.-PHOS.-Puls.-SULPH.
Catarrh, Mucous discharge, (in general).—ARS.-BELL.-Bry.-CHAM.-HEP.-IPEC.-LACH.-MERC.-NUX.-Phos.-PULS.-Rhus.-SULPH.
———— Asthmatic Affections, (with).—ARS.-Bry.-IPEC.-Nux.-Sulph.
———— of the Chest.—Ars.-Bry.-CHAM.-Ipec.-MERC.-NUX.-Phos.-PULS.-Rhus.-SULPH.
———— in Children.—Acon.-Bell.-CHAM.-IPEC.-Nux.
———— Chronic.—Ars.-Calc.-CARB.-PHOS.-SULPH.
———— with Fever.—ACON.-ARS.-Bry.-CHAM.-MERC.-NUX.-PHOS.
———— Suffocative.—ARS.-Chin.-IPEC.-Puls.
———— Suppressed.—Ars.-BRY.-Ipec.-Nux.-SULPH.

The principal uses in the treatment of—
*Carbuncle.
Ars.—Malignant. When occasioned by infection. Burning pains. Tendency to gangrene.
Bell.—Red hot swelling of the diseased part.

Chaps on the Skin.—CALC.-HEP.-MERC.-Puls.-SULPH.
Chest, Anxiety in the.—ACON.-ARS.-Phos.-Sulph.-Verat.
—— **Burning in the.**—Ars.-Bry.-Calc.-SULPH.
—— **Coldness in the.**—Ars.
—— **Compression or Constriction in the.**—Arn.-ARS.-IPEC.-Nux.-Phos.-Puls.-Rhus.-Verat.
—— **Cramps in the.**—Phos.-Verat.
—— **Excoriation, Rawness in the.**—ARS.-Calc.-CARB.-PHOS.-Rhus.-Sulph.
—— **Fulness in the.**—Acon.-Calc.-PHOS.-Sulph.
—— **Heat in the** (Sensation of).—Ars.-BRY.
—— **Inflammation.**—*See Pleurisy.*
—— **Oppression of the.**—Arn.-ARS.-Bell.-BRY.-CHAM.-Chin.-Ipec.-LACH.-Nux.-PHOS.-Puls.-RHUS.-Sulph.-Verat.
—— **Pains, Bruise, as from a.**—ARN.-Chin.
—— —— **Burning.**—Bry.-Carb.-Phos.
—— —— **Cramplike.**—Phos.-Puls.
—— —— **Rheumatic.**—Bell.-Bry.
—— —— **Stitching and Shooting.**—ACON.-ARN.-BRY.-Calc.-Cham.-PHOS.-Puls.-Rhus.-SULPH.

The principal uses in the treatment of—
Chaps on the Skin.
Calc.—Rough and dry skin. Especially of those who work in water, &c.
Hep.—Cracks and chaps of the hands and feet. Unhealthy skin. Even slight injuries produce suppuration and ulceration, &c.
Merc.—Deep and bleeding, &c.
Sulph—Skin cracks very readily. Pains as from excoriation, &c.

Chest, Pressure in the.—BELL.-Bry.-Chin.-Sulph.-Verat.
———— **Spasms in the.**—Phos.-Puls.-Sulph.-Verat.
———— **Tightness in the.**—Acon.-ARS.-Calc.-CARB.-Chin.-IPEC.-LACH.-PHOS.-PULS.-Sulph.
———— **Weakness in the.**—Phos.-Rhus.-SULPH.
———— **Weight in the** (Sensation of).—Acon.-PHOS.-SULPH.
*****Chickenpox.**—Acon.-Puls.-RHUS.
†**Chilblains.**—Arn.-Ars.-Phos.-PULS.-Rhus.-SULPH.
‡**Cholera, Asiatic.**—Ars.-Ipec.-VERAT.

The principal uses in the treatment of—
*****Chickenpox.**
Acon.—During the inflammatory period.
Puls.—If the eruption is slow, with gastric symptoms.
Rhus.—When the vesicles are fully matured.
†**Chilblains.**
Arn.—When the swelling is hard, shining, and painful, &c.
Ars.—When there is a tendency to ulceration. Acute burning pains, &c.
Phos.—If the chilblains should be very painful. If they break and discharge a watery fluid, &c.
Puls.—If blue, red, swollen, or inflamed, &c.
Rhus.—Very great irritation and the formation of blisters, &c.
Sulph.—Old standing chilblains. Great inflammation and itching, &c.
‡**Cholera, Asiatic.**
Ars.—Violent pains in the stomach with great distress and burning. Icy coldness of skin and clammy perspiration. Great prostration. Diarrhœa and violent vomiting. The lips and tongue are dry, blackish, and cracked. Small, weak, intermittent, or trembling pulse, &c.
Ipec.—If the vomiting is most prominent, &c.
Verat.—Violent evacuations upwards and downwards. Icy coldness and great debility. Cramps in the legs. In the worst stages, &c.

Cholera Morbus.—Ars.-Cham.-IPEC.-VERAT.
Choleric Colic.—CHAM.-VERAT.
——— **Diarrhœa.**—Ipec.-VERAT.
——— **Vomiting.**—IPEC.-Verat.
Cholerine, (Diarrhœa preceding Cholera).—ARS.-Verat.
*****Cold or Chill,** Sufferings from a.—ACON.-Ars.-Bell.-
 BRY.-CHAM.-MERC.-NUX.-PHOS.-
 Puls.-RHUS.-Sulph.-Verat.
Cold, Against a disposition to take.—Acon.-Calc.-CARB.-
 Cham.-MERC.-NUX.-Phos.-Puls.-Rhus.-
 SULPH.
✝**Cold in the Head,** (In general).—ARS.-Bell.-Bry.-
 CHAM.-MERC.-NUX.-PULS.-Sulph.

The principal uses in the treatment of—
*****Cold or Chill,** Sufferings from a.
 Acon.—In faceache, toothache, and other kinds of neuralgiæ, where there is much fever heat, &c.
 Ars.—In asthmatic or gastric affections with pains in the stomach, &c.
 Bell.—In headache, dimness of sight, sore throat, gastric symptoms, feverish heat, &c.
 Bry.—For spasmodic cough with nausea, pains in the limbs, diarrhœa, &c.
 Cham.—For headache, toothache, earache and other kinds of very painful neuralgiæ, &c.
 Merc.—For pains in the limbs, sore throat, sore eyes, toothache, earache, and painful diarrhœa, &c.
 Nux.—In dry cold in the head, dry cough, constipation, dysentery, &c.
 Puls.—For fluent cold, moist cough, earache, fever, diarrhœa, &c.
 Rhus.—For toothache, or pains in the limbs, &c.
 Sulph.—In obstinate pains in the limbs, colic, slimy diarrhœa, profuse cold in the head, sore eyes, &c.
✝**Cold in the Head.**
 Ars.—Stoppage of the nose with copious discharge of a watery mucus. Excoriation of the adjacent parts. Relief by warmth, &c.

MEDICAL INDEX. 37

Cold in the Head, Chronic.—Ars.-Phos.-Puls.-Sulph.
—— Dry.—Bry.-Calc.-Cham.-NUX.-PHOS.-Sulph.
—— Dry and Fluent alternately.—NUX.
—— Fluent.—ARS.-Calc.-Cham.-MERC.-PULS.-Rhus.
—— Secretion, Acrid, with.—ARS.-Cham.-MERC.-Nux.-Puls.
———— ———— Bloody.—Chin.-Phos.-Sulph.
———— ———— Burning.—ARS.
———— ———— Mucous.—ARS.-Bell.-Bry.-Calc.-Chin.-MERC.-Nux.-PHOS.-Puls.-Sulph.
———— ———— Offensive.—Ars.-Bell.-CALC.-Merc.-PULS.-Sulph.
———— ———— Purulent.—Bell.-CALC.-Chin.-MERC.-PHOS.-PULS.-Rhus.-Sulph.
———— ———— Thick.—Calc.-Phos.-PULS.
———— ———— Viscous.—Ars.-Phos.

The principal uses in the treatment of—
Cold in the Head, continued.
Bell.—When the sense of smelling is too acute, or too dull, &c.
Cham.—Principally in children. Watery discharge. Shiverings with thirst, &c.
Merc.—In most cases of ordinary catarrh. Copious discharge of serous mucus. Soreness of nose. Offensive smell of mucus, &c.
Nux.—Suppression of discharge with stoppage of nose. Heaviness in the forehead, &c.
Puls.—Discharge of a yellowish, green, thick, and fetid mucus. Heaviness of the head especially in the evening and in a warm room, with obstruction of the nose, &c.
Sulph.—Stoppage and great dryness of the nose, or copious secretion of a thick, yellowish, and purulent mucus. In chronic cases, or where there is a constitutional susceptibility, &c.
See Cold in the Head, Dry, &c.; with Secretion, Acrid, &c.

Cold in the Head, Secretion, Watery, with.—
ARS.-CHAM.-MERC.-Nux.-Sulph.
Coldness, External.—Arn.-Ars.-Calc.-MERC.-Nux.-PHOS.-Puls.-RHUS.-VERAT.
——— **Internal.—**ARS.-Bell.-Bry.-Calc.-CARB.-Chin.-NUX.-Phos.-Puls.-Sulph.-VERAT.
——— **Shivering, with.—**Acon.-Ars.-BRY.-Cham.-CHIN.-Ipec.-Nux.-Rhus.-Verat.
——— **Thirst, with.—**ACON.-Arn.-Ars.-BRY.-Calc.-CHAM.-CIN.-NUX.-Rhus.-Verat.
——— **Thirst, without.—**ARS.-Bell.-Chin.-Nux.-PULS.-Rhus.-Sulph.
***Colic** (In general).—Ars.-BELL.-CHAM.-Ipec.-NUX.-PULS.-Verat.

The principal uses in the treatment of—
***Colic.**
Acon.—Violent cramp-pains. Great sensitiveness of the abdomen, &c.
Ars.—Great pain with great distress in the abdomen. Intolerable burning. Great debility. Spasmodic pains. Especially at night or after eating and drinking, &c.
Bell.—As if the bowels were grasped with the nails. Spasmodic constriction in the abdomen, &c.
Carb.—Distension of the abdomen. Incarcerated flatulence. Constipation. Worse after the slightest meal, &c.
Cham.—Tearing, drawing pains with great restlessness. Bitter vomiting, or bilious diarrhœa. Incarcerated flatulence. Fulness and tension in the pit of the stomach, caused by flatulence. Particularly at night or after a meal, &c.
Chin.—Extreme distension of the abdomen, with fulness and pressure as from a hard body. Incarceration of flatulence, &c.
Merc.—Shooting or violent contracting pains, especially around the navel, with nausea. Slimy diarrhœa, &c.

MEDICAL INDEX. 39

Colic, Chill or Cold, from a.—CHAM.-Merc.-Nux.
——— Flatulent.—Bell.-CARB.-CHAM.-CHIN.-NUX.-PULS.-VERAT.
——— Gastric Derangement (from).—Bell.-NUX.-PULS.
——— Hysterical.—Bell.-NUX.
——— Inflammatory.—ACON.-Bell.-Bry.-MERC.-NUX.
——— Menstrual.—CHAM.-Nux.-PULS.
——— Spasmodic.—BELL.-Cham.-Ipec.-NUX.
——— Worms (from).—CIN.-Merc.
Concussion, Effects of a.—Acon.-ARN.-Bell.-Bry.-RHUS.
*Congestion, Abdomen, in the.—Bell.-Merc.-NUX.-Puls.-SULPH.
†——————— Brain.—ACON.-Arn.-BELL.-NUX.

The principal uses in the treatment of—
Colic, continued.
Nux.—Obstinate constipation. Pressure as from a stone. The clothes feel too tight. Contractive or compressive pains. Rumbling. Pressure on the bladder and rectum, &c.
Puls.—Disagreeable tension and distension. Pains worse by sitting or lying. Rumbling, &c.
Verat.—Cutting as from knives in the abdomen, which is very painful to the touch. Burning in the whole abdomen, &c.
See Abdomen, Pains in the.
*Congestion, Abdomen, in the.
Nux.—Particularly useful for those leading a sedentary life, or occupied with study. Constipation, &c.
Sulph.—In the generality of cases, even the most obstinate, &c.
†Congestion, Brain, in the.
Acon.—At the commencement. In serious cases. If caused by fright or chagrin, &c.

Congestion, Chest, in the.—ACON.-BELL.-Chin.-
Merc.-NUX.-PHOS.-Puls.-Rhus.-Sulph.
———————— **Eyes.**—Acon.-Bell.
†———————— **Head.**—ACON.-Arn.-BELL.-Bry.-
Merc.-NUX.

The principal uses in the treatment of—
Congestion, Brain, in the, continued.
Arn.—If arising from a fall, shock, or blow, &c.
Bell.—Veins of the head much distended. Violent headache aggravated by noise, light, and every motion, &c.
Nux.—If from study, sedentary habits, or spirituous liquors. Worse in the open air, or after a meal, &c.
*Congestion, Chest, in the.
Acon.—Violent pressure with palpitation of the heart, &c.
Bell.—Beatings of the heart which go even to the head, &c.
Chin.—If arising from debilitating losses, &c.
Merc.—Anxious oppression with desire to take a long breath, &c.
Nux.—Heavy pressure as from a weight with uncomfortable feel from the clothes on the chest. If from suppression of piles, &c.
Phos.—Weight, tension, violent oppression, and sense of fulness in the chest, &c.
Puls.—If from suppression of the menses, or piles, &c
†Congestion, Head, in the.
Acon.—Frequent giddiness, especially when stooping Ringing in the ears. When occurring in children during dentition, or in young girls or persons leading a sedentary life, &c.
Arn.—If arising from external injuries, &c.
Bell.—Aggravation at every step or movement, or through the least noise or light. Disposition to sleep, &c.
Bry.—Sensation as if everything would fall out of the forehead when stooping, &c.
Merc.—Feeling as if the head were compressed by a band. Worse at night, &c.
Nux.—If arising from spirits, sedentary habits, or overexcitement. Worse after eating, or taking coffee, or in the open air, &c.

Congestion, Heart, in the.—Acon.-Bell.-PULS.-SULPH.

*****Constipation** (In general).—Bell.-BRY.-Calc.-Merc.-NUX.-Phos.-SULPH.-Verat.

———————— Chronic.—Bry.-CALC.-SULPH.

———————— **Inactivity of the bowels** (from).—Arn.-Bry.-Chin.-HEP.-NUX.-Sulph.-Verat.

———————— **Sedentary Persons** (in).—Bry.-NUX.

†**Consumption.**—Ars.-Bell.-CALC.-CHIN.-PHOS.-PULS.-Sulph.

The principal uses in the treatment of—
*****Constipation.**
Bell.—Constipation, with distension of abdomen and heat in the head, &c.
Bry.—In persons subject to rheumatism. Especially in summer. From a sedentary life. In cases of long disposition to constipation, &c.
Calc.—Constipation increasing from day to day, &c.
Merc.—Bitter taste. Painful gums. No loss of appetite, &c.
Nux.—Sensation as if the anus was narrower than usual. Ineffectual desire to evacuate the bowels. From a sedentary life, abuse of spirituous liquors, or derangement of the stomach. In habitual constipation. In persons subject to piles, &c.
Phos.—In old people, or when connected with consumption, &c.
Sulph.—Frequent but ineffectual desire to go to stool. Habitual costiveness. From a sedentary life. Unfitness for intellectual labour, &c.
Verat.—From inactivity and torpor of the bowels. Abdomen very tender to the touch, &c.
†**Consumption.**
Ars.—Burning in the chest and difficulty of breathing. Exhausting night sweats with creeping chills. Exhausting offensive diarrhœa, &c.
Bell.—Suitable to scrofulous children with cough at night. Shortness of breathing and mucous rattling, &c.

Convulsions.—Acon.-Ars.-BELL.-Bry.-Cham.-Ipec.-Merc.-NUX.-Sulph.-Verat.—*See Spasms.*

———— **Hysterical.**—Bell.-BRY.-NUX.

***Corns.**—Bry.-CALC.-Phos.-Rhus.-SULPH.

Corpulency.—CALC.-Puls.-Sulph.

‡**Cough, Dry.**—ACON.-ARN.-ARS.-BELL.-BRY.-CALC.-Cham.-Chin.-IPEC.-LACH.-MERC.-NUX.-PHOS.-Puls.-Rhus.-SPONG.-SULPH.-Verat.

‡———— **with Expectoration.**—ARS.-Bell.-BRY.-CALC.-Chin.-Ipec.-MERC.-Nux.-PHOS.-PULS.-SULPH.

The principal uses in the treatment of—
Consumption, continued.

Calc.—In the first stage; particularly in the case of plethoric young people who are affected with congestions of blood, bleeding at the nose, &c.; also to young girls with profuse and too frequent menstruation, &c.

Chin.—If the patient has suffered from bleeding, or pulmonary hæmorrhage, &c.

Phos.—In incipient as well as confirmed cases. Bloated appearance under the eyes. Tendency to diarrhœa, &c.

Sulph.—Useful in the second stage; also in incipient cases, where the inflammatory symptoms have been removed by other medicines, &c.

***Corns.**

Bry.—⎱ If troublesome during wet weather.
Rhus.—⎰

Phos.—Piercing pains.

Calc.—To eradicate a tendency to corns. With burning pains, or as from excoriation or pain of the whole foot.

Sulph.—Inflamed corns. Stitches in the corns. To eradicate a tendency to corns.

‡**Cough.**

Acon.—Short dry cough with constant irritation. Stitches in the chest, &c.

Arn.—Cough, mostly dry, caused by a titillation in the windpipe early in the morning. In children after crying, &c.

Cough, Fatiguing.—Ars.-Calc.-Merc.-Nux.-Phos.-Puls.-Sulph.

The principal uses in the treatment of—
Cough, continued.
Ars.—Difficult expectoration. Viscid mucus in the larynx and bronchia. Worse in evening or at night after lying down, &c.
Bell.—Spasmodic cough which allows no time for breathing. Worse at night, or in the evening, or on movement, &c.
Bry.—Spasmodic or suffocative cough. Vomiting of food. Stitches in the side, or pains in the head on coughing. With yellowish expectoration, &c.
Calc.—Tickling cough as from feather dust in the throat. With a thick, yellowish, and fetid expectoration, &c.
Cham.—Dry cough occasioned by constant titillation in the larynx and chest. Worse at night in bed, &c.
Chin.—Nocturnal suffocative cough with pain in the chest, causing one to cry out. Violent cough after eating, excited by laughing. Blood-streaked expectoration, &c.
Ipec.—Suffocative feeling as from accumulation of mucus, &c.
Lach.—At night during sleep. Excited by the least pressure on the throat, &c.
Merc.—Dry and shaking cough. Disposition to perspire. Excited by tickling or feeling of dryness in the throat. Roughness and hoarseness. Worse at night, &c.
Nux.—Rough, dry, and deep cough. Feeling of rawness in the throat. Accumulation of tenacious mucus in the throat, which will not be detached. Pains in the stomach on coughing, &c.
Phos.—Dry cough with tickling in the throat. Stitches in the throat. Pains or soreness in the chest, &c.
Puls.—Racking cough. Worse in the evening, or at night, and on lying down, &c.
Rhus.—Cough in the morning on awaking, with bitter taste or vomiting of food taken, &c.
Spong.—Hollow barking dry cough. Cough day and night, with burning in the chest, which abates after eating and drinking, &c.

44   MEDICAL INDEX.

Cough, **Hacking.**—Acon.-Arn.-ARS.-Calc.-DROS.-Merc.-Nux.
——— **Hollow.**—Bell.-Nux.-SPONG.-Verat.
——— **Hooping.**—Acon.-Ars.-Bell.-DROS.-IPEC.-Verat.
——— **Racking.**—Ipec.-LACH.-Merc.-NUX.-PULS.-Sulph.
——— **Rattling.**—Bell.-Ipec.-Puls.
——— **Shaking.**—Ars.-Bell.-Chin.-Ipec.-MERC.-Nux.-Phos.-PULS.-Sulph.
——— **Short.**—ACON.-Arn.-Ars.-Merc.-Sulph.
——— **Spasmodic.**—Acon.-Bell.-BRY.-CHIN.-DROS.-IPEC.-Merc.-NUX.
——— **Suffocating.**—Ars.-BRY.-Chin.-DROS.-IPEC.
——— **Violent.**—Bell.-Bry.-Calc.-Chin.-Ipec.-Merc.-Phos.-Puls.
Cough, **Expectoration, Acrid, with.**—ARS.-Merc.-Phos.-Puls.
——— ——— **Bitter, with.**—ARS.-CHAM.-Merc.-Nux.-PULS.-Verat.
——— ——— **Blood.**—Acon.-ARN.-Ars.-Bell.-Bry.-Chin.-IPEC.-Merc.-PHOS.-PULS.-Rhus.-Sulph.
——— ——— **Blood, Coagulated.**—Arn.-Bell.-Cham.-Chin.-Ipec.-PULS.-RHUS.

The principal uses in the treatment of—
Cough, continued.
Sulph.—In chronic cases. Expectoration of much thick whitish mucus. Dry cough with nausea. In the evening, or at night on lying down, &c.
Verat.—Cough deep and hollow as though it came from the abdomen, &c.
See Cough Fatiguing, &c. : with Expectoration, Acrid, &c.

Cough, Expectoration, Blood, Dark, with.—
Arn.-Cham.-Chin.-Nux.-PULS.
——— ——— ——— **Pale.**—BELL.-Phos.-Rhus.
——— ——— ——— **Streaked Mucus** (of).—
Arn.-ARS.-Bell.-BRY.-CHIN.-Ipec.-Phos.
——— ——— **Difficult.**—ARS.-Cham.-Chin.-Nux.-Puls.
——— ——— **Disgusting.**—Arn.-Calc.-DROS.-Merc.-Nux.-PULS.-Sulph.
——— ——— **Frothy.**—ARS.-PHOS.-PULS.
——— ——— **Mucous.**—ARS.-Bell.-Bry.-CALC.-Cham.-Chin.-Ipec.-Nux.-PHOS.-PULS.-Sulph.
——— ——— **Offensive.**—Ars.-Bell.-CALC.-Puls.-Sulph.
——— ——— **Profuse.**—Puls.-Sulph.
——— ——— **Purulent.**—CALC.-CHIN.-PHOS. Puls.-Rhus.-Sulph.
——— ——— **Salt.**—ARS.-Chin.-PHOS.-Puls.
——— ——— **Sour.**—Ars.-Bell.-CALC.-Cham.-Chin.-Nux.-PHOS.-Puls.-Sulph.
——— ——— **Sweetish.**—PHOS.-Puls.-Rhus.
——— ——— **Thick.**—Bell.-Calc.-PULS.-Sulph.
——— ——— **Viscous.**—Ars.-Cham.-Nux.-Phos.-Spong.
——— ——— **Watery.**—Cham.-Merc.-Sulph.
Cough, Asthma, with.—ARS.-IPEC.-Phos.
——— **Blueness of the Face, with.**—IPEC.
——— **Burning in the Larynx, with.**—Acon.-Phos.-Spong.
——— **Choking, with.**—ARS.-IPEC.
——— **Cold in the Head, with.**—Bell.-Merc.-Nux.-SPONG.-Sulph.

MEDICAL INDEX.

Cough, Drinking, from.—Ars.-Bry.
— Headache, with.—Bell.-Bry.-Merc.-Nux.-Phos.-Puls.-Sulph.
— Headache, as if the Head would split (with).—BRY.-Merc.-NUX.
— Hoarseness, with.—CHAM.-MERC.-PHOS.-Nux.-SPONG.
— Lying down, from.—ARS.-PULS.-Sulph.
— Meal, after a.—Bry.-Nux.
— Movement, from.—Bell.-Nux.
— Open Air, in the.—ARS.
— Pains in the Chest, with.—BRY.-Merc.-PHOS.-Puls.-SULPH.
— Periodical.—Ars.-Nux.
— Rattling in the Chest, with.—Bell.-Bry.-Cham.-Ipec.-Puls.-Sulph.
— Rawness in the Chest, with.—Calc.-CARB.-Merc.-PHOS.-SULPH.
— Sleep, during.—Arn.-BELL.-Cham.-Merc.
— Sore Throat, with.—Acon.-MERC.-Nux.-PHOS.
— Talking, from.—Chin.-Merc.
— Tickling in the Chest, from.—PHOS.-Rhus.-Verat.
— ———————— Larynx, from.—Acon.-Arn.-Bell.-CHAM.-DROS.-IPEC.-LACH.-Merc.
— ———————— Throat, from.—Bry.-Chin.-Lach.-Nux.-Phos.-Puls.
— Vomiting, with.—CARB.-DROS.-Ipec.-Merc.-Nux.-Phos.-Puls.-Verat.

Cramps.—BELL.-Bry.-Cham.-Ipec.-Merc.-Phos.-Verat.

Critical Age (of Women), In general.—LACH.-Puls.

MEDICAL INDEX. 47

*Croup.—ACON.-HEP.-Phos.-SPONG.

†Deafness (In general).— BELL.-CALC.-Nux.-Phos.-
PULS.-SULPH.-Verat.
———— Catarrhal.—Ars.-Calc.-Merc.-Puls.
———— Congestive.—Bell.-Merc.-Phos.
———— Measles, from.—Bell.-CARB.-Merc.-
PULS.
———— Scarlatina, from.—BELL.-Merc.
———— Severe Illness, from.—Arn.-Phos.-
Verat.
———— Small Pox, from.—MERC.-Puls.-Sulph.

The principal uses in the treatment of—
*Croup.
Acon.—During the inflammatory period.
Hep.—If the croup symptoms are attended with rattling of mucus. Cough moist, &c.
Phos.—In cases where *Acon.* and *Spong.* give only partial relief. To cure a disposition to croup.
Spong.—Hoarse hollow barking and crowing cough. Slow loud wheezing and sawing breathing; or fits of choking. In the worst cases, &c.
†Deafness.
Bell.—If from tendency of blood to the head, or after apoplexy, inflammation of the brain, typhus, &c.
Calc.—Constant dryness of the ears, or purulent discharge, &c.
Merc.—Loud reverberation of all the sounds in the ear. If from swelling of the tonsils, &c.
Phos.—Loud reverberation of all sounds, especially words, in the ears extending deep into the head, &c.
Puls.—The ears as it were stopped, with roaring, and whizzing, or ringing. If the consequence of the suppression of a discharge from the ears, &c.
Sulph.—Deafness especially to the human voice, or on one side only. If caused by inveterate eruptions, &c.

48   MEDICAL INDEX.

Deafness, Suppressed Eruptions (from).—Ars.-Bry.-SULPH.
*****Delirium Tremens.**—BELL.-NUX.-Verat.
†**Diarrhœa** (In general).—Acon.-ARS.-BRY.-Calc.-CARB.-CHAM.-CHIN.-Ipec.-MERC.-Nux.-Phos.-PULS.-Rhus.-SULPH.-VERAT.
———— **Chill or Cold, from a.**—Ars.-BRY.-Cham.-MERC.-Verat.

The principal uses in the treatment of—
*****Delirium Tremens.**
Bell.—Congestion of blood to the head. Heat and pain in the head. Pulsation of the temporal arteries. Boisterous delirium, &c.
Nux.—Especially useful in the first stage.
Verat.—Great anxiety. Madness, &c.
†**Diarrhœa.**
Ars.—Watery or slimy or brownish evacuations. After eating and drinking. Great debility. Emaciation. Violent thirst. At night, after midnight, &c.
Bry.—If in the heat of summer. From cold drinks, &c.
Calc.—Chronic diarrhœa of scrofulous children, &c.
Cham.—Watery, bilious, or slimy, or like stirred up eggs. Especially in children, &c.
Chin.—Undigested or brownish stools. At night, &c.
Ipec.—Watery or slimy yellow diarrhœa, &c.
Merc.—Watery, slimy, frothy, bilious or bloody evacuations. Chills and shivering. Especially at night, &c.
Nux.—Frequent but scanty evacuations, &c.
Phos.—Chronic with painless evacuations, &c.
Puls.—Slimy or whitish evacuations. Consequence of indigestion, &c.
Rhus.—Especially at night with tearing in the limbs, headache, colic, &c.
Sulph.—In obstinate cases. Frequent slimy, whitish, or greenish stools. Emaciation. If in scrofulous individuals, &c.
Verat.—Feeling of coldness in the abdomen. Debility, &c.
See Diarrhœa with Evacuations, Acrid, &c.

MEDICAL INDEX. 49

Diarrhœa, Chronic.—Calc.-PHOS.-SULPH.
——— Cold Drinks, from.—ARS.-Bry.
——— Colic, with.—ARS.-Bry.-CHAM.-IPEC.-
 MERC.-Nux.-PULS.-Rhus.-Sulph.-
 VERAT.
——— Constipation, alternating with.—
 Ars.-Bry.-NUX.-Rhus.
——— Consumptives (in).—CHIN.-PHOS.
——— Feeble Persons, in.—Calc.-CHIN.-
 Phos.
——— Fruit, from eating.—Ars.-Puls.
——— Gastric Derangement (from).—Ipec.-
 Nux.-PULS.
——— Old People, in.—Bry.-PHOS.
——— Painless.—ARS.-Bell.-Chin.-PHOS.-
 Sulph.-Verat.
——— Straining, griping, with.—Acon.-
 Ars.-Bell.-MERC.-NUX.-Rhus.-SULPH.
——— Violent.—ARS.-VERAT.
——— Vomiting, with.—ARS.-IPEC.-Phos.-
 Puls.-VERAT.
——— Weakness, with.—ARS.-Phos.-VERAT.
Diarrhœa, Evacuations, Acrid, with.—ARS.-
 Cham.-MERC.-Puls.-Sulph.
——— —— Bilious.—Ars.-CHAM.-Chin.-Ipec.-
 MERC.-Puls.-Verat.
——— —— Blackish.—ARS.-Bry.-Chin.-Ipec.-
 Merc.
——— —— Bloody.—ARS.-Ipec.-MERC.-Nux.-
 Puls.-Rhus.-Sulph.
——— —— Dysenteric.—ARS.-Bell.-Ipec.-
 MERC.-Nux.-Rhus.-Sulph.
——— —— Fermented, as if.—IPEC.
——— —— Greenish.—ARS.-CHAM.-Chin.-
 IPEC.-MERC.-PHOS.-PULS.-Sulph.-
 Verat.

Diarrhœa, Evacuations, Involuntary, with.— Arn.-ARS.-BELL.-Chin.-PHOS.-Sulph.-VERAT.

―――― ―― **Mucous.**—Arn.-Ars.-Bell.CHAM.-Chin.-Ipec.-MERC.-NUX.-Phos.-PULS.-Rhus.-SULPH.

―――― ―― **Purulent.**—Arn.-Chin.-MERC.-Puls.

―――― ―― **Putrid.**—Ars.-CARB.-CHIN.-MERC.-Nux.

―――― ―― **Scanty.**—Acon.-Bell.-Merc.-NUX.

―――― ―― **Sour.**—Calc.-CHAM.-Merc.-Sulph.

―――― ―― **Undigested.**—Arn.-Ars.-CHIN.-PHOS.-Sulph.

―――― ―― **Watery.**—Acon.-Ars.-CHAM.-CHIN.-Ipec.-NUX.-Phos.-PULS.-Rhus.-Verat.

Dislocations.—ARN.-Phos.-RHUS.

Dreams, Frightful.—Acon.-ARN.-Ars.-BELL.-Bry.-CALC.-CHIN.-Merc.-NUX.-PHOS.-PULS.-RHUS.-SULPH.-Verat.

*****Dropsy.**—ARS.-Bell.-Bry.-CHIN.-Merc.-Rhus.-SULPH.

―――― **Abdomen, in the.**—ARS.-Bry.-CHIN.-Merc.-Sulph.

The principal uses in the treatment of—
*****Dropsy.**
Ars.—Face livid, pale, or greenish. Great debility and prostration. Internal sensation of heat, &c.
Bry.—Especially when the swelling increases in the day time and diminishes at night, &c.
Chin.—Great weakness. From debilitating losses. Tendency to perspire on the least exertion, &c.
Merc.—General heat and sweat. When connected with some affection of the liver. Symptoms of jaundice, &c.
Sulph.—If the sequela of acute eruptions, &c.

*Dropsy, Chest, in the.—ARS.-Bry.
———— Debilitating Losses, from.—CHIN.
———— Spirituous Liquors, from.—ARS.-CHIN.-Sulph.
†Drunkards, Sufferings of.—Ars.-Bell.-Calc.-Chin.-LACH.-NUX.-Puls.-Rhus.-Verat.
‡Dysentery.—Acon.-Ars.-Bry.-Cham.-Ipec.-MERC.-NUX.-Puls.-Rhus.-Sulph.

The principal uses in the treatment of—
*Dropsy, Chest, in the.
Ars.—Great difficulty of breathing. Constriction and compression of the chest. Shootings, burning and anguish in the chest with cold perspiration, &c.
Bry.—Attacks of difficult respiration. Pressure as from a weight in the chest. Pain, anxiety, and tightness in the chest, &c.
†Drunkards, Sufferings of.
Ars.—Mental alienation. Chronic effects, &c.
Bell.—Difficult deglutition. Violent thirst, &c.
Calc.—Frightful delirium, &c.
Chin.—Debility. Dropsy, &c.
Lach.—Debility and tremor of the hands, &c.
Nux.—Headache. Worse in the open air. Constipation. Tremor of the limbs, &c.
Puls.—Derangement of the stomach. Relief in the open air, &c.
Verat.—Great anxiety. Madness, &c.
‡Dysentery.
Acon.—Violent chills, heat, and thirst, &c.
Ars.—Great debility. Involuntary evacuations, &c.
Bry.—When from taking cold drinks or in the heat of summer, &c.
Cham.—Great heat, rheumatic pains in the head, restlessness, &c.
Ipec.—Bilious stools, afterwards bloody mucus. Especially in dysentery occurring in autumn, &c.
Merc.—Violent straining, especially after stool. Discharge of pure blood. Chilliness and shuddering, &c.
Nux.—Frequent small stools. Discharge of bloody mucus, &c.

Dysentery, Colic (with).—Ars.-Cham.-MERC.-NUX.
───────── **Distension of the Abdomen** (with).—Acon.-ARS.-Cham.-MERC.-Nux.-Puls.-Verat.
───────── **Sensibility** (painful) **of the Abdomen,** (with).—ACON.-Ars.-Bell.-Cham.-MERC.-NUX.-Puls.

***Dyspepsia,** (Chronic Indigestion).—ARN.-Bry.-CALC.-CHIN.-HEP.-Merc.-NUX.-Phos.-Puls.-Rhus.-SULPH.

The principal uses in the treatment of—
Dysentery, continued.
Puls.—Desire to vomit, or else vomiting of mucus. Frequent chills. Mucus streaked with blood, &c.
Rhus.—Involuntary stools at night, &c.
Sulph.—Often in desperate cases. Blood-streaked mucus. Violent straining, especially at night, &c.
    See *Diarrhœa, with Evacuations, Bloody, &c.*

***Dyspepsia.**
Arn.—Great sensitiveness and irritation of the nerves. Frequent eructations sometimes with the taste of rotten eggs. Yellowish livid complexion, &c.
Bry.—If in summer time, or in damp and warm weather. Frequent eructations, especially after a meal. Regurgitation or vomiting of food. Inability to bear the tight pressure of the clothes. Loathing of food. Painful sensitiveness of the region of the stomach to contact. Constipation, &c.
Calc.—Fits of canine hunger. Heartburn and acidity. Accumulation of mucus in the stomach. Stool only every two, three, or four days, &c.
Chin.—Malaise. Drowsiness. Fulness and distension. Weakness after every meal. Easily disturbed sleep. After debilitating losses, &c.
Hep.—In chronic dyspepsia, especially in persons who have taken much mercury. Liability to derange the stomach in spite of the most careful diet. Frequent nausea, especially in the morning, with desire to vomit and eructations. Accumulation of mucus in the throat. Hard, difficult dry stools, &c.

*Earache (In general).—BELL.-CHAM.-Merc.-PULS.
———— Chill, from a.—CHAM.-Merc.-Puls.
———— Inflammatory.—BELL.-Bry.-Merc.-Nux.-PULS.

The principal uses in the treatment of—
Dyspepsia, continued.
Merc.—Pressure in the pit of the stomach; eructations; heartburn. Aversion to solid food. Foul, sweetish, or bitter taste, especially early in the morning. Painful sensitiveness, pressure and tension in the region of the stomach, &c.
Nux.—Often at the commencement of the treatment. Regurgitation of food. Dulness of the head; giddiness. Distension. Heartburn. Constipation. Vomiting of food. Fulness and tension in the region of the stomach with great sensitiveness to the touch. The clothes feel tight. If caused by a sedentary life, study, or spirituous liquors. Accumulation of mucus in the stomach, &c.
Puls.—Adapted to females or persons of easy temperament. Absence of thirst. Frequent diarrhœic stools. Eructations tasting of food. Waterbrash. Nausea. If caused by fat things, &c.
Rhus.—If sleep, fulness, or eructations set in after eating. Empty, violent, and painful eructations, &c.
Sulph.—In most cases of chronic dyspepsia. Acidity, heartburn, and waterbrash. If caused by a sedentary life, or study. Heavy breathing, nausea, pain in the stomach, regurgitation or actual vomiting. Frequent eructations, &c.
*Earache.
Bell.—Tearing and shooting extending to the throat. Great sensibility to the least noise, &c.
Cham.—Stabbings as with knives, &c.
Merc.—Shooting pains with chilly feeling in the ears. Worse by the warmth of the bed, &c.
Nux.—Tearing shooting pains extending to the forehead and temples, with tearing in the facial bones, &c.
Puls.—Pains as if something would penetrate through the ears. Redness, swelling, and heat of the external ear, &c.
See Ears, Pains in the.

Earache, Rheumatic.—BELL.-MERC.-Nux.-PULS.
*****Ears, Discharge from the.**—Bell.-Calc.-MERC.-PULS.-SULPH.
—— —————— **Acute Inflammation, after.**—Merc.-Puls.
—— —————— **Catarrhal.**—MERC.-PULS.
—— —————— **Suppressed.**—Bell.-Bry.-Merc.-PULS.
—— **Excoriation in the.**—MERC.
—— **Humming in the.**—Acon.-BELL.-Bry.-Calc.-Merc.-NUX.-PULS.-SULPH.
†—— **Inflammation in the.**—BELL.-Cham.-MERC.-Nux.-PULS.
—— **Obstruction in the.**—Merc.-PULS.
—— **Pains, Boring, in the.**—Bell.
—— —— **Drawing.**—Merc.
—— —— **Shooting.**—Arn.-BELL.-CHAM.-Merc.-NUX.-Phos.-Puls.-Sulph.

The principal uses in the treatment of—
*****Ears, Discharge from the.**
Bell.—After scarlet fever, &c.
Calc.—If from the sudden suppression of eruptions of long standing, &c.
Merc.—Purulent or of wax. After a chill or an acute inflammation, &c.
Puls.—Purulent or mucous or bloody. After measles, scarlatina, an acute inflammation, or a chill, &c.
Sulph.—Purulent. In chronic and tedious cases, &c.
†**Ears, Inflammation in the.**
Bell.—Determination of blood to the head. Tearing or shooting pains extending to the throat, fever and great sensibility to the least noise, &c.
Merc.—Soreness of the orifice, and discharge. Swelling of the glands, &c.
Puls.—Especially when the external ear is much affected, &c.

MEDICAL INDEX. 55

Ears, Pains, Tearing, in the.—BELL.-CHAM.-Chin.-Merc.-NUX.-Phos.-PULS.-Sulph.
———— **Swelling of the.**—Merc.-PULS.-Rhus.
Emaciation.—ARS.-Bell.-CALC.-CHIN.-Merc.-NUX.-Phos.-Rhus.-SULPH.
†Epilepsy.—Ars.-BELL.-CALC.-CIN.-Ipec.-Nux.-Sulph.
Eructations (In general).—ARN.-BELL.-BRY.-Chin.-MERC.-Nux.-PHOS.-PULS.-RHUS.-SULPH.-VERAT.
———————— **Abortive.**—Bell.-PHOS.
———————— **Bitter.**—Ars.-BRY.-Chin.-MERC.-NUX.-PULS.-Verat.
———————— **Putrid.**—Arn.-Merc.-Nux.
———————— **Sour.**—Bry.-Calc.-Cham.-Chin.-Merc.-Nux.-Phos.-Puls.-Sulph.
———————— **Violent.**—Merc.-Verat.
Eruptions, Acute.—Acon.-BELL.-BRY.-MERC.-PULS.-RHUS.
———————— **Burning.**—ARS.-Bell.-Bry.-Merc.-Nux.-RHUS.-Sulph.
———————— **Chronic.**—Ars.-Calc.-Rhus.-SULPH.

The principal uses in the treatment of—
†Epilepsy.
Ars.—Burning in the stomach, spine, and abdomen.
Bell.—Congestion of the head with giddiness, redness, heat, and bloatedness of the face. Dilated pupils. Cramps in the throat with danger of suffocation. Complete loss of consciousness. Lethargic sleep. Renewal on the slightest contact or contradiction, &c.
Calc.—In chronic cases. Nocturnal paroxysms. If connected with teething, &c.
Cin.—When arising from worms.
Nux.—Sensation of torpor and numbness in the limbs, &c.
Sulph.—In cases of long standing, or when excited by the sudden suppression of an eruption, &c.
See Spasms.

Eruptions, Dry.—ARS.-CALC.-Merc.-Phos.-VERAT.
———— Humid.—CARB.-RHUS.-SULPH.
———— Itching.—Bry.-Merc.-RHUS.-Sulph.
———— Miliary.—Acon.-Ars.-Bell.-BRY.-Ipec.-MERC.-Rhus.-Sulph.-Verat.
———— ———— Purple.—ACON.
———— ———— Scarlet.—ACON.-BRY.-Ipec.-Merc.
———— ———— White.—ARS.-Bry.
———— Painful.—Arn.-BELL.-Merc.-Verat.
———— Purulent.—MERC.-RHUS.
———— Pustulous.—Ars.-Bell.-Chin.-MERC.-PHOS.-Puls.-RHUS.-Sulph.
———— Scabby.—Ars.-CALC.-RHUS.-Sulph.
———— Scaly.—Ars.-Merc.-PHOS.-Sulph.
———— Scurfy.—CALC.-Phos.-RHUS.-Sulph.
———— Suppressed.—Ars.-BRY.-Cham.-IPEC.-Phos.-Puls.-Sulph.
*Erysipelas.—ACON.-Arn.-Ars.-BELL.-Bry.-Cham.-Merc.-Phos.-RHUS.-Sulph.

The principal uses in the treatment of—
*Erysipelas.
Acon.—Fever. Skin dry and burning, &c.
Arn.—Erysipelas of the feet and knees, &c.
Ars.—When there is a tendency to gangrene, &c.
Bell.—Erysipelatous inflammation. Headache. Delirium, &c.
Bry.—When the joints are chiefly affected, &c.
Cham.—Swelling of the cheeks with redness. Gnawing pains in the bones, sometimes accompanied with bitter taste, thirst, &c.
Merc.—Worse at night in bed. If terminating in abscesses, &c.
Rhus.—Vesicular erysipelas.
Sulph.—In obstinate cases, or cases which recur frequently.

MEDICAL INDEX. 57

Erysipelas, Gangrenous.—ARS.
——————— **Pustulous.**—Ars.-Bell.-RHUS.
Evacuations, Hard.—BRY.-Merc.-NUX.-Sulph.
——————— **Knotty.**—MERC.-Nux.-SULPH.
See Diarrhœa with Evacuations.
Excoriation of the Skin.—ARN.-Ars.-Calc.-Cham.-
Chin.-Puls.-SULPH.
Eyelids, Agglutination of the.—Calc.-CHAM.-
Merc.-Phos.-PULS.-RHUS.-Sulph.
*——— **Inflammation of the.**—Acon.-BELL.-
Calc.-CHAM.-Chin.-MERC.-Nux.-PULS.-
Rhus.-Sulph.-Verat.
——— **Paralysis of the.**—Bell.-VERAT.
——— **Styes on the.**—PULS.-Sulph.
——— **Swelling of the.**—Acon.-Calc.-MERC.-
NUX.-Puls.-Rhus.-SULPH.

The principal uses in the treatment of —
*****Eyelids, Inflammation of the.**
Acon.—Eyelids swollen, hard and red, with heat, burning and dryness. Great dread of light, &c.
Bell.—The margins are turned up. Inflammation of the external surface and margins, &c.
Calc.—Cutting pains, especially when reading, &c.
Cham.—Spasmodic closing or great weight of the lids, &c.
Chin.—Creeping on the internal surface with lachrymation, &c.
Merc.—Shootings; burning pains and itching, or else no pain, &c.
Nux.—Burning itching of the lids, especially on the margins, &c.
Puls.—Inflammatory redness of the margins. Styes, &c.
Rhus.—Stiffness of the lids, as if paralysed, with burning itching, &c.
Sulph.—Ulceration of the margins. Great redness. When the external surface is inflamed, &c.
Verat.—Great dryness of the lids with lachrymation, difficulty of moving them and great heat in the eyes, &c.

E

MEDICAL INDEX.

Eyelids, Trembling of the.—Bell.-CALC.-Ipec.
——— **Twitching of the.**—CHAM.-NUX.-Sulph.
Eyes, Bleeding of the.—BELL.-Cham.
——— **Burning in the.**—BELL.-Bry.-CARB.-MERC.-Nux.-PHOS.-Sulph.-Verat.
——— **Convulsions in the.**—BELL.-Cham.
——— **Double Vision.**—BELL.-Puls.-Verat.
——— **Dryness in the.**—BELL.-Nux.-Sulph.
——— **Fixed Look.**—Ars.-BELL.
——— **Flames before the** (appearance of).—BELL.-Puls.
——— **Heat in the.**—Bell.-MERC.-Verat.
*——— **Inflammation of the** (Ophthalmia).—ACON.-Arn.-Ars.-BELL.-Bry.-Calc.-CHAM.-MERC.-NUX.-Phos.-PULS.-Rhus.-SULPH.-Verat.

The principal uses in the treatment of—
*__Eyes, Inflammation of the.__

Acon.—In most cases of acute inflammation. Redness of the eyes with dark redness of the vessels. Intolerable burning stitching pains. Violent dread of light, &c.

Arn.—If from an injury.

Ars.—Burning pains as from hot coals. Intolerable pains with anguish so that the patient cannot remain still, &c.

Bell.—Painful sensitiveness to light. Aching pains round the eyes, or to a depth in the orbits and in the head. The pains are aggravated by motion. Vivid redness of the eyes, &c.

Bry.—Lids swollen, with pains in the head when the eyes are opened. In rheumatic inflammation, &c.

Calc.—Specks and ulcers on the cornea. Dread of light. Spots before the eyes when reading or in any other exertion of the eyes, &c.

Cham.—Especially in children, and when the pains are *intolerable*, with great impatience, &c.

Eyes, Inflammation of the, Chronic.—Calc.-Phos.-SULPH.
———— ———————— **Scrofulous.**—Ars.-Bell.-CALC.-HEP.-Merc.-Puls.-Rhus.-SULPH.
———— **Intolerance of Light.**—ACON.-ARS.-BELL.-Bry.-Calc.-Cham.-Chin.-Merc.-Nux.-Puls.-Rhus.-SULPH.-Verat.
———— **Itching in the.**—Bell.-Calc.-MERC.-NUX.-Sulph.
———— **Neuralgic Pains in the.**—BELL.-Chin.
———— **Pains, Aching, in the.**—Bell.-Rhus.
———— ———— **Bruise, as from a.**—Arn.-Chin.-Rhus.-Verat.
———— ———— **Drawing.**—Ars.-Bell.-Nux.-Puls.
———— ———— **Pressive.**—Ars.-Cham.-Nux.-Phos.-PULS.
———— ———— **Sand, as from.**—Bry.-Phos.-Puls.-Sulph.

The principal uses in the treatment of—
Eyes, Inflammation of the, continued.
Merc.—Cutting pains. Sensation as from sand under the eyelids. Great sensibility to the light of the fire. Itching and shooting. Worse in the evening, or in the warmth of the bed, &c.
Nux.—Pressing pains as if there were sand in the eye. Violent and pressive headache. Worse in the morning, &c.
Puls.—Pressure; tearing, shooting, cutting, or boring pains in the eyes. Copious lachrymation, or great dryness of the eyes. Swelling of the eyelids, &c.
Rhus.—In damp weather, or when the eye continues to burn, with lachrymation and erysipelatous swelling of the lids, &c.
Sulph.—Sensation as from sand under the eyelids, with burning and smarting. Vesicles, ulcers, and pustules round the eyes or on the cornea. Great dryness of the eyes, or lachrymation, &c.
Verat.—Tearing pains with violent headache, dread of light, heat, and feeling of dryness in the eyes, &c.

Eyes, Pains, Shooting, in the.—Acon.-Ars.-Bell.-Bry.-CALC.-Merc.-PULS.
———— ———— **Smarting.**—MERC.-NUX.
———— **Pressure in the.**—Bry.-CALC.-CARB.-MERC.-PHOS.-Sulph.
———— **Prominent.**—Arn.-Ars.-BELL.
———— **Pupils, Contracted.**—Arn.-Bell.-Cham.-Phos.-Puls.-Sulph.-Verat.
———— ———— **Dilated.**—ACON.-Ars.-BELL.-CALC.-Chin.-CIN.-Ipec.-Nux.-Verat.
———— **Redness of the.**—ACON.-Arn.-Ars.-BELL.-Bry.-Calc.-Chin.-MERC.-NUX.-Rhus.-Sulph.
———— **Shortsightedness.**—Calc.-PHOS.-PULS.-Sulph.
———— **Sight Illusory, Mist before the.**—Bell.-CALC.-Sulph.
———— ———— ———— **Reflection round the Candle.**—Bell.-Phos.-Puls.-SULPH.
———— ———— ———— **Spots before the.**—Bell.-Calc.-Chin.-Merc.-Phos.
———— **Sparkling.**—Acon.-BELL.
———— **Spots on the Cornea.**—BELL.-Calc.-PULS.
———— **Watery.**—Arn.-Bell.-Calc.-Merc.-Nux.-Phos.-PULS.-Rhus.-SULPH.-Verat.

Face, Bloated.—Arn.-ARS.-BELL.-BRY.-CHAM.-Ipec.-Merc.-Phos.-Puls.
———— **Burning in the.**—Arn.-Bell.-Bry.-Nux.-Puls.-Verat.
———— **Colour, Bluish.**—Acon.-ARS.-Bell.-Bry.-Ipec.-Verat.
———— ———— **Pale.**—Acon.-ARS.-Calc.-CHIN.-CIN.-Ipec.-Merc.-Nux.-Phos.-Puls.-Rhus.-SULPH.-Verat.

Face, Colour, Pale (Semilateral).—Acon.-CHAM.-Verat.
— — **Red.**—ACON.-Arn.-BELL.-BRY.-CHAM.-Chin.-Merc.-NUX.-Puls.-Rhus.-Sulph.-Verat.
— — **Sallow.**—Ars.-Bry.-CHIN.-MERC.-Nux.-Phos.
— — **Yellow.**—Ars.-Bry.-Cham.-Chin.-Merc.-NUX.-Phos.-SULPH.-Verat.
— **Convulsions of the.**—Bell.-Cham.-Ipec.
— **Distortion of the.**—Ars.-Bell.-Cham.-Ipec.-Merc.-Rhus.-Verat.
— **Eruptions on the.**—Ars.-Bell.-Bry.-Calc.-Merc.-Phos.-RHUS.-Sulph.-Verat.
*— **Erysipelas in the.**—BELL.-CHAM.-LACH.-RHUS.-Sulph.
†— - **Pains in the** (Faceache).—ACON.-Arn.-ARS.-BELL.-Bry.-Calc.-Cham.-Chin.-HEP.-Merc.-NUX.-PHOS.-Puls.-Rhus.-Sulph.-Verat.
— **Pains in the** (Inflammatory).—ACON.-MERC.
— — **Burning.**—Ars.-Rhus.-Sulph.
— — **Drawing.**—Ars.-Bell.-NUX.-PHOS.
— — **Semilateral.**—Acon.-Cham.-Nux.
— — **Shooting.**—Acon.-Ars.-Bell.
— — **Tearing.**—Bell.-Chin.-MERC.-NUX.-PHOS.

The principal uses in the treatment of—
***Face, Erysipelas in the.**
Bell.—Delirium. Stitching headache. Great thirst, &c.
Cham.—Swelling of the cheeks with redness. Gnawing pains in the bones, sometimes accompanied with bitter taste, thirst, &c.
Lach.—If the head symptoms do not yield to *Bell.*
Rhus.—In vesicular erysipelas or of the scalp.
†**Face, Pains in the.**—*See Neuralgia. Tic-Doloreux.*

Face, Pains, Tensive, in the.—Bell.-Verat.
—— —— **Throbbing.**—Bell.-Merc.
—— **Scabs on the.**—ARS.-CALC.-MERC.-RHUS.-Sulph.
—— **Swelling of the.**—Arn.-Ars.-BELL.-BRY.-CHAM.-MERC.-NUX.-PULS.-Sulph.
—— **Swelling, Hard.**—Arn.-Ars.-Bell.-Cham.
—— —————— **Hot.**—Arn.-Bell.-Bry.-Cham.
*****Fainting** (In general).—ACON.-Arn.-Ars.-Bell.-CHAM.-CHIN.-Ipec.-NUX.-Phos.-VERAT.
—————— **Debilitating Losses** (from).—CHIN.
—————— **Fright** (from).—ACON.
—————— **Hysterical.**—CHAM.-Nux.
†**Fatigue, Sufferings from.**—ARN.-Ars.-BRY.-CALC.-Cham.-Merc.-Phos.-RHUS.-Verat.

The principal uses in the treatment of—
*****Fainting.**
Acon.—Violent palpitation of the heart. Deadly paleness of the face. When rising from a recumbent posture. If from violent pain, &c.
Cham.—If from violent pain, &c.
Chin.—If from loss of blood, &c.
Nux.—In the morning or after a meal. With nausea and clouded sight, or pain in the stomach. In persons addicted to spirituous liquors, or fatigued with study, &c.
Verat.—When the paroxysms set in after the least motion, or are preceded by great anguish, despondency, &c.
†**Fatigue.**
Arn.—If from labour or bodily exertion.
Bell.—For headache after too much study, &c.
Bry.—If after heating or running, stitches remain in the side, &c.
Calc.—If the least exertion or conversation fatigues very much, &c.
Chin.—After bodily exertion with profuse sweat, &c.
Nux.—For the consequences of long night-watching, too much study, or a sedentary life. Worse in the open air, &c.

Fatigue, Mind (of the).—Bell.-CALC.-Chin.-NUX.-Puls.-Sulph.
Fear, Sufferings from.—ACON.-Nux.-Puls.
Feet, Burning in the.—CALC.
— Coldness of the.—Calc.-PHOS.-Sulph.-Verat.
— Cramps in the.—CALC.-Sulph.
— Inflammation of the.—Arn.-Bry.
— Paralysis of the.—Bell.-Rhus.-Sulph.
— Perspiration on the.—CALC.-Merc.-Sulph.
— Swelling of the.—ARS.-Bry.-CHIN.-LACH.-PHOS.-PULS.
— Swelling, Dropsical.—Ars.-Chin.-Sulph.
Fevers.—*See their respective heads.*
Fever, Simple.—ACON. *See Inflammatory Fever.*
—— with Constipation.—Bry.-Calc.-Nux.-Verat.
—— —— Delirium.—ACON.-BELL.-BRY.-Cham.
—— —— Headache.—Acon.-Arn.-Ars.-Bell.-NUX.-Puls.-Sulph.
Fingers, Chaps in the.—MERC.
—— Deadness of the.—CALC.-Phos.-Sulph.
—— Pains, Drawing, in the.—PULS.
—— —— Jerking.—Chin.-Puls.
—— —— Tearing.—Acon.-Chin.-Sulph.
—— Swelling of the.—Rhus.-Sulph.
Fistula.—CALC.-PULS.

The principal uses in the treatment of—
Fatigue, continued.
Puls.—For the consequences of excessive study, or long night-watching. Relief in the open air, &c.
Rhus.—From lifting or carrying great loads, &c.
Verat.—When the least work fatigues even to fainting, &c.

Flatulence (In general).—Bell.-CARB.-Cham.-CHIN.-
Nux.-Phos.-Puls.-Verat.

*——— (Pent-up).—Calc.-CARB.-CHAM.-CHIN.-
NUX.-Phos.-PULS.

†**Flooding, Uterine.**—Arn.-BELL.-CHAM.-CHIN.-
IPEC.-Puls.

——— Accouchement or Miscarriage, after.—Arn.-
BELL.-Bry.-CHAM.-Chin.-IPEC.

——— **Critical Age, at the.**—Lach.-Puls.

——— **Serious and Extreme Cases, in.**—
CHIN.-Ipec.

The principal uses in the treatment of—
***Flatulence.**
Carb.—Especially when arising from taking the smallest quantity of food, &c.
Cham.—Incarceration of flatulence with pressure upwards, &c.
Chin.—In consequence of flatulent food. After eating fat meats or fruits. With distension of the abdomen, &c.
Nux.—Abundant. After a meal or drinking, &c.
Puls.—After fat meats or rich food, &c.
Sulph.—In obstinate cases, &c.
See *Eructations. Sufferings after a Meal.*
†**Flooding.**
Arn.—If from missing a step, straining, or after any other over-exertion, &c.
Bell.—Blood of a natural colour. Violent pressive pains in the abdomen. Sensation as of a forcing outwards through the parts. Active hæmorrhage, &c.
Cham.—Dark red or black fetid blood with lumps, the discharge taking place by fits and starts. Labour-like pains, &c.
Chin.—In the most serious and severe cases. The blood gushes at intervals, with spasmodic pains, &c.
Ipec.—Copious and uninterrupted discharge of fluid and bright red blood, &c.
Puls.—Discharge thick and black. By fits and starts, &c. See *Hæmorrhage.*

MEDICAL INDEX. 65

Freckles.—CALC.-PHOS.-Puls.-SULPH.

---

*Gangrene.—ARS.-CHIN.
†Gastric Derangement.—ARN.-Ars.-BRY.-Calc.-Chin.-IPEC.-Merc.-NUX.-PULS.

The principal uses in the treatment of—
*Gangrene.
Ars.—Fetid smell. Fetid watery discharge. Great burning heat, &c.
Chin.—Itching and burning, gnawing pains, &c.
†Gastric Derangement.
Arn.—If from external injuries. From continual watching and mental exertions. Eructations tasting of putrid eggs. Great nervousness, &c.
Ars.—Violent thirst and desire to drink frequently but little at a time. Burning pains in the stomach and abdomen. Vomiting of bilious, greenish substances. Great nausea, &c.
Bry.—Especially in summer and in hot and damp weather. Bilious vomiting. Tension and fulness in the region of the stomach, &c.
Calc.—Acid rising off the stomach. Insipid taste. Loss of appetite. Slimy mouth and tongue, &c.
Chin.—Frequent discharge of fetid flatulence. Undigested stools, &c.
Ipec.—Vomiting of food or of slimy substances, easy but with great force. Cutting in the abdomen and diarrhœic stools of a yellow colour, &c.
Merc.—Offensive, foul, and bitter taste. Bilious, mucous vomiting. Painful sensitiveness of the abdomen. Drowsiness in the day time, sleeplessness at night, &c.
Nux.—Pressive spasms in the stomach. Painful pressure and tension. Constipation, ineffectual urging to stool. Dulness of the head with giddiness. Bitter eructations. Constant nausea. Vomiting of food, &c.
Puls.—Slimy diarrhœa. Chilliness. Regurgitation of food. Aversion to food. Vomiting of food. Foul, flat, or bitter taste, &c.

*Gastric Fever.—Bry.-IPEC.-Merc.-NUX.-PULS.-Verat.

†Giddiness (In general).—ACON.-Arn.-BELL.-Bry.-CALC.-Cham.-Chin.-Ipec.-NUX.-PHOS.-PULS.-RHUS.-Sulph.-Verat.

The principal uses in the treatment of—
*Gastric Fever.
Bry.—Stitches in the head. Constipation. Great debility. Violent heat with burning thirst, or chilliness and shuddering over the whole body, &c.
Ipec.—Loathing of all food with desire to vomit. Regurgitation and vomiting of undigested food. Diarrhœic yellowish stools. Headache in the forehead. Pale yellow colour of the skin, &c.
Merc.—Nauseous, foul, or bitter taste. Vomiting of mucus. Painfulness of the pit of the stomach and stomach. Drowsiness in the day time and sleeplessness at night. Burning thirst, &c.
Nux.—Vomiting of undigested food. Painful pressure and tension in the whole region of the stomach. Constipation, with frequent but ineffectual urging to stool. Pressive pains in the forehead with giddiness. Red and hot, or yellow and livid face, &c.
Puls.—Regurgitation and vomiting of food. Vomiting of slimy and whitish, bitter and greenish substances. Diarrhœic white slimy, or bilious and greenish stools. Frequent chills without thirst, &c.
Verat.—Great debility after every evacuation, &c.

†Giddiness.
Acon.—On raising the head when lying or stooping. Sensation as if the brain were moved. Redness of face. Heat. Cloudiness before the eyes, &c.
Arn.—If during dinner or after a hearty meal, &c.
Bell.—Cloudiness of sight. Partial loss of consciousness. Staggering. Swimming in the head. Fulness and violent pressure on the forehead, &c.
Bry.—On stooping, or when rising from a recumbent position, &c.
Calc.—When ascending an eminence, or with trembling before breakfast, &c.

MEDICAL INDEX. 67

Giddiness, Confused Sight, with.—ACON.-Cham.-Merc.-NUX.-Puls.

——— Congestion to the Head (from).—ACON.-Arn.-BELL.-CHIN.-Merc.-NUX.-Puls.-Rhus.-Sulph.

——— Fainting, with.—LACH.-NUX.

——— Gastric Derangement, from.—Ars.-NUX.-PULS.-Rhus.

——— Loss of Consciousness, with.—Acon.-BELL.-LACH.-NUX.

——— Nausea, with.—ACON.-Ars.-Phos.-Sulph.

——— Nervous Affections, from.—Arn.-Bell.-NUX.-Phos.-Puls.

——— Stooping, from.—Bell.-Bry.-NUX.-PULS.

——— Whirling.—ARN.-BELL.-Bry.-NUX.-Phos.-Verat.

Glands, Burning in the.—ARS.-BELL.-Merc.-Phos.

The principal uses in the treatment of—
Giddiness, continued.

Cham.—Accompanied with attacks of fainting, &c.

Chin.—During movement, or after debilitating losses, &c.

Merc.—In the morning on arising, or in the evening with nausea, dimness of sight, &c.

Nux.—During or after meals. When walking in the open air. With wavering in the head, danger of falling, buzzing in the ears, or cloudiness of sight. If from wine, coffee, excessive mental exertions, &c.

Phos.—Giddiness with vanishing of ideas, &c.

Puls.—When raising the eyes. Relief in the open air. Paleness of the face. Nausea. Palpitation of the heart. If from fat meats, rich food, &c.

Rhus.—When lying down in the evening, with fear of dying, &c.

Sulph.—When sitting, or ascending an eminence, or after a meal in the morning, &c.

Glands, Induration of the.—Bell.-Cham.-Chin.-Phos.-Sulph.
——— **Inflammation of the.**—Acon.-BELL.-Bry.-Cham.-MERC.-Nux.-PHOS.-Puls.-Sulph.
——— **Pain in the.**—ARN.-BELL.-Chin.-MERC.-Phos.-Puls.-Sulph.
——— **Pains, Cutting, in the.**—BELL.
——— ——— **Drawing.**—Arn.-Bell.-Chin.-Sulph.
——— ——— **Jerking.**—Bell.-Calc.-Puls.
——— ——— **Pressive.**—Bell.-Merc.
——— ——— **Pricking.**—Bell.-Merc.-Puls.
——— ——— **Tearing.**—Arn.-Bell.-CHIN.-Sulph.
——— **Pulsation in the.**—Calc.-MERC.-Phos.-Sulph.
——— **Sensibility** (Painful) of the.—PHOS.
——— **Swelling of the.**—Ars.-BELL.-Bry.-Calc.-Cham.-MERC.-Nux.-PHOS.-PULS.-RHUS.-SULPH.
——— **Swelling, Hard.**—Bry.-Phos.-Puls.-Rhus.-Sulph.
——— ——— **Hot.**—Acon.-Arn.-BELL.-Bry.-MERC.-PHOS.-Sulph.
——— ——— **Inflammatory.**—Acon.-Arn.-Bell.-Bry.-Cham.-MERC.-Phos.-Puls.
——— ——— **Painful.**—Arn.-Bell.-Chin.-Nux.-Puls.
——— **Tightness in the.**—Arn.-Bry.-PHOS.-Puls.-Rhus.-Sulph.
——— **Ulcers in the.**—ARS.-Bell.-PHOS.-Sulph.
Glands, Salivary, (beneath the Ear) Inflammation of.—Bell.-CHAM.-MERC.-Rhus.
——— ——— **Swelling.**—Bell.-CHAM.-MERC.-RHUS.

Glands of Neck.—*See Neck.*

Goitre.—Calc.-SPONG.

*****Gout** (In general).—Acon.-ARN.-Bell.-BRY.-Calc.-Chin.-Merc.-Nux.-Phos.-PULS.-RHUS.-Sulph.

———— **Acute.**—ACON.-Arn.-Bell.-BRY.-Chin.-Nux.-PULS.

———— **Ankles, in the.**—Bry.-Calc.-Sulph.

———— **Arms, in the.**—BRY.-RHUS.

———— **Chronic.**—Arn.-CALC.-Rhus.-SULPH.

———— **Feet, in the.**—Sulph.

———— **Hips, in the.**—BELL.-Bry.-Calc.-MERC.-Rhus.-Sulph.

The principal uses in the treatment of—
*****Gout.**

Acon.—Throbbings in the foot. Hot swelling and shining redness. Great sensibility to the touch, &c.

Arn.—Sore and aching pains, or as if bruised and sprained, &c.

Bell.—When the redness spreads very much and is very deep. Shooting, burning pains, &c.

Bry.—Swelling with redness and heat. Worse when moving the part. Shooting in the toes, &c.

Calc.—Burning, followed by coldness and numbness of the soles of the feet. Burning pain. Gouty nodosities, &c.

Chin.—Extreme sensibility to the touch. Worse by the least contact, &c.

Nux.—If from abuse of spirituous liquors. Torpor and swelling of the part. Swelling, burning, and itching of the toes. For the precursors of gout, &c.

Puls.—Hot swelling. Torpor. Wandering gout. Worse when rising from a seat or lying down, &c.

Rhus.—Drawing and tearing pains. Numbness and insensibility in the feet. Worse during rest, &c.

Sulph.—Contraction of the toes. Crawlings in the ends of the toes. Frequently required during the treatment. Large and shining swelling of the toes, &c.

See Rheumatism, Pains in the joints, &c.

Gout, Knees, in the.—Bry.-Chin.-Puls.-Rhus.-Sulph.
——— Legs, in the.—Bry.-Puls.
——— Toes, in the.—Arn.-SULPH.
Grief, Sufferings from.—Puls.
*Gullet, Inflammation of the.—Ars.-BELL.-Bry.-MERC.
——— Paralysis of the.—Bell.-Lach.
†Gumboil.—CALC.-Sulph.
Gums, Bleeding of the.—Calc.-CARB.-Merc.
——— Inflammation of the.—BELL.-Chin.-MERC.-Nux.-Sulph.
——— Mercurial Affections.—CARB.-CHIN.
——— Painful.—Ars.-MERC.-PULS.
——— Scurvy of the.—CARB.-Chin.-Merc.-Sulph.
——— Swelling of the.—Bell.-Calc.-Chin.-Merc.-Nux.-Phos.-Sulph.
——— Ulcers on the.—Merc.

The principal uses in the treatment of—
*Gullet, Inflammation of the.

Ars.—Excessive burning in the throat with spasmodic constriction and inability to swallow, as from paralysis of the parts. Sensation of great dryness. Burning thirst, &c.

Bell.—Complete inability to swallow even liquids. Constant inclination to swallow with a spasmodic constriction of the throat, &c.

Bry.—Pressure in the gullet as from a hard body. Sticking sensation when swallowing, turning the head, or touching the throat, &c.

Merc.—Shooting pains when swallowing. Pressure in the gullet or pains as from excoriation and ulceration. Painful difficult spasmodic deglutition, &c.

†Gumboil.—*See Abscess or Boil, and treat accordingly.*

Hæmorrhage, Active.—ACON.-BELL.-Chin.-IPEC.-Puls.
———— **Blood, Coagulated, with.**—Bell.-CHAM.-Chin.-Ipec.-Puls.-RHUS.
———— ———— **Dark.**—Arn.-Cham.-Nux.-Puls.
———— ———— **Pale.**—BELL.-Phos.-Rhus.
———— **Debility, arising from.**—CHIN.-Ipec.
———— **Mechanical Injuries, from.**—ARN.-Chin.-Phos.
———— **Pulmonary.**—Acon.-Bell.-CHIN.-Ipec.-PHOS.-Rhus.
———— **Uterine.**—*See Flooding.*
———— **Wounds, from.**—Arn.-PHOS.
Hands, Cramp in the.—BELL.
———— **Deadness of the.**—CALC.
———— **Jerking in the.**—BELL.
———— **Pains, Burning, in the.**—Bry.-PHOS.
———— ———— **Drawing.**—PULS.
———— ———— **Tearing.**—Chin.-PHOS.-Puls.-SULPH.
———— ———— **Wrenching.**—Bry.-Calc.-Phos.-Puls.-Sulph.

The principal uses in the treatment of—
*Hæmorrhage.
Acon.—Profuse bleeding and inflammatory state of the blood. When there is imminent danger. Blood bright red, &c.
Bell.—From the eyes and mouth. Blood bright red. Coagulated, &c.
Chin.—When the blood gushes at intervals. In passive hæmorrhages, &c.
Ipec.—Violent hæmorrhage. Continuous. Blood bright red, &c.
Puls.—Blood pale, watery, or dark red, &c.

Hands, Swelling of the.—Bell.-Bry.-CALC.-PHOS.-RHUS.-Sulph.

——— **Trembling of the.**—LACH.-PHOS.-SULPH.

——— **Weakness of the.**—Arn.-Merc.-Sulph.

Head, Bewildered Sensation.—Acon.-BELL.-Bry.-NUX.-Puls.-Rhus.

——— **Burning in the.**—Arn.-Merc.-Nux.-Rhus.

——— **Coldness** (Sensation of) in the.—CALC.-Sulph.-Verat.

——— **Crawling in the.**—RHUS.

——— **Emptiness** (Sensation of) in the.—PULS.

——— **Expansion** (Sensation).—BELL.-Bry.-NUX.

——— **Fluctuation in the.**—Acon.-BELL.-Nux.

——— **Fulness in the.**—ACON.-BELL.-BRY.-Chin.-Rhus.-Sulph.

——— **Heaviness in.**—BELL.-Bry.-CARB.-Cham.-NUX.-Rhus.-Sulph.

——— **Intoxicated** (Sensation as if).—Acon.-Bell.-NUX.-PULS.-Rhus.

——— **Pains, Aching, in the.**—Arn.-Bell.-Chin.-Ipec.-Nux.-Phos.

——— ——— **Bruise, as from a.**—CHIN.-NUX.-PULS.-VERAT.

——— ——— **Cramplike.**—Acon.-Arn.-Calc.-Chin.-Merc.-Puls.

——— ——— **Digging.**—Bry.-Calc.-Merc.-Puls.

——— ——— **Drawing.**—Bell.-Cham.-MERC.-NUX.-Puls.

——— ——— **Jerking.**—Arn.-Bell.-CHIN.-NUX.-PULS.

——— ——— **Shooting.**—Arn.-BELL.-Bry.-Ipec.-Merc.-NUX.-Puls.-Rhus.-Sulph.

——— ——— **Spasmodic.**—Acon.-Arn.-Nux.

Head, Pains, Split Open (as if the Head would).—
BELL.-Bry.-CHIN.-Merc.-NUX.

—— —— **Stupefying.**—Acon.-Bell.-Calc.-PHOS.

—— —— **Tearing.**—BELL.-Bry.-Cham.-Merc.-NUX.-PULS.-Sulph.

—— —— **Tensive.**—Acon.-MERC.-PULS.-Sulph.

—— —— **Throbbing.**—BELL.-Bry.-Calc.-SULPH.-VERAT.

—— **Soreness of the.**—ARS.-CHIN.-Merc.-Nux.-Sulph.-VERAT.

—— **Water** (Sensation of), in the.—Acon.-BELL.

*****Headache** (In general).— Acon.-Arn.-BELL.-BRY.-Cham.-Chin.-IPEC.-MERC.-NUX.-Phos.-PULS.-Rhus.-Sulph.-Verat.

The principal uses in the treatment of—
*****Headache.**

Acon.—Violent, stupefying, compressive pains. Burning pains through the brain, or contractive pains, especially over the root of the nose. Red and bloated face, &c.

Arn.—Heat in the head, with coldness of the body, &c.

Bell.—Great fulness and violent pressing and distending pains as if the head would split open, or as if everything would issue through the forehead. Pains above the eyes. Violent throbbing. Excessive sensibility to the least noise, motion, or light. Waverings, shocks, and undulations in the head as of water, &c.

Bry.—Distending pressure, or compressive sensation in the head. Shootings, especially on one side. Aggravated by motion. When produced by heat or bad weather, &c.

Cham.—Tearing and jerking in one side of the head down to the jaws. Heaviness. Great sensibility to pain, &c.

Chin.—Aching pains at night which prevent sleep. Aggravation by contact. Painful sensitiveness of the scalp, &c.

Ipec.—With nausea and vomiting. Sensation extending to the tongue as if the brain were bruised, &c.

F

Headache, Anger, from.—Acon.-CHAM.-NUX.
─────── **Catarrhal.**—CHAM.-MERC.-NUX.-Sulph.
─────── **Cold Drinks, from.**—Acon.-ARS.-Bell.
─────── **Congestive.**—ACON.-ARN.-BELL.-BRY.-MERC.-NUX.
─────── **Gastric Derangement, from.**—Ipec.-NUX.-PULS.-Sulph.
─────── **Heat, from.**—ACON.-BRY.
─────── **Hysterical.**—Cham.-Nux.-Verat.
─────── **Intellectual Fatigue, from.**—NUX.-SULPH.
─────── **Movement, aggravated by.**—Acon.-Bell.-BRY.-Chin.-Nux.-Sulph.

The principal uses in the treatment of—
Headache, continued.

Merc.—Tearing, shooting pains. Aggravation at night or by the warmth of the bed. Semilateral tearing with stitches in the ears, &c.

Nux.—Pain as if a nail were driven into the head. Great heaviness of the head, especially when moving the eyes and whilst thinking, with sensation as if the skull would burst. Sensation as if the brain were bruised. Worse after eating, or in the open air, or when stooping. Constipation. If from spirituous liquors, excessive study, &c.

Puls.—Semilateral tearing pains. Heaviness in the head. Humming, tearing, and shootings in the ears. Paleness of the face. Shocks and stitches. Worse in the evening or during rest. Relief in the open air, &c.

Rhus.—Doubting and wavering of the brain at every step, and creeping in the head, &c.

Sulph.—Inability to think. Fulness, pressure, and heaviness, especially on one side. Worse in the open air, or by thinking, &c.

Verat.—Great debility even to fainting. Great malaise. Pains so violent as to cause delirium and frenzy, &c.

See Pains in the Head. Headache, Catarrhal, &c.

MEDICAL INDEX. 75

Headache, Moving the Eyes, aggravated by.—Bell.-BRY.-Nux.
———— **Nausea, with.**—Acon.-Bry.-IPEC.-NUX.-Verat.
———— **Nervous.**—Acon.-Arn.-Ars.-Bell.-BRY.-CALC.-Cham.-CHIN.-Ipec.-NUX.-PHOS.-PULS.-RHUS.-Sulph.-VERAT.
———— **Pain in one Spot, with.**—ACON.-BRY.
———— **Periodical.**—BELL.-Calc.-Nux.-Sulph.
———— **Rheumatic.**—ACON.-Cham.-CHIN.-MERC.-Nux.-PULS.-SULPH.
———— **Semilateral.**—ARS.-Bell.-BRY.-CALC.-Cham.-CHIN.-MERC.-NUX.-PULS.-Sulph.-VERAT.
———— **Sick.**—IPEC.-NUX.-Verat.
———— **Spirituous Liquors, from.**—NUX.
———— **Vomiting, with.**—Bry.-IPEC.-NUX.-Puls.-VERAT.
———— **Wavering** (Sensation of) in the Head, with.—ACON.-BELL.-Calc.-CHIN.-NUX.-Rhus.-SULPH.
Heart, Congestion in the.—Acon.-Bell.-PULS.-SULPH.
———— **Inflammation of the.**—ACON.-Ars.
*———— **Rheumatism of the.**—ACON.-BELL.-Bry.-LACH.

The principal uses in the treatment of—
*****Heart, Rheumatism of the.**
Acon.—Palpitation with great anguish. Feverish heat. The heart beats rapidly while the pulse is slow and intermittent, &c.
Bell.—Palpitation with intermitting pulse. Great anguish, tremor, and pain. Oppression of the chest, &c.
Bry.—Respiration impeded by stitches in the chest, with palpitation and violent oppression, &c.
Lach.—Irregularity of the pulse. Great anguish with heaviness on the chest. Weakness, &c.

Heartburn.—CALC.-Chin.-NUX.-Phos.-Puls.-SULPH.

Heat, Dry.—ACON.-Arn.-ARS.-Bell.-BRY.-LACH.-MERC.-Nux.-PHOS.-PULS.-Rhus.-Sulph.

—— **External.**—Acon.-Arn.-ARS.-BELL.-Bry.-Merc.-Nux.-Phos.-Puls.-RHUS.-Sulph.

—— **Internal.**—ACON.-Arn.-ARS.-BELL.-BRY.-Calc.-Cham.-NUX.-Phos.-Puls.-RHUS.-Verat.

—— **Thirst, with.**—ACON.-Arn.-ARS.-Bell.-Bry.-CALC.-Cham.-HEP.-MERC.-RHUS.-SULPH.

—— **Thirst, without.**—ARS.-Chin.-Ipec.-Puls.

Heaviness in the Limbs.—ARN.-Bell.-Cham.-CHIN.-NUX.-Phos.-PULS.-RHUS.-Sulph.

*****Hectic Fever.**—Ars.-Bell.-Calc.-CHIN.-PHOS.-Sulph.

Hiccough (In general).—Acon.-Bell.-Bry.-NUX.-Puls.-Verat.

————— **Violent.**—BELL.-NUX.

†**Hip Gout.**—Acon.-BELL.-MERC.-Rhus.

The principal uses in the treatment of—
*****Hectic Fever.**

Ars.—Great debility. Night sweats. Thirst obliging one to drink frequently, but little at a time, &c.

Calc.—Frequent paroxysms of flushes of heat. Sweat breaking out easily. Great fear about one's health, &c.

Chin.—Great hunger. Fever attendant on consumption. If from debilitating losses or violent diseases, &c.

Phos.—Debilitating diarrhœa. Exhausting, clammy night sweats, &c.

Sulph.—Sharply circumscribed redness of the cheeks. Loose and slimy evacuations. Sour and fetid night sweats, &c.

†**Hip Gout.**

Acon.—Fever. Great inflammation, &c.

*Hip-joint Disease.—BELL.-MERC.-Rhus.
†Hoarseness (In general).—BELL.-Calc.-CARB.-Cham.-Merc.-Nux.-PHOS.-Puls.-SPONG.-SULPH.-Verat.
——————— Catarrhal.—Bell.-CHAM.-Merc.-Nux.-Phos.-Puls.-SULPH.
——————— Chronic.—Calc.-CARB.-PHOS.-SULPH.
——————— Cold Damp Weather, from.—CARB.-SULPH.

The principal uses in the treatment of—
Hip Gout, continued.
Bell.—Shooting and burning pains in the hip-joint. Worse from the least contact, &c.
Merc.—Sharp and cutting pains. Worse during movement or at night. Profuse nocturnal sweating, &c.
Rhus.—Pains with tension and stiffness. Worse during rest, &c.
*Hip-joint Disease.
Bell.—When there is great pain, &c.
Merc.—Little or no pain. Sallow complexion, &c.
Rhus.—Pains with tension and stiffness. Worse during rest, &c.
†Hoarseness.
Bell.—With tenacious mucus in the chest. With great soreness, redness, and dryness of the larynx. Voice weak, very hoarse, &c.
Carb.—Painful scraping of the voice. Worse after talking, or in damp and cold weather, &c.
Cham.—A good deal of phlegm in the throat. Tickling in the throat-pit, &c.
Merc.—Sometimes amounting to loss of voice. Worse in the evening. The throat feels dry. Nocturnal perspiration, &c.
Phos.—Roughness of the throat. Violent catarrh with hoarseness, &c.
Sulph.—Creeping in the larynx. Deep rough voice. Roughness. With pressure as from a plug or from a tumour in the throat, &c.
See Hoarseness, Catarrhal, &c.

Hoarseness, Cold in the Head, with.—CHAM.-Merc.-PULS.

——————— **Sore Throat, with.**—Bell.

*****Hooping Cough** (In general).—BELL.-DROS.-IPEC.-Puls.-Verat.

——————— ——— **Catarrhal Stage.**—Acon.-BELL.-Cham.-IPEC.-Nux.-Puls.-Verat.

——————— ——— **Convulsive Stage.**—DROS.-IPEC.-VERAT.

†**Hypochondriasis.**—CALC.-Chin.-NUX.-Phos.-SULPH.

The principal uses in the treatment of—
*****Hooping Cough.**
Acon.—With fever. Constant desire to cough. With anxiety and short breath. With burning pains in the larynx, &c.
Bell.—Spasmodic cough with marked head symptoms. Vomiting and bleeding from nose and mouth, &c.
Dros.—When fully developed, with vomiting of food or mucus, and bleeding from the mouth and nose. No fever, or else high fever, &c.
Ipec.—If from commencement, the cough is attended with suffocative symptoms and bluish face, &c.
Puls.—Cough moist with easy expectoration of serous mucus, &c.
Verat.—Great weakness. Vomiting of food. Suffocative fits. If *Dros.* has not perfectly sufficed, &c.
†**Hypochondriasis.**
Calc.—Despair about one's health. In scrofulous individuals. Incapacity for thought or any mental exertion whatever, &c.
Chin.—A fixed idea of being unhappy. Weak digestion with distension of the abdomen. Unrefreshing sleep. If from debilitating losses. Great apathy, &c.
Nux.—Disposition to be angry. Bewilderment of the head, with pressive pains as from a nail driven into the brain. Constipation. Constant desire to lie down. If from sedentary habits, &c.

*Hysterics.—Bell.-Bry.-Cham.-NUX.-PULS.-Sulph.

†Indigestion (In general).—Arn.-Bry.-IPEC.-Nux.-PULS.

——————— **Acids, Sufferings from.**—ARS.-CARB.-Puls.

——————— **Coffee, from.**—CHAM.-NUX.-Puls.-Sulph.

——————— **Cold Food, from.**—ARS.-NUX.-Rhus.-Verat.

——————— **Fat Meats, from.**—CARB.-Ipec.-PULS.

——————— **Fruits, from.**—ARS.-BRY.-CHIN.-PULS.-Verat.

——————— **Hot Food, from.**—Bry.-Phos.-PULS.

——————— **Pastry, from.**—PULS.

——————— **Wine, Spirits, &c., from.**—Ars.-NUX.-SULPH.

The principal uses in the treatment of—
Hypochondriasis, continued.
Phos.—Especially suited to thin slender constitutions. If arising from excesses, &c.
Sulph.—Painful anxiety of mind. Great bodily and mental indolence. Pressive headache. Constipation. Bewilderment of the head with unfitness for intellectual exertion, &c.

See Mental Emotions.

*Hysterics.
Nux.—Aching and dulness in the head. Constipation, &c.
Puls.—Especially when caused by suppression of the menses, or milk, &c.
Sulph.—Especially when complicated with liver complaints, or when arising from suppression of piles, &c.

†Indigestion.
If recent, see Sufferings from Acids, Coffee, &c.; also Sufferings after or during a Meal. If chronic, see Dyspepsia, also Gastric or Bilious Derangement, Headache, &c.

Indigestion, Chronic.—*See Dyspepsia.*
——————— **Debility, from.**—CHIN.-Nux.-Sulph.
*——————— **Flatulence from.**—CHIN.-NUX.-PULS.
†——————— **Spasms from.**—Bry.-NUX.-PULS.
‡**Infants, Acidity of.**—Bell.-CHAM.-Sulph.
§——————— **Asthma.**—Acon.-Bell.-CHAM.-IPEC.-PULS.

The principal uses in the treatment of—
*****Indigestion, Flatulence from.**
Chin.—With contraction of the intestines. In consequence of flatulent food. After eating pork or fat meats, &c.
Nux.—Abundant. Pressure in the stomach, &c.
Puls.—After fat meats. In hysterical females, &c.

†Indigestion, Spasms from.
Bry.—Painful pressure or disagreeable fulness, relieved by eructations or external pressure, &c.
Nux.—Contractive, pressive, and spasmodic pains. As if the stomach was clutched. The clothes feel tight, &c.
Puls.—Shooting spasmodic pains. Shiverings. Worse on movement, &c.
See Spasms in the Stomach.

‡Infants, Acidity of.
Bell.—Violent retching of mucous matter. Spasmodic hiccough, &c.
Cham.—Bitter vomiting. Bitter risings. Tossings about and restlessness, &c.
Sulph.—Continued empty eructations, &c.

§Infants, Asthma of.
Acon.—When the attack occurs suddenly at night with suffocating cough. Fever, &c.
Bell.—Great painfulness in the larynx with danger of suffocation when touching or turning the throat, coughing, or taking breath, &c.
Cham.—Distension of the stomach. Restlessness, &c.
Ipec.—Oppression of the chest with accumulation of mucus. Danger of suffocation. Bluish face. Rattling of mucus, &c.

*Infants, Cold in the Head of.—Cham.-NUX.-Sulph.
† ———— Colic.—Bell.-CHAM.-Ipec.
‡ ———— Constipation.—BRY.-NUX.
§ ———— Convulsions.—BELL.-CHAM.
‖ ———— Crying.—BELL.-CHAM.
¶ ———— Diarrhœa.—Calc.-CHAM.-Ipec.-Merc.-Sulph.

The principal uses in the treatment of—
Infants, Asthma of, continued.
Puls.—Worse at night, or when lying down, with desire to vomit and difficult expectoration of mucus, &c.
***Infants, Cold in the Head of.**
Cham.—Discharge of water from the nose, &c.
Nux.—Dry stoppage of the nose, &c.
Sulph.—If only temporary relief is obtained, &c.
†**Infants, Colic of.**
Bell.—If the face is pale, &c.
Cham.—If the legs are drawn up and the face is red, &c.
Ipec.—If with fermented diarrhœa and violent crying, &c.
‡**Infants, Constipation of.**
Bry.—Hard tough stool. Large-sized and passed with difficulty, &c.
Nux.—As if from inactivity of the bowels. Anxious and ineffectual urging to stool, &c.
§**Infants, Convulsions of.**
Bell.—Comatose condition. Dilated pupils, &c.
Cham.—Involuntary movement of the head. Redness of one cheek, &c. *See Spasms.*
‖**Infants, Crying of.**
Bell.—If the child cries for no perceptible cause.
Cham.—If there is headache, earache, &c.
¶**Infants, Diarrhœa of.**
Calc.—In obstinate cases, or in scrofulous or weakly children, &c.
Cham.—Colic. Red face. Greenish stools, &c.
Ipec.—If in summer time or with vomiting, &c.
Merc.—Griping before or during stool. Straining after each evacuation, &c.
Sulph.—In obstinate cases, &c.

***Infants, Excoriation of.**—Calc.-CHAM.-Chin.-Merc.-SULPH.
† ——— **Indigestion.**—IPEC.-Nux.-PULS.
‡ ——— **Jaundice.**—Cham.-Chin.-MERC.
§ ——— **Ophthalmia.**—ACON.-Cham.-Sulph.
‖ ——— **Red Gum** (Infant Rash).—ACON.-Cham.-BRY.-Sulph.
——— **Regurgitation of Milk.**—Cham.

The principal uses in the treatment of—
***Infants, Excoriation of.**
Cham.—Easily excoriated with great sensitiveness to the touch, &c.
Merc.—Violent itching. Worse at night or by the warmth of the bed, &c.
Sulph.—In obstinate cases, or if connected with a rash, &c.
†**Infants, Indigestion of.**
Ipec.—Vomiting with diarrhœa, &c.
Nux.—Vomiting with constipation, &c.
Puls.—If arising from pastry or rich foods, or if *Ipec.* is insufficient, &c.
‡**Infants, Jaundice of.**
Cham.—If from a chill or fit of passion, &c.
Chin.—If of an intermittent character or from abuse of mercury, &c.
Merc.—In most ordinary cases, &c.
§**Infants, Ophthalmia of.**
Acon.—If cold or exposure to a strong light is the cause. Eyes very red and inflamed, &c.
Cham.—Redness, swelling, and agglutination of the lids, &c.
Sulph.—In all kinds of obstinate inflammations, &c.
‖**Infants, Red Gum of.**
Acon.—Fever. Restlessness, &c.
Cham.—Great fretfulness and excitement, &c.
Bry.—Constipation, and distension of the bowels. Languor. White miliary eruptions, &c.
Sulph.—In most stages of the ailment, &c.

MEDICAL INDEX. 83

*Infants, Restlessness of.—ACON.-BELL.-CHAM.-COFF.
†————— Sleeplessness.—BELL.-COFF.
————— Weakness of Joints.—CALC.-Sulph.
For other Affections, refer under head in regular order.
Inflammation (In general).—ACON-Arn.-Ars-BELL.-BRY.-Cham.-MERC.-NUX.-PHOS.-Puls.-Sulph.
‡Inflammatory Fever.—ACON.-BELL.-BRY.-Cham.-Merc.-Nux.-Phos.-Puls.

The principal uses in the treatment of—
*Infants, Restlessness of.
Acon.—If from feverishness.
Bell.—Drowsiness with inability to sleep, &c.
Cham.—If with colic and screaming, &c.
Coff.—If from excitement, &c.
†Infants, Sleeplessness of.
Bell.—If the child seems inclined to sleep and cannot, but starts and cries. If from no perceptible cause, &c.
Coff.—In most cases suitable. Excitability, &c.
‡Inflammatory Fever.
Acon.—Burning heat. Skin dry. Burning thirst. Great restlessness. Full, hard, or suppressed pulse. Hot and red face, or alternately red and pale when the patient raises himself. Oppression of the chest with short breathing. Palpitation of the heart. Nightly delirium, &c.
Bell.—Internal and external heat. Loss of consciousness. Violent delirium. Dilated pupils. Dread of light. Burning thirst. Sleepiness in the day time with sleeplessness at night. Sudden starting during sleep. Deep redness of the face and eyes, &c.
Bry.—Great heat or chill with chattering of teeth. Delirium day and night. Great general debility, &c.
Cham.—Heat of face and redness of cheeks or only of one cheek. Burning thirst. Great anguish, tension, and pressure in the region of the stomach. Bitter taste, &c.
Merc.—Chills alternating with heat. Burning thirst. Stitching and aching pains in the head, &c.

*Influenza.—Acon.-ARS.-Bell.-Merc.-Nux.

†Intermittent Fever (Ague).—Acon.-ARS.-Bell.-Bry.-Calc.-CHIN.-Ipec.-NUX.-Puls.-RHUS.-Sulph.

The principal uses in the treatment of—
Inflammatory Fever, continued.

Nux.—Heat especially in the face. Dry and white tongue. Pressive headache aggravated by stooping. Constipation. Excitability of the whole nervous system. Pressive pain in the stomach. Sensation as if the limbs had been beaten, &c.

Puls.—Total absence of, or insatiable thirst, &c.

See Bilious, Gastric, Hectic, or Typhus Fever, &c.

*Influenza.

Acon.—In a decided inflammatory stage, &c.

Ars.—Fluent and corrosive discharge from the nose. Great debility, &c.

Bell.—Spasmodic cough. Violent headache, &c.

Merc.—Rheumatic pains in the head, face, ears, and teeth. Fluent cold in the head. Violent shaking cough, &c.

Nux.—Cough with rattling of thick mucus. Heaviness of the head. Nausea. Giddiness, &c.

†Intermittent Fever.

Acon.—Violent heat and chill, &c.

Ars.—Burning heat. Heat and chilliness slightly developed. Great debility. Violent pains in the stomach, also in the limbs, &c.

Bell.—Chill and cold of some parts with heat in other parts of the body, &c.

Bry.—If heat prevails, with subsequent chilliness. Headache and giddiness. Coated tongue. Very great thirst, &c.

Chin.—Thirst generally before or after the chill and heat, or during the sweating, or during the entire duration of the paroxysm; or else no thirst, tendency of blood to the head, headache, and paleness of face during the chill. Yellow skin. When sweating is the prevailing symptom, &c.

Ipec.—If the chill is increased by external heat. Vomiting and other gastric symptoms, &c.

*Itch (In general).—Ars.-CARB.-MERC.-SULPH.-Verat.
—— Bleeding.—MERC.-Sulph.
—— Dry.—Calc.-MERC.-Sulph.-Verat.
—— Suppressed.—Chin.-Merc.-Sulph.

†Jaundice (In general).—Acon.-Bell.-Bry.-Cham.-Chin.-MERC.-NUX.-Sulph.

The principal uses in the treatment of—
Intermittent Fever, continued.
Nux.—In case of great debility and loss of power at the commencement. Coldness and blueness of the skin. Heat about the head and face, red cheeks and thirst, &c.
Puls.—Aggravation in the afternoon or evening. Gastric or bilious symptoms, &c.
Rhus.—Pains in the limbs during the chill. Convulsive twitchings of the limbs, &c.
Sulph.—Ague following the suppression of eruptions, or after the abuse of quinine, &c.
*Itch.
Ars.—In watery itch, &c.
Carb.—Dry, rash-like itch. If the vesicles are small, &c.
Merc.—Violent itching at night. Readily bleeding itch, &c.
Sulph.—A specific in uncomplicated itch, aided by *sulphur ointment* externally.
Verat.—Dry itch with nightly itching, &c.
†Jaundice.
Acon.—If the fever is high, &c.
Bell.—Convulsions; spasms; violent fever, &c.
Bry.—If caused by passion, or arising from chronic inflammation of the liver. For the dyspeptic symptoms which sometimes remain, &c.
Cham.—If caused by chagrin, irregular diet, cold, &c.
Chin.—When the region of the liver is painful to the touch. Want of appetite, &c.
Merc.—In most cases useful.
Nux.—If from sedentary habits, or spirituous liquors. Constipation, &c.
Sulph.—In obstinate cases, &c.

Jaundice, Anger, from.—Acon.-CHAM.-NUX.
———— Mercury, from.—CHIN.-Sulph.
Jaw, Hanging down of the.—BELL.
——— Spasms of the.—BELL.-Nux.-Verat.
Joints, Pains, Bruise as from a, in the.—ARN.-CHIN.-NUX.-PULS.
————— ————— Cramplike.—Bell.-Bry.-CALC.-Merc.-Sulph.
————— ————— Drawing.—Acon.-Calc.-Chin.-MERC.-Phos.-RHUS.-SULPH.
————— ————— Gouty, Rheumatic.—Arn.-Bell.-BRY.-Calc.-MERC.-Phos.-Puls.-RHUS.
————— ————— Pricking.—Arn.-Bell.-CALC.-MERC.-Phos.-RHUS.-Sulph.
————— ————— Shooting.—Bell.-MERC.-Puls.-RHUS.-SULPH.
————— ————— Sprain, as from a.—ARN.-Bry.-Calc.-Merc.-PHOS.-PULS.-RHUS.-SULPH.
————— ————— Tearing.—ACON.-Bry.-CALC.-Chin.-MERC.-Phos.-RHUS.-SULPH.
————— Rigidity of the.—Bell.-BRY.-Chin.-Nux.-RHUS.-Sulph.
————— Weakness in the.—Acon.-ARN.-Bry.-CALC.-CHIN.-MERC.-Nux.-Phos.-RHUS.-SULPH.

*Kidneys, Inflammation of the.—Bell.-CANTH.-NUX.-Puls.
————————— Pains, Pressive, in the.—Nux.
————————— ————— Shooting.—Bell.-CANTH.-Chin.

The principal uses in the treatment of—
*Kidneys, Inflammation of the.
Bell.—Shooting pains in the kidneys extending to the bladder, with great anguish and colic, &c.
Canth.—Shooting, tearing, and cutting with painful discharge of urine by drops. Urine mixed with blood. Cramplike pains in the bladder, &c.

MEDICAL INDEX. 87

*Knee, Inflammation of the.—Arn.-Calc.-Puls.-Sulph.
——————— Serous Effusion, with.—Merc.-Rhus.-SULPH.
——————— Suppuration, with.—Hep.-Merc.-Rhus.
—— Pains, Shooting, in the.—Acon.-Calc.-Puls.-Sulph.
—— —— Tearing.—Acon.-Bell.-Chin-Phos.-Puls.-Sulph.
—— Rigidity of the.—Bry.-Rhus.-Sulph.
—— Swelling of the.—Bry.-Calc.-Chin.-Puls.-Sulph.
—— Weakness of the.—Chin.-Puls.
Knee-joint, Dropsy of the.—Merc.-SULPH.

†Labour, Pains ceasing during.—Bell.-Cham.-Nux.-PULS.

The principal uses in the treatment of—
Kidneys, Inflammation of the, continued.
Nux.—When caused by suppression of piles or congestion to the abdomen, with tension, distension, and pressure, &c.
Puls.—Bloody urine with purulent sediment. When accompanied with suppressed or scanty menstruation in delicate females, &c.
*Knee, Inflammation of the.
Arn.—Gouty inflammation. Pale swelling of the knee, &c.
Calc.—Shootings in the knees. Swelling of the knee, &c.
Puls.—Lacerating pains in the knees like jerks. Hot swelling of the knee with stinging, &c.
Sulph.—Gouty inflammation. Large and shining swelling of the knees with shootings, &c.
†Labour-Pains.
Cham.—Fruitless, spasmodic, labour pains. Convulsions or spasms during the pains. Too acute and too long. Pressure towards the parts, &c.

MEDICAL INDEX.

Labour-Pains, strong, too.—Bell.-CHAM.-COFF.-Nux.
———————— **weak, too.**—Bell.-Cham.-Nux.-PULS.
Labour, Spasms during.—BELL.-Cham.-Ipec.
Larynx & Bronchia, (*Upper part of the Windpipe.*)
———————— **Burning in the.**—Ars.-Lach.-Merc.-Phos.-Spong.
———————— **Dryness in the.**—Ars.-PHOS.-SPONG.
***Larynx, Inflammation of the.**—ACON.-Cham.-HEP.-Nux.-Phos.-SPONG.

The principal uses in the treatment of—
Labour-Pains, continued.
Coff.—Violent pains driving the patient to despair, &c.
Nux.—Pains without progress of the labour and accompanied by a constant urging to stool or to urinate. Cramplike contractive pains and pressure towards the parts, &c.
Puls.—Inactivity of the uterus after the birth; the removal of the afterbirth does not take place duly. Labour pains succeeding each other slowly with violent spasms, &c.

***Larynx, Inflammation of the.**
Acon.—Fever. Oppressed respiration. Croupy cough, &c.
Cham.—Worse at night. Tittilation from phlegm in the air passages, &c.
Hep.—Hoarseness, pain, and great sensitiveness of the larynx, with weak and rough voice, &c.
Nux.—Cough rough and dry, and attended with bruised pain in the abdomen which is painful to the touch, &c.
Phos.—Heat and dryness of the larynx. Cough with bloody mucus, &c.
Spong.—Hoarseness with cough and cold. Pain in the larynx on touching it, and on turning the head. Weak voice which fails in singing and in conversation, &c.

MEDICAL INDEX.

Larynx, Inflammation, Chronic, of the.—Ars.-Calc.-Nux.-PHOS.
— Mucus in the.—Ars.-Calc.-CHAM.-Nux.-Phos.-Sulph.
— Pains, Shooting, in the.—PHOS.
— Plug (Sensation as of a) in the.—BELL.
— Roughness in the.—Nux.-PHOS.-Puls.-SULPH.

Legs, Cramps in the.—CALC.-CHAM.-Sulph.-Verat.
— Pains, Aching, in the.—Acon.-Bry.-Calc.-Merc.-Nux.-Verat.
— — Burning.—CARB.
— — Drawing.—Bry.-Calc.-Cham.-Chin.-MERC.-Phos.-Puls.-Rhus.-SULPH.
— — Shooting.—Bry.-Sulph.
— — Tearing.—Chin.-Merc.-Phos.-Rhus.-Sulph.
— Paralysis of the.—Bell.-Nux.-RHUS.
— Rigidity of the.—Bry.-Calc.-Nux.-Rhus.
— Swelling of the.—BRY.-Calc.-LACH.-Merc.-Puls.
— Tension in the.—Bry.-Puls.-Rhus.
— Trembling of the.—Ars.-BELL.-Nux.-Puls.
— Weakness of the.—Nux. Phos.-Sulph.

*Leucorrhœa (Whites), In general.—Ars.-CALC.-Chin.-Merc.-Phos.-PULS.-Sulph.

The principal uses in the treatment of—
*Leucorrhœa.

Ars.—Acrid, corrosive, thick, or yellowish leucorrhœa, &c.

Calc.—Burning, itching leucorrhœa. Like milk. Flowing before the menses. Flowing by fits, &c.

Chin.—Bloody. With painful pressure on the groin and anus, &c.

G

Lips, Bloated.—Arn.-BELL.-Bry.-Merc.-Rhus.
— **Chaps in the.**—Arn.-Ars.-Bry.-Calc.-Cham.-Chin.-MERC.-Nux.-Puls.-Verat.
— **Convulsions of the.**—Bell.-Cham.-Ipec.
— **Dryness of the.**—Acon.-Bell.-BRY.-CHIN.-Merc.-NUX.-PHOS.-Rhus.-Sulph.-Verat.
— **Ulceration of the.**—Ars.-Bell.-Merc.-Sulph.
Liver, Induration of the.—Ars.-CHIN.-Nux.-Sulph.
*— **Inflammation of the.**—ACON.-Bell.-BRY.-Cham.-Chin.-MERC.-NUX.-Puls.-Sulph.
— —————— **Chronic.**—Bry.-Calc.-Chin.-NUX.-SULPH.

The principal uses in the treatment of—
Leucorrhœa, continued.
Merc.—Mild or acrid, whitish, purulent, or corrosive. Discharge of mucous and purulent flocks, &c.
Phos.—Mucous, &c.
Puls.—Thick. Corrosive and burning, or with cutting, shivering, and pains in the back. When occurring during the menses, &c.
Sulph.—Corrosive or yellowish. Preceded by cutting colic or pinching around the navel, &c.
***Liver, Inflammation of the.**
Acon.—Violent inflammatory fever. Shooting pains, &c.
Bell.—Great thirst, tossing about, and sleeplessness. Aching pains extending to the chest and shoulder, &c.
Bry.—Violent oppression of the chest with hurried and anxious breathing. Worse during motion, &c.
Cham.—When there are dull, aching pains not aggravated by external pressure, motion or breathing. Yellow colour of the skin. When brought on by violent chagrin or cold, &c.
Chin.—Shooting and pressing pains, swelling and hardness in the region of the liver, &c.
Merc.—Pressive pains which do not allow to lie on the right side. Very yellow colour of the skin and eyes, &c.
Nux.—Excessive tenderness of the region of the liver. Pressure in the stomach. Constipation, &c.

Liver, Painful Sensibility in the.—ACON.-MERC.-NUX.
—— Pains, Burning, in the.—Acon.-Bry.-Merc.
—— —— Pressive.—Chin.-Nux.
—— —— Shooting.—Acon.-Bry.-Chin.-Merc.-Nux.-Sulph.
—— Pressure in the.—Acon.-Chin.-Nux.
*Lock-jaw.—Arn.-Ars.-BELL.-Nux.-Verat.
Loins, Pains in the.—Bry.-CALC.-NUX.-Puls.-Sulph.
—— —— Bruise, as from a.—Acon.-Arn.-Chin.-Merc.-NUX.-Phos.-Verat.
—— —— Rheumatic.—Nux.-Sulph.
—— —— Shooting.—Puls.-Sulph.
—— Rigidity of the.—Rhus.-Sulph.
—— Swelling of the.—Bell.-Rhus.-Sulph.
†Lumbago.—Bry.-NUX.-Puls.-RHUS.-Sulph.

The principal uses in the treatment of—
Liver, Inflammation of the, continued.
Puls.—Frequent attacks of anguish, especially at night, with diarrhœa, &c.
Sulph.—Shootings in the side. In obstinate cases, &c.
*Lock-jaw.
Arn.—If arising from an injury, &c.
Bell.—Constriction in the throat. Spasmodic clenching of the jaws. Distortion of the mouth, &c.
Nux.—Lock-jaw with perfect consciousness, &c.
See Spasms.
†**Lumbago.**
Bry.—Pains worse during motion, &c.
Nux.—Constipation. Indigestion. Back feels fatigued, &c.
Puls.—If caused by menstrual suppression or irregularity, &c.
Rhus.—If caused by exposure to wet or suppressed perspiration, &c.

92   MEDICAL INDEX.

*Lungs, Hæmorrhage from the.—ACON.-Arn.-Chin.-IPEC.-PHOS.-Puls.-Sulph.

———— **Inflammation of the.**—*See Pneumonia.*

Lying-in (After Confinement).—*See After-Pains.*

———— **Colic.**—Bell.-Bry.-CHAM.-Nux.-Puls.-Verat.

———— **Constipation.**—BRY.-NUX.

———— **Convulsions.**—Bell.-Cham.

———— **Debility.**—Calc.-Chin.

For other Affections refer under head in regular order.

Meal, Sufferings after or during a.

———— **Diarrhœa.**—ARS.-CHIN.-Verat.

———— **Distension.**—Calc.-CARB.-Cham.-CHIN.-LACH.-Merc.-NUX.-Phos.-Rhus.-Sulph.

———— **Eructations.**—Bry.-Calc.-Chin.-Merc.-Nux.-Phos.-Sulph.-Verat.

The principal uses in the treatment of—
Lumbago, continued.

Sulph.—Chronic. Frequently useful during the treatment, &c.

See Rheumatism.

*Lungs, Hæmorrhage from the.

Acon.—When there is congestion of blood in the chest. Profuse expectoration of blood at intervals, excited by a very slight cough. When there is imminent danger, &c.

Arn.—If caused by a blow, fall, or mechanical injury, &c.

Chin.—In extremely dangerous cases. For the debility following, &c.

Ipec.—If after *Acon.* a constant taste of blood, with short cough remains. Also in serious cases, &c.

Phos.—In consumptive young people, with great irritation of the bronchia and dry irritating cough, &c.

Puls.—Discharge of black coagulated blood. Difficulty of breathing. If from the suppression of the menses, &c.

Sulph.—Frequently to prevent relapses, &c.

See Hæmorrhage.

Meal, Headache (after or during a).—Chin.-NUX.

—— **Heartburn.**—Calc.-Chin.-Merc.-NUX.-SULPH.

—— **Lassitude.**—Chin.-Phos.-SULPH.

—— **Nausea.**—Ars.-Bry.-NUX.-Phos.-PULS.-Rhus.-Sulph.

—— **Pains in the Abdomen.**—ARS.-Bry.-Chin.-NUX.-PULS.-Rhus.-Sulph.

—— —————— **Stomach.**—Acon.-ARS.-Bell.-Bry.-Calc.-Phos.-Puls.

—— **Regurgitation.**—BRY.-Merc.-NUX.-Phos.-Puls.

—— **Vertigo** (Giddiness).—Cham.-LACH.-NUX.-PULS.

—— **Vomiting.**—ARS.-NUX.-Puls.-Sulph.-Verat.

—— **Waterbrash.**—SULPH.

—— **Weakness.**—Chin.-SULPH.

*****Measles** (In general).—ACON.-Bell.-Bry.-Ipec.-Phos.-PULS.-Rhus.

The principal uses in the treatment of—
*****Measles.**

Acon.—Fever. Sleeplessness. Dread of light. Short, dry and hollow cough. Shootings in the side and chest. In the early stage of the disease, &c.

Bell.—Sore throat. Aching pains in the forehead. Delirium. Violent thirst, &c.

Bry.—Rheumatic pains in the limbs. Cough and stitches in the chest, &c.

Ipec.—Gastric symptoms with fever. Coated tongue. Nausea, &c.

Phos.—Typhoid symptoms with loss of consciousness. Watery diarrhœa. Great debility, &c.

Puls.—In almost every stage of the disease. To facilitate the eruption. Catarrhal affections. Internal and external inflammation of the ear. Dread of light, &c.

Rhus.—Typhoid symptoms, livid colour of the skin, fading away and unhealthy character of the eruption, &c.

MEDICAL INDEX.

Measles, Eruption (to facilitate the).—ACON.-PULS.
—————— Gastric Derangement, with.—Cham.-Ipec.-PULS.
—————— Head Symptoms, with.—BELL.-Merc.
—————— Intolerance of Light, with.—Acon.-BELL.-Phos.-Puls.-Rhus.
—————— Malignant.—Ars.-Phos.-Puls.-Rhus.-Sulph.
—————— Retrocession of.—Ars.-BRY.-Phos.-Puls.
—————— Typhoid Symptoms.—BELL.-Nux.-Phos.-RHUS.

Menstruation, Delay of.—PULS.-SULPH.
—————————— too Late.—Acon.-Merc.-Phos.-PULS.-SULPH.
—————————— too Long.—Acon.-Bry.-Chin.-NUX.-Phos.-Rhus.
*————————— Painful.—Ars.-Bell.-CHAM.-NUX.-Phos.-PULS.

The principal uses in the treatment of—
*Menstruation, Painful.

Bell.—Pressing down in the abdomen as if everything would press out. Colic and cloudiness of sight preceding the menses, &c.

Cham.—When the pains resemble labour-pains, with pressure from the small of the back extending to the abdomen and downwards, &c.

Nux.—Forcing pains. Nausea with fainting, especially early in the morning, Congestion of blood in the head, giddiness, great debility, &c.

Puls.—Nausea. Colic. Pain in the small of the back. Discharge of black and coagulated blood. Sour or mucous vomiting, &c.

MEDICAL INDEX.

*Menstruation, Profuse.—Acon.-Ars.-BELL.-Bry.-CALC.-Cham.-Chin.-IPEC.-Merc.-NUX. Phos.-Verat.

———————— too Short.—Phos.-PULS.-Sulph.

———————— too Small in quantity.—Nux.-PULS.-SULPH.

———————— too Soon.—Bell.-CALC.-Cham.-Ipec.-NUX.-PHOS.-RHUS.-Sulph.-Verat.

†———————— Suppressed.—Acon.-Ars.-Bry.-Cham.-Merc.-PULS.-SULPH.

Menstruation, Discharge, Coagulated.—Bell.-CHAM.-Chin.-Ipec.-Puls.-Rhus.

The principal uses in the treatment of—
*Menstruation, Profuse.

Acon.—Especially in plethoric constitutions.

Bell.—When too profuse with violent pressure downwards, with pains in the small of the back, &c.

Calc.—In obstinate cases, &c.

Cham.—Blood dark and clotted; flowing at intervals. Labourlike pains, &c.

Chin.—Great weakness. Faintness. Gushing at intervals with spasmodic pains, &c.

Ipec.—Where the discharge is profuse and continued. Flooding, &c.

Nux.—Spasms in the abdomen. Nausea and fainting. Pains in the limbs, &c.

Verat.—When attended with diarrhœa, &c.

†Menstruation, Suppressed.

Acon.—Especially in young girls who lead a sedentary life. In plethoric individuals. If from fright, &c.

Ars.—Great debility. Pale, livid complexion, &c.

Bry.—Stitches in the chest. Vertigo. Constipation, &c.

Cham.—Great sensitiveness of the abdomen. Greenish diarrhœa. Desire to vomit. Bitter taste in mouth, &c.

Merc.—Great languor and debility, with trembling and rushes of blood to the head after the least exertion, &c.

Puls.—From getting wet or catching cold. Palpitation of the heart. Leucorrhœa. In individuals of a mild disposition. Nausea or actual vomiting, &c.

Menstruation, Discharge, Dark Coloured.—Bry.-CHAM.-Nux.-Puls.

——————— ——————— **Offensive.**—BELL.-Bry.-Cham.

——————— ——————— **Pale.**—BELL.-Phos.-Rhus.

Menstruation, Headache before.—SULPH.-Verat.

——————— **Nausea, with.**—Ars.-Nux.-Puls.

——————— **Pains** in the Abdomen (with).—Calc.-PULS.

——————— **Pains in the Loins.**—Ars.-Phos.-Puls.-Sulph.

——————— **Spasms, with.**—Cham.-Puls.

——————— **Vomiting, with.**—Ars.-Puls.

——————— **Weakness, with.**—Calc.-Nux.-Phos.

Mental and Moral Emotions.

—— **Absence of Mind.**—Acon.-CHAM.-Nux.-PULS.

—— **Anxiety.**—ACON.-Arn.-ARS.-Bell.-Bry.-Calc.-CHAM.-Chin.-Merc.-Nux.-Phos.-PULS.-Rhus.-Sulph.-Verat.

—— **Consciousness Lost.**—Arn.-BELL.-Nux.-Puls.-Rhus.

—— **Delirium.**—Acon.-Arn.-Ars.-BELL.-BRY.-Verat.

—— **Excitement.**—Cham.-COFF.-Nux.

—— **Fearfulness.**—ACON.-ARS.-Bell.-BRY.-Calc.-Nux.-Phos.-Puls.-Verat.

The principal uses in the treatment of—
Menstruation, Suppressed, continued.

Sulph.—Pressive and tensive headache, especially at the back part of the head. Diarrhœic mucous stools, or constipation. Great languor particularly in the lower limbs. Pressure, feeling of fulness and weight in the stomach, &c.

MEDICAL INDEX. 97

Mental and Moral Emotions.
——— Fretful.—Bell.-Calc.-CHAM.-Merc.-Nux.-Phos.-PULS.-SULPH.
——— Irritability.—Ars.-Bell.-Bry.-CHAM.-COFF.-NUX.-Phos.-Sulph.-Verat.
——— Madness.—Ars.-BELL.-Merc.-Sulph.-VERAT.
——— Passionate.—CHAM.-Merc.-NUX.-Phos.
——— Raving.—BELL.-Bry.-Puls.-Verat.
——— Sadness.—ACON.-Calc.-Phos.-Puls.-Rhus.
——— Variableness.—ACON.-Puls.-Sulph.
*Mercury, Sufferings from.—Bell.-Calc.-CARB.-Chin.-HEP.-LACH.-Puls.-Rhus.-SULPH.
†Miliary Fever.—ACON.-Ars.-Bell.-BRY.-Cham.-IPEC.-MERC.-Puls.-Rhus.

The principal uses in the treatment of—
*Mercury, Sufferings from.
Carb.—Affections of the mouth and gums. Sore throat. Rheumatic pains. Great sensitiveness to change of weather, &c.
Hep.—Falling off of the hair. Ulcerated gums. Disposition of the skin to ulcerate. Nervous debility and excitement, &c.
Lach.—Sore throat. Nervous debility. Ulcers, &c.
Sulph.—Ulcers. Affections of the bones. Rheumatic pains. Sore throat. Affections of the gums, &c.
†Miliary Fever.
Acon.—Heat, thirst, and inflammatory symptoms, &c.
Ars.—If the breaking out of the eruption is accompanied with great distress, &c.
Bell.—If the head is affected, &c.
Bry.—When it occurs in lying-in women. Constipation, &c.
Cham.—In infants, &c.
Ipec.—Sudden suppression or tardy developement of the eruption with asthmatic sufferings, &c.
Merc.—Irritation, aggravated by warmth, &c.
Puls.—If with gastric symptoms, &c.

Milk, Deficient.—Acon.-CALC.-Puls.-Rhus.

‡—— **Excessive flow of.**—BELL.-BRY.-CALC.-Phos.-PULS.-Rhus.

—— **Offensive to the Child.**—MERC.

*—— **Suppression of.**—Bell.-Bry.-PULS.-Rhus.

—— **Stop (to) the Secretion of** (when Weaning).—Calc.-PULS.-Rhus.

†**Milk-Crust.**—Bell.-Calc.-Merc.-RHUS.

The principal uses in the treatment of—
‡**Milk, Excessive flow of.**
Bell.—When the breasts are full and hard and there are pulsations in them. Inflammation, &c.
Bry.—Breasts swollen, hard, and knotty, &c.
Calc.—When the breasts are constantly loaded with milk. When connected with a debilitated state of the system, &c.
Puls.—If accompanied with scanty or retarded menstruation, &c.
Rhus.—Painful distension of the breasts, with rheumatic pains throughout the system, &c.
***Milk, Suppression of.**
Bell.—If caused by a chill, or if the abdominal organs become affected, &c.
Bry.—If the breasts become hard and knotty, &c.
Puls.—From a chill. In most cases. Chronic effects, &c.
Rhus.—For the chronic consequences of the retrocession of the milk, &c.
†**Milk-Crust.**
Bell.—If the eruption suddenly dries up and the child becomes drowsy with head symptoms, &c.
Calc.—When dry and tedious, &c.
Merc.—Great irritation. Readily bleeding after scratching, &c.
Rhus.—If the eruption is on a dry surface. Burning itching, &c.

*Milk Fever.—ACON.-BRY.-Cham.-COFF.-Puls.-Rhus.
Milk-Leg.—Ars.-Bell.-BRY.-Puls.-RHUS.-Sulph.
†Miscarriage, Disposition to.—CALC.-SULPH.
‡——————— Precursors of, for the.—Bell.-CHAM.-Ipec.
——————— the Consequences of.—Bell.-Cham.-CHIN.-Ipec.
Morning (Sufferings worse in the), In general.— Acon.-Arn.-CALC.-CARB.-NUX.-PHOS.-Rhus.-Verat.
Mouth, Dryness in the.—Acon.-Ars.-BELL.-BRY.-CHAM.-Nux.-Phos.-Puls.-Rhus.-Verat.

The principal uses in the treatment of—
*Milk Fever.
Acon.—Deficiency of milk with tension, redness, and pulsations in the breasts, and fever, &c.
Bry.—Oppressed and laboured breathing, great headache, and constipation. Rheumatic pains in the breasts, &c.
Cham.—If caused by a violent emotion or a chill. Great nervous excitement, &c.
Coff.—If arising from violent mental emotions.
Puls.—If from taking cold, &c.
Rhus.—Extreme fulness, tension, and painfulness of the breasts with excessive secretion of milk. Rheumatic pains, &c.
†Miscarriage, Disposition to.
Calc.—Disposition to leucorrhœa. In plethoric persons in whom the menses are too profuse and premature, &c.
Sulph.—Premature and profuse menstruation, or where the discharge is scanty and retarded, with leucorrhœa. Disposition to piles, &c.
‡Miscarriage, Precursors of, for the.
Bell.—Violent pressive pains in the whole of the abdomen, the small of the back feels broken, &c.
Cham.—Violent cutting pains from the loins to the abdomen, with frequent desire to pass urine, or to go to stool, &c.
Ipec.—In case of spasms without loss of consciousness, &c.

Mouth, Excoriation of the.—Merc.-Phos.
———— **Frothing at the.**—BELL.-Cham.-Verat.
———— **Inflammation of the.**—Bell.-MERC.-Nux.
———— **Mucus in the.**—BELL.-MERC.-NUX.-Phos.-Puls.-Rhus.-Sulph.
———— **Saliva** (accumulation of) in the.—BELL.-Bry.-Calc.-MERC.-Nux.-PHOS.-Puls.-Rhus.-Sulph.-Verat.
*———— **Scurvy of the.**—MERC.-NUX.
———— **Ulcers in the.**—MERC.-Nux.

Movement (Sufferings increased by) In general.—ACON.-Arn.-BELL.-BRY.-Cham.-Chin.-Ipec.-Merc.-NUX.-Phos.
————— (Sufferings relieved by) In general.—Ars.-Chin.-LACH.-Puls.-RHUS.

Mucous Fever.—Ipec.-MERC.-Nux.-PULS.

†**Mumps.**—Bell.-MERC.-Nux.-Puls.
———— **Head symptoms, with.**—BELL.

Muscles, Jerking of the.—Bell.-Cham.-Chin.-Nux.-Phos.-RHUS.-SULPH.
———— **Pains, Cramp-like, in the.**—Arn.-BELL.-CALC.-CIN.-MERC.-RHUS.-Sulph.

The principal uses in the treatment of—
***Mouth, Scurvy of the.**
Merc.—Red, spongy, receding, ulcerated gums. Burning pains at night. Loose teeth. Inflamed, sore, ulcerated tongue and mouth. Fetid and even bloody saliva, &c.
Nux.—Foul and painful swelling of the gums. Fetid odour from the mouth. In sedentary habits. Constipation, &c.

†**Mumps.**
Bell.—Erysipelatous inflammation. Fever. Delirium, &c.
Merc.—Inflammatory swelling and painful sensibility of the glands, &c.

Muscles, Pains, Pricking, in the.—Arn.-BELL.-BRY.-CALC.-CHIN.-MERC.-Phos.-PULS.-RHUS.-SULPH.
— — **Shooting.**—ACON.-ARN.-Bell.-BRY.-Calc.-Chin.-MERC.-Nux.-Phos.-PULS.-RHUS.-SULPH.
— — **Tearing.**—Ars.-Bell.-Bry.-CALC.-CARB.-CHIN.-MERC.-Phos.-PULS.-SULPH.
— **Relaxation of the.**—Acon.-CALC.-Cham.-Sulph.
— **Tension of the.**—ACON.-NUX.-PHOS.-Rhus.-Sulph.

Nausea (In general).—ARS.-Bell.-Cham.-Chin.-IPEC.-LACH.-Merc.-NUX.-Phos.-PULS.-Rhus.-SULPH.-VERAT.
— **Headache, with.**—Acon.-Merc.-Nux.
— **Meal, after a.**—Ars.-Bry.-NUX.-Phos.-PULS.-Rhus.-Sulph.

Near-Sightedness.—Calc.-PHOS.-PULS.-Sulph.

Neck, (Glands of the) Inflamed.—Bell.-MERC.-Phos.
— — **Painful.**—Arn.-BELL.-MERC.-Phos.
— — **Swelling.**—BELL.-Cham.-MERC.-PHOS.-Sulph.
— **Pains Rheumatic in the.**—Bry.
— **Stiffness of the.**—BELL.-BRY.
— — **Nape of the.**—Acon.-BELL.-Bry.-CARB.-PHOS.-Rhus.-Sulph.
— **Swelling of the Nape of the.**—BELL.-Puls.
— **Tension in the Nape of the.**—Bry.-Puls.

***Nervous Debility.**—Bell.-Calc.-CHIN.-NUX.-PHOS.-PULS.-Rhus.-Sulph.-Verat.

†**Nervous Excitement.**—Acon.-BELL.-CHAM.-Chin.-COFF.-Merc.-NUX.-Puls.-Sulph.

‡**Nettlerash.**—ACON.-Ars.-Bell.-BRY.-Calc.-Puls.-RHUS.-SULPH.-Verat.

The principal uses in the treatment of—
***Nervous Debility.**
Chin.—Great debility with trembling. Excessive sensibility of the whole nervous system. If from debilitating losses, &c.
Nux.—Inclination to remain lying down. Repugnance to the open air. If from study, a sedentary life, wine, spirits, &c.
Phos.—Excessive sensibility of all the senses. Tendency to start. If arising from excesses, &c.
Puls.—Most suitable for females or persons of a mild and easy temperament, &c.
†**Nervous Excitement.**
Acon.—Excitability of the organs of sight and hearing. Agitation and tossing about. Palpitation of the heart. In young girls of a plethoric habit and leading a sedentary life, &c.
Bell.—Great irritability of the senses. Immoderate laughter, &c.
Cham.—Tendency to faint from the least suffering. Disconsolate, with tossing about, &c.
Coff.—Extreme sensitiveness to the least pain. Sleeplessness. Excessive mirthfulness and liveliness, &c.
Nux.—Extreme excitement. Timidity, &c.
See Mental Emotions.
‡**Nettlerash.**
Acon.—Fever, &c.
Ars.—In very severe cases. After eating unripe fruit,&c.
Bell.—If the head is affected. Headache, &c.
Bry.—If the eruption suddenly disappears and is followed by difficulty of breathing. In infants. In lying-in women. Especially round the joints, &c.
Calc.—If the rash passes off in the cool air, &c.

Nettlerash, Chronic.—ARS.-CALC.-HEP.-Rhus.-Sulph.

*Neuralgia.—ACON.-Arn.-ARS.-Bell.-Bry.-Cham.-Chin.-Merc.-NUX.-Phos.-PULS.-Rhus.-Verat.

The principal uses in the treatment of—
Nettlerash, continued.

Hep.—When attended with severe catarrhal symptoms, &c.

Puls.—If caused by eating rich or fat food, &c.

Rhus.—When produced by fish or unwholesome articles of diet. If caused by damp weather, &c.

Sulph.—If not permanently relieved by other medicines, &c.

*Neuralgia.

Acon.—Intolerable pains, especially at night. Feverishness. Great sensibility of the whole nervous system. Fear of death. In plethoric persons, &c.

Arn.—In neuralgia depending upon a mechanical cause. Aching, bruised pains. Worse by the least exertion or noise, &c.

Ars.—Burning, tearing, pains, so unbearable as to drive one to despair. Great weakness. Sensation of coldness or of burning heat in the parts affected, &c.

Bell.—Shooting, burning pains, worse by motion, light, or noise. Violent cutting pains when rubbing the part. In plethoric persons, &c.

Bry.—Aching or drawing and tearing pains. Worse during movement. Disposition to rheumatism, &c.

Cham.—Drawing and pulsative pains with torpor of the part affected. Great sensibility to the least pain. Fainting. Restlessness, &c.

Chin.—Great sensitiveness of the skin. Worse by the least touch. If arising from abuse of mercury, &c.

Merc.—In persons subject to rheumatism. Worse at night. Tearing and shooting pains, &c.

Nux.—In persons of sedentary habits. Drawing and jerking pains. After eating, or in the morning. Worse in the open air, &c.

Neuralgia after a Cold.—ACON.-CHAM.-MERC.-PULS.

Night (Sufferings worse at) In general.—ACON.-Arn.-ARS.-Bell.-Bry.-CHAM.-CHIN.-MERC.-Phos.-Puls.-Rhus.-Sulph.

*****Nightmare.**—ACON.-Bell.-NUX.-PULS.-Sulph.

†**Nipples, Excoriation of the.**—ARN.-Calc.-CHAM.-Merc.-Puls.-SULPH.

———— **Ulceration of the.**—CHAM.-Merc.

The principal uses in the treatment of—
Neuralgia, continued.

Phos.—Tearing and stitches in the cheek from the jaws to the ears, &c.

Puls.—Shooting and pulsative pains. Semilateral pains. Worse in the evening or when lying down. Relief in the open air, &c.

Rhus.—Pressing cutting pains in the cheek bones, with heat and roughness of the skin of the cheeks, &c.

Verat.—Insupportable pains which almost drive the patient to distraction. Great weakness even to fainting, &c. See *Tic Doloreux. Face, Pains in the. Pains in general. Sensibility to Pain, &c.*

*****Nightmare.**

Acon.—Fever. Palpitation. Oppression of the chest, &c.

Bell.—Face flushed. Eyes bright. Starting as if in a fright, &c.

Nux.—If the result of spirituous liquors, ales, too hearty meals, a sedentary life, study, indigestion, &c.

Puls.—In the case of females. Stertorous inspiration. Anxious, sad dreams. From rich living, &c.

Sulph.—Too light, unrefreshing sleep with aching and beating pains in the head. Eyes sometimes half open, &c.

†**Nipples, Excoriation of the.**

Arn.—For simple soreness.

Cham.—If the nipples are inflamed or ulcerated, &c.

Sulph.—If *Arn.* does not suffice.

MEDICAL INDEX.

*Nose, Bleeding from the.—Acon.-ARN.-BELL.-Bry.-CALC.-Chin.-Ipec.-MERC.-Nux.-Phos.-PULS.-RHUS.-Sulph.

—— Bloated.—Ars.-BELL.-Bry.-Calc.-Cham.-Chin.-Merc.-Nux.-Phos.-PULS.-RHUS.

—— Discharge Purulent from the.—Bell.-Calc.-MERC.-Puls.-Sulph.

—— Dryness in the.—Bry.-CALC.-Merc.-PHOS.-SULPH.

—— Inflammation of the.—BELL.-Bry.-Merc.-Sulph.

—— Stoppage of the.—Bry.-Calc.-CARB.-NUX.-PHOS.-Puls.-Rhus.-Sulph.

—— Swelling of the.—Arn.-Bell.-BRY.-Merc.-Phos.-SULPH.

—— Ulceration in the.—Bry.-Calc.-PULS.-Sulph.

The principal uses in the treatment of—
*Nose, Bleeding from the.
Acon.—Violent bleeding. If from blood to the head or from being overheated, &c.
Arn.—If from physical exertion, a contusion, or a blow, &c.
Bell.—If from congestion to the head, &c.
Bry.—If from overheating during warm weather, or at night during sleep, &c.
Calc.—Disposition to bleed at the nose. Amounting to fainting. From physical exertion, &c.
Chin.—Violent hæmorrhage. For debilitated persons, &c.
Ipec.—Profuse bleeding, &c.
Merc.—If arising from worms, &c.
Nux.—If from the use of spirituous liquors, &c.
Puls.—If from scanty or suppressed menstruation, &c.
Rhus.—From bodily exertion or lifting a heavy weight, &c.
Sulph.—Disposition to bleed at the nose, &c.
See Hæmorrhage.

Pains, In general (Neuralgic, Gouty, Rheumatic, &c.)—
    Aching.—ARN.-BELL.-Calc.-CARB.-CHIN.-MERC.-Nux.-Phos.-Puls.-Sulph.-Verat.

—— —— **Bruise, as from a.**—Acon.-ARN.-BRY.-CHIN.-CIN.-Merc.-NUX.-Phos.-PULS.-Rhus.-VERAT.

—— —— **Burning.**—Acon.-Arn.-ARS.-Bell.-BRY.-Calc.-CANTH.-CARB.-MERC.-NUX.-PHOS.-RHUS.-SULPH.-Verat.

—— —— **Cramp-like.**—Arn.-BELL.-CALC.-CARB.-Chin.-CIN.-Merc.-Nux.-Puls.-Rhus.-Sulph.

—— —— **Cutting.**—Bell.-CALC.-CANTH.-MERC.-Rhus.

—— —— **Dull.**—CHIN.

—— —— **Paralytic.**—Acon.-Bell.-Bry.-Cham.-CHIN.-CIN.-Nux.-Phos.-PULS.-Rhus.-Sulph.

—— —— **Pressing.**—Acon.-Ars.-BELL.-Calc.-CHIN.-Merc.-Nux.-Sulph.-Verat.

—— —— **Pricking.**—Acon.-ARN.-BELL.-BRY.-CALC.-CANTH.-CHIN.-MERC.-Phos.-PULS.-RHUS.-SULPH.

—— —— **Pulsative.**—Acon.-Ars.-BELL.-CALC.-Cham.-PHOS.-PULS.-Sulph.-Verat.

—— —— **Shooting.**—ACON.-ARN.-Ars.-Bell.-BRY.-CALC.-Chin.-Merc.-Nux.-Phos.-PULS.-Rhus.-SULPH.

—— —— **Tearing.**—Acon.-Arn.-Bell.-BRY.-Calc.-Cham.-CHIN.-MERC.-Nux.-Phos.-PULS.-RHUS.-SULPH.

—— —— **Violent (insupportable).**—ACON.-ARS.-Cham.-COFF.

—— —— **Wandering.**—Arn.-Bell.-Chin.-PULS.-Sulph.

Palate, Inflammation of the.—BELL.-CALC.-CHIN.-MERC.-NUX.

———— ———— ———— of the Soft.—Bell.-MERC.-Nux.

———— Swelling of the.—Chin.-NUX.

*Palpitation of the Heart (In general).—ACON.-Ars.-BELL.-Calc.-CHIN.-MERC.-Nux.-PHOS.-PULS.-Rhus.-Sulph.-VERAT.

———— Anxiety, with.—ACON.-Ars.-CALC.-Cham.-Chin.-LACH.-Merc.-PHOS.-PULS.-Sulph.-VERAT.

———— Congestion of Blood (from).—ACON.-BELL.-Nux.-Phos.-Sulph.

———— Debilitating Losses, from.—Calc.-CHIN.-Nux.

———— Fainting, with.—Acon.

———— Fear, from.—ACON.-Verat.

———— Meal, after a.—CALC.

———— Nervous persons, in.—Cham.-Nux.-PULS.

The principal uses in the treatment of—
*Palpitation of the Heart.

Acon.—In plethoric persons. Great heat of body chiefly of the face, and great weariness of the limbs, &c.

Ars.—In chronic cases, or in old people, or from the sudden healing of an old sore, &c.

Bell.—Violent throbbings in the chest and heart which sometimes are felt in the head. From plethora, &c.

Chin.—If from great loss of blood or vanishing of milk, &c.

Nux.—In robust constitutions. In the morning. After a meal. With nausea and sense of heaviness, &c.

Phos.—With congestion in the chest and sensation of heat which ascends to the throat, &c.

Puls.—In hysterical females. Especially at night, &c.

Sulph.—If from suppression of an eruption, or piles, &c.

Verat.—When arising from fear or anguish, &c.

Palpitation of the Heart, Suppressed Eruptions, from.—Ars.-Sulph.

————— **Violent.**—ARS.-Bell.-PULS.

***Paralysis.**—BELL.-NUX.-PHOS.-Puls.-RHUS.

————— **Debilitating Losses, from.**—CHIN.-Sulph.

————— **Semilateral.**—Bell.-Rhus.

Perspiration, Clammy.—ARS.-Cham.-Merc.-PHOS.-Verat.

————— **Debilitating.**—Ars.-Bry.-Calc.-Chin.-Phos.-Sulph.

————— **Easy.**—Bry.-CALC.-Merc.-SULPH.

————— **Nocturnal.**—Ars.-Bell.-Bry.-CALC.-CARB.-Chin.-Merc.-Nux.-PHOS.-Puls.-Rhus.-SULPH.

————— **Sour Smelling.**—Bry.-CHAM.-Merc.-Sulph.

————— **Suppressed.**—Acon.-BELL.-Bry.-Calc.-CHAM.-CHIN.-Merc.-Nux.-Phos.-Puls.-Rhus.-SULPH.

The principal uses in the treatment of—
Paralysis.
Bell.—After apoplexy. Paralysis of the tongue, gullet, anus, or bladder. Incontinence of urine and fæces. With shooting aching pains in the parts affected, &c.
Nux.—In paralysis unaccompanied with inflammatory or congestive symptoms. Rheumatic paralysis without fever, &c.
Phos.—Paralysis of the spinal cord with loss of feeling and moving power, &c.
Rhus.—Of the lower extremities with numbness and insensibility, &c.
Sulph.—Often to commence the treatment. If from suppressed eruptions, &c.

*Pharynx (Upper part of the Gullet), **Inflammation of the.**—ACON.-BELL.-MERC.

†Piles (In general).—Ars.-Calc.-LACH.-NUX.-Phos.-PULS.-SULPH.

——— **Bleeding profusely.**—ACON.-Bell.-Calc.-IPEC.-Sulph.

——— **Burning or painful.**—ARS.-Nux.

The principal uses in the treatment of—
*Pharynx, Inflammation of the.
Acon.—Scraping and pricking pains in the pharynx, with thirst, redness of throat, and fever. Simple inflammation, &c.
Bell.—Inflammatory swelling with pains of excoriation and shootings in the throat. Inability to swallow. Great dryness and burning in the throat, &c.
Merc.—Pressive pains. Pains as from excoriation and ulceration. Inflammatory swelling of the back parts of the mouth. Painful, difficult spasmodic deglutition. Sensation of enlargement in the throat, &c.
†Piles.
Acon.—Bleeding piles with stitches in the anus. Feeling of fulness in the abdomen, &c.
Ars.—Burning and heat. Great debility, &c.
Calc.—If *Sulph.* is not sufficient and if the piles should often bleed, &c.
Lach.—Shooting pains and urging to stool. Bleeding piles, &c.
Nux.—For blind and bleeding piles. In persons who lead a sedentary life, use much coffee or spirits, or in pregnant females. Constipation, with ineffectual urging to stool. Bruised pain in the back so that the patient is unable to raise himself. Disposition to piles, &c.
Phos.—Bleeding freely during evacuation, &c.
Puls.—Discharge of blood and mucus with pains in the back, especially in sensitive individuals. In suppressed piles, &c.
Sulph.—Constipation alternating with discharges of bloody mucus. Frequent protrusion of piles. In obstinate cases. Constitutional disposition to piles, &c.

Piles, Chronic.—NUX.-SULPH.

—— **Inflamed.**—ARS.-NUX.-PULS.-Sulph.

—— **Mucous discharge, with.**—Nux.-Puls.-Sulph.

—— **Pains in the Loins, with.**—Acon.-Bell.-Nux.

—— **Protruding.**—Phos.-PULS.-SULPH.

—— **Swollen.**—CARB.

—— **Ulcerated.**—Cham.

***Pimples.**—BELL.-Nux.-Sulph.

—————— **of Young people.**—BELL.-Calc.-Sulph.

†**Pleurisy.**—ACON.-BRY.-Sulph.

‡—————— **Bastard** (Rheumatic).—ARN.-Bry.-Puls.

The principal uses in the treatment of—
***Pimples.**
Bell.—Chiefly on the face, neck, chest, abdomen, and hands. Red, hot, swelling, and painful pustules, &c.
Calc.—If humid and scabby. From excesses. In form of clusters, &c.
Nux.—Pricking, burning, and itching. From wine, spirituous liquors, &c.
Sulph.—Itching. From excesses, drinking, &c.
See Eruptions.
†**Pleurisy.**
Acon.—During the febrile symptoms, &c.
Bry.—If the pains in the side still continue.
Sulph.—To complete the cure if necessary.
‡**Pleurisy, Bastard.**
Arn.—Shootings or pains as from a bruise. When moving, coughing, &c.
Bry.—If the patient is very restless and feverish. Tension and pressure on the chest, &c.
Puls.—Worse towards evening, &c.

Pneumonia (In general).—ACON.-Bell.-BRY.-Merc.-PHOS.-Rhus.-Sulph.

———— First Stage.—ACON.-Bell.-BRY.-PHOS.

———— Second Stage.—Acon.-Bry.-PHOS.-SULPH.

———— Third Stage.—Chin.-PHOS.

Polypus (In general).— CALC.-PHOS.

———— Nose, in the.—Calc.-Phos.-Puls.

†**Pregnancy, Colic during.**—Bell.-Bry.-CHAM.-NUX.-Puls.

The principal uses in the treatment of—
*Pneumonia.
Acon.—In the first and second stages. Fever, thirst, and heat, &c.
Bell.—Spasmodic constriction of the chest, with dry, hacking cough, &c.
Bry.—Cough with shootings in the chest and aching pains in the head. Expectoration of slimy or dirty reddish mucus, or of yellow colour, or of pure blood. When the fever is abated, &c.
Merc.—Expectoration of bloody mucus. Hoarse cough. Purulent expectoration. If complicated with bronchitis, &c.
Phos.—Sensation as if the chest was raw. Purulent, greenish expectoration, or slimy mucus with blood. Great oppression and cough. In most stages, &c.
Rhus.—In typhoid pneumonia. Great debility and loss of appetite. Face red, &c.
Sulph.—Whenever an amelioration takes place and is not permanent. The sequelæ of pneumonia, &c.
†**Pregnancy, Colic during.**
Bell.—Pain as if clutched with the nails, &c.
Cham.—Flatulence. Anguish and pressure in the pit of the stomach. From a chill, &c.
Nux.—Constipation, &c.
See *Colic. Pains in the Abdomen.*

- **Pregnancy, Constipation during.**—BRY.-NUX.
† ——— ——— **Convulsions.**—BELL.-Cham.
——— ——— **Diarrhœa.**—Cham.-Puls.-Phos.-SULPH.
——— ——— **Dyspepsia.**—Ipec.-Nux.-Puls.
——— ——— **Headache.**—Bell.-Bry.-Nux.-Puls.
——— ——— **Nausea.**—Ars.-Ipec.-Nux.-Puls.
‡ ——— ——— **Toothache.**—Bell.-Cham.-Nux.-Puls.
§ ——— ——— **Uterine Hæmorrhage.**—Bell.-CHAM.-Ipec.

The principal uses in the treatment of—
*Pregnancy, Constipation during.
Bry.—Hard, tough stool. If occurring in warm weather, &c.
Nux.—Inactivity of the bowels. From sedentary habits. Ineffectual urging to stool, &c.
†Pregnancy, Convulsions during.
Bell.—Will mostly remove the danger.
Cham.—May be employed if *Bell.* does not succeed.
‡Pregnancy, Toothache during.
Bell.—Congestion to the head. Worse at night. In feverish, congestive, and inflammatory toothaches, &c.
Cham.—Pains which seem insupportable and almost drive the patient to desperation, &c.
Nux.—In nervous and spasmodic toothaches. Worse from wine, coffee, or mental exertions. Worse in the morning, &c.
Puls.—Worse in the evening, in a warm room, or from warm things, &c.
See *Toothache. Pains in the Teeth.*
§Pregnancy, Uterine Hæmorrhage during.
Bell.—Pressure to the parts as though everything would force out. Pains in the back as though it would break, &c.
Cham.—If with labour-like pains, &c.
Ipec.—If the flow is copious and continuous, &c.

Pregnancy, Varicose Veins during.—ARN.-PULS.-Sulph.

*———— **Vomiting.**—Ars.-IPEC.-LACH.-NUX.-Puls.

Proud Flesh.—ARS.-Phos.-Sulph.

†**Puerperal Fever.**—ACON.-BELL.-BRY.-Cham.-Merc.-Nux.-Puls.-Rhus.

Pulse, Feeble.—Ars.-Chin.-Merc.-Rhus.-Verat.

The principal uses in the treatment of—
***Pregnancy, Vomiting during.**

Ars.—Excessive vomiting after eating and drinking. Great weakness, &c.

Ipec.—In simple and uncomplicated cases. Bilious vomiting, &c.

Lach.—Vomiting of food or bilious vomiting. Inclination to vomit early in the morning in bed, &c.

Nux.—Nausea and vomiting every morning on rising. Headache. Constipation, &c.

Puls.—Sour vomiting. White coated tongue, &c.

†**Puerperal Fever.**

Acon.—Violent fever. Dread of death, &c.

Bell.—Violent spasmodic colic, or painful pressing downwards towards the parts. The abdomen is sensitive to contact. Furious delirium, &c.

Bry.—Abdomen distended, extremely sensitive to the touch. Constipation. Violent fever, &c.

Cham.—Discharge of blood not too profuse. Worse at night. Great restlessness. Nervous excitability, &c.

Merc.—In many cases where *Bell.* is not sufficient, especially when the head symptoms are less marked than those of the abdomen, &c.

Nux.—If the discharge has ceased suddenly with feeling of heaviness. Constipation. Pressure in the head with giddiness and fainting, &c.

Puls.—Useful to modify the gastric symptoms, &c.

Rhus.—If from the commencement the nervous system has been affected. If the least contradiction aggravates the symptoms, &c.

Pulse, Full.—ACON.-Arn.-BELL.-Bry.-Nux.-Phos.
——— **Hard.**—ACON.-Arn.-BELL.-BRY.-NUX.-Phos.
——— **Imperceptible.**—ARS.-CARB.-VERAT.
——— **Intermittent.**—Ars.-Bry.-CHIN.-Sulph.
——— **Irregular.**—Acon.-Ars.-CHIN.
——— **Quick.**—ACON.-Ars.-Bell.-BRY.-Chin.-MERC.-Nux.-PHOS.-Puls.-Rhus.
——— **Slow.**—Bell.-Verat.
——— **Small.**—ACON.-Ars.-Bell.-CARB.-Chin.-Nux.-Phos.-Puls.-Rhus.-VERAT.
——— **Trembling.**—ARS.-Bell.-CALC.-LACH.-Rhus.
***Purple Rash.**—ACON.-Bell.

†**Quinsy.**—BELL.-Calc.-MERC.

Regurgitation (In general).—Bry.-Calc.-NUX.-Sulph.
——————— **Bitter.**—Ars.-Nux.
——————————— **Eating (after).**—BRY.-Merc.-NUX.-Phos.-Puls.

The principal uses in the treatment of—
***Purple Rash.**
  Acon.—Fever. Tossing about, &c.
  Bell.—Inflammation of the throat. Delirium, &c.
†**Quinsy.**
  Bell.—Inflammation and swelling of the throat, palate, uvula, and tonsils. Complete inability to swallow. Excoriation or shooting pains in the throat. Choking and spasmodic constriction of the throat, &c.
  Calc.—Sore throat as from an internal swelling extending into the ears. Swelling of the tonsils and palate, &c.
  Merc.—Violent stitches in the throat and tonsils extending to the ears and glands. Inflammatory redness of the affected parts. Difficult swallowing. Salivation, &c.
      See Sore Throat.

Regurgitation, Food (of).—BRY.-LACH.-NUX.-PHOS.-Puls.-SULPH.

──────── **Sour.**—Calc.-CARB.-NUX.-PHOS.-Sulph.

Rest, (Sufferings increased by) In general.—LACH.-PULS.-RHUS.-Sulph.

──── (Sufferings relieved by) In general.—Acon.-Arn.-BELL.-BRY.-Merc.-NUX.-Phos.

Restlessness.—ACON.-ARS.-BELL.-Bry.-Calc.-CHAM.-Chin.-MERC.-Nux.-Phos.-Puls.-Rhus.-Sulph.

Retching (effort to vomit).—Acon.-Arn.-BELL.-Bry.-Chin.-IPEC.-NUX.-PULS.-VERAT.

*****Rheumatism** (In general).—Acon.-Arn.-Bell.-BRY.-Cham.-Merc.-Nux.-PULS.-RHUS.-Sulph.-Verat.

The principal uses in the treatment of—
*****Rheumatism.**

Acon.—Violent fever. Shooting pains. Intolerable at night, &c.

Arn.—Pains as from a sprain or contusion. Violent pains in the affected parts as if resting upon something very hard, &c.

Bell.—Shooting, burning pains. Worse at night. Congestion to the head. Swelling of the part, with widely spreading redness, &c.

Bry.—Tearing, shooting pains worse in the muscles than in the bones. Shining swelling of the part affected. Bilious symptoms. Worse on movement, &c.

Cham.—Sensation of numbness or lameness. Fever with burning heat in the part. Tossing about. Worse at night, &c.

Merc.—Worse in cold and damp weather, or in bed. Perspiration which affords no relief, &c.

Nux.—Tensive, jerking or pulling pains, especially in the back, loins, chest, or joints. Numbness in the affected parts. Bilious sufferings, &c.

MEDICAL INDEX.

Rheumatism, Acute.—ACON.-Arn.-Bell.-BRY.-Cham.-Merc.-Nux.-Puls.-Rhus.

——————— **Chill, from the least.**—Acon.-Calc.-Merc.

——————— **Chronic.**—PHOS.-Puls.-Rhus.-SULPH.-Verat.

——————— **Fever (with).**—ACON.-BELL.-BRY.-Cham.-Merc.-Puls.-Rhus.

——————— **Wandering Pains (with).**—Arn.-Bry.-Chin.-Nux.-PULS.

*****Rickets.**—Bell.-CALC.-Merc.-Sulph.

Rigidity of the Body.—BELL.-IPEC.

——————— **Limbs.**—Ars.-Merc.-NUX.

The principal uses in the treatment of—
Rheumatism, continued.

Puls.—Pains shifting from one joint to another. Drawing and jerking pains. Worse at night, &c.

Rhus.—Rigidity of the parts affected. Wrenching pains and paralytic weakness. Worse during rest, and in bad weather, &c.

Sulph.—In most cases of chronic rheumatism and the obstinate continuance of acute cases, &c.

Verat.—Pains as if bruised, with weakness and trembling of the affected part, &c.

See *Joints and Muscles, Pains in the.*

*****Rickets.**

Bell.—Hardness and distension of the abdomen with unsteady staggering gait, &c.

Calc.—Where the spine appears too weak to carry the weight of the body. Softening and distortion of the bones. Swelling and enlargement of the head in children, &c.

Merc.—Especially useful to those disposed to glandular enlargements, &c.

Sulph.—In all stages of the disease, especially where there is curvature of the spine, &c.

MEDICAL INDEX.

*Ringworm.—Calc.-Rhus.-Sulph.
†Rose Rash.—ACON.-Bell.-BRY.-Merc.-PULS.-Rhus.
‡Rupture (In general).—Acon.-NUX.-SULPH.-Verat.
——— Children (in).—NUX.-VERAT.
——— Strangulated.—NUX.-Sulph.
——— Umbilical (Navel).—NUX.-Verat.

§ Scald Head (Ringworm of the Scalp).—CALC.-HEP.-RHUS.-SULPH.

The principal uses in the treatment of—
*Ringworm.
Calc.—In obstinate cases and in persons of a scrofulous habit, &c.
Rhus.—Burning as if ulcerated. Skin hot. Crusty eruption in the face, &c.
Sulph. When there is a general predisposition to the affection, &c.
†Rose Rash.
Acon.—Feverish symptoms.
Bell.—Head symptoms. Sore throat, &c.
Bry.—If connected with oppression, and hurried breathing, &c.
Puls.—Eruption like measles. When accompanied with acidity, nausea, diarrhœa, &c.
Rhus.—Great irritation and itching, &c.
‡Rupture.
Acon.—Violent inflammation. Bitter bilious vomiting.
Nux.—Tumour not very painful. Vomiting less violent, but great difficulty of breathing. If caused by cold, irregular living, &c.
Sulph.—If the bilious vomitings turn to sour. In chronic cases.
Verat.—If the vomiting is attended with cold sweat and coldness of the extremities, &c.
§Scald Head.
Calc.—Inveterate scabs, clammy perspiration, scaling off of the skin and painful sensibility of the roots of the hair. In scrofulous individuals. Falling off of the hair, &c.

Scald Head, Dry.—Ars.-CALC.-Rhus.-SULPH.
———— **Moist.**—RHUS.-Sulph.
*****Scarlatina** (Scarlet Fever).—ACON.-Ars.-BELL.-Bry.-Merc.-Sulph.
———————— **Malignant.**—ARS.-Bell.
———————— **Retrocession of the Eruption.**—Bry.-Sulph.
———————— **Sore Throat (with).**—BELL.-MERC.
———————— **Vomitings (with).**—Acon.-Ars.-Bell.-Ipec.
†**Sciatica.**—ACON.-Ars.-NUX.-PULS.

The principal uses in the treatment of—
Scald Head, continued.
Hep.—If the face and neck become involved or the eyes inflamed, &c.
Rhus.—Thick scabs which destroy the hair. Greenish pus and violent itching, &c.
Sulph.—Dry, thick, yellowish scabs with secretion of fetid pus and great itching. When the eruption begins to dry up and scale off, &c.
*****Scarlatina.**
Acon.—Violent fever. Bilious vomiting. Congestion to the head. Sleeplessness, &c.
Ars.—Complete prostration. Gangrenous inflammation of the throat. For dropsy after scarlatina, &c.
Bell.—Violent inflammation of the throat with spasmodic contraction. Danger of suffocation. Pains in the head, &c.
Bry.—For retrocession of the eruption.
Merc.—In case of inflammation and swelling of the tonsils with salivation or ulcers, &c.
Sulph.—If the head symptoms do not yield to *Bell.* Lethargic sleep. Starts, convulsions, or continued delirium, &c.
†**Sciatica.**
Acon.—When fever is present. Intolerable pains, &c.
Ars.—In cases of long standing. Burning pains. Acute drawings in the hip extending to the thighs, obliging one to move the limb constantly, &c.

*Scrofula.—ARS.-BELL.-CALC.-MERC.-RHUS.-SULPH.

†Scurvy.—Ars.-CARB.-MERC.-NUX.-Sulph.

The principal uses in the treatment of—
Sciatica, continued.
Nux.—Torpor and paralytic weakness. Sharp and shooting pains in the thighs. If caused by indigestion, wine, &c. Worse in the morning, &c.
Puls.—If from rich living. Worse in the evening, &c.
*Scrofula.
Ars.—Wasting. Great debility. Pale bloatedness, &c.
Bell.—Hard, swollen, and ulcerated glands. Pale bloatedness. Inflammation of the eyes. Intolerance of light, &c.
Calc.—In case of curvature of the spine and ricketty affections. Glandular affections. Emaciation with voracity, &c.
Merc.—In case of diseased nutrition, great bodily and mental weakness. Slimy diarrhœa, &c.
Rhus.—Swelling of the glands. Scald head and other eruptions forming scurfs, &c.
Sulph.—In most cases at the commencement of treatment. Swelling, induration, or ulceration of glands. Diarrhœa with colic. Constipation. Disposition to take cold. Physical and intellectual weakness, &c.
†Scurvy.
Ars.—Ulceration of the gums. Burning pains. Great prostration, &c.
Carb.—If arising from mercury. Sore and ulcerated gums. Gums bleed profusely, &c.
Merc.—Teeth loose, ready to fall out. Gums fungous, bleed easily, livid and ulcerated, &c.
Nux.—Fetid ulcers. Fetid smell. Putrid taste, &c.
Sulph.—Thrush. Fetid and sour smell from mouth. Sensation of looseness, bleeding and swelling of the gums with throbbing pains, &c.
See Gums, Bleeding. Mouth, Scurvy in the, &c.

*Sea Sickness.—Ars.-Ipec.-Nux.-Sulph.

Sensibility of the Body (Excessive), In general.
—ACON.-Arn.-Ars.-Bell.-CANTH.-Cham.-CHIN.-COFF.-Merc.-NUX.-Phos.

——————————— **Cold, to.**—ARS.-Bry.-Nux.-PHOS.-RHUS.-Verat.

——————————— **Damp Air, to.**—CALC.-LACH.-MERC.-Rhus.-Sulph.-Verat.

——————————— **Noise, to.**—Acon.-Arn.-BELL.-Calc.-Cham.-COFF.-NUX.

——————————— **Pain, to.**—ACON.-Arn.-CHAM.-Chin.-COFF.-Nux.-PHOS.

†**Shingles.**—Ars.-MERC.-RHUS.

Shoulders, Pains, Drawing, in the.—Bry.-Puls.-Sulph.

——————— ——— **Tearing.**—Bell.-Bry.-MERC.-Phos.-Puls.-Rhus.-SULPH.

‡**Sickness, Green** (of females).—Bell.-CALC.-Chin.-Phos.-PULS.-SULPH.

The principal uses in the treatment of—
*Sea Sickness.
Ars.—Great weakness. Violent retching. &c.
Ipec.—Frequent vomiting without feeling very weak, &c.
Nux.—Giddiness. Headache. Great nausea. Useful to take before going on board ship, &c.
Sulph.—Vomiting of food with trembling. Sour vomiting, &c.
†**Shingles.**
Ars.—Nocturnal burning, &c.
Merc.—May be used after *Rhus.* Violent burning itching, particularly after scratching and at night, &c.
Rhus.—Should be first administered.
‡**Sickness, Green.**
Bell.—Congestion of the head and chest. Violent throbbing of the blood vessels of the neck, &c.
Calc.—Pallid countenance. Loss of appetite. Costive bowels or diarrhœa. Great emaciation, &c.

Sight, Dimness of.—Bell.-Calc.-Chin.-Merc.-PHOS.-
  Rhus.-Sulph.
Skin, Blue.—ARS.-Nux.-Verat.
—— **Burning.**—ACON.-ARS.-BELL.-Bry.-Calc.-
  Cham.-LACH.-MERC.-Nux.-PHOS.-
  Puls.-RHUS.-Sulph.

The principal uses in the treatment of—
Sickness, Green, continued.
Chin.—Dropsical swellings, particularly of the feet. Distension of the abdomen. Bad digestion. If arising from debilitating losses, &c.
Phos.—Menses not entirely suppressed, but irregular. Nausea. Oppression of breathing. Giddiness, &c.
Puls.—At the commencement. Menses feeble or retarded. Complexion pale and muscles flabby, &c.
Sulph.—In green sickness generally. In all stages, &c.
*Sight, Dimness of.
Bell.—Dilated and insensible pupils. Dread of light. Flames. Black spots and points. Red appearance of all objects. Pressive pains even to the orbits. Nocturnal blindness as soon as the sun is set. If from doing fine work, congestion to the head, &c.
Calc.—Dim sight as through a mist. Great intolerance of light. Pupils very much dilated. In scrofulous subjects, &c.
Chin.—Dilated pupil with insensibility to light, or slightly contracted pupil with the sensation of a white cloud before the eyes, &c.
Merc.—Momentary attacks of sudden blindness. Great sensibility of the eyes, especially for the glare of the fire or the day light, &c.
Phos.—Sudden paroxysms of blindness. Everything seems to be covered with a grey veil. Great sensibility to light. Black spots before the eyes, &c.
Rhus.—Sensation of a gauze before the eyes, &c.
Sulph.—Dimsightedness as through a mist. Paroxysms of sudden blindness in the day. Copious tears especially in the open air, or great dryness in the room. Dread of light especially in the sunshine. If from a rheumatic cause, or the retrocession of an eruption, &c.

  See Eyes. Attacks of Blindness, &c.

Skin, Chapped.—CALC.-MERC.-PULS.-SULPH.
— **Cold.**—ARS.-IPEC.-Nux.-RHUS.-Sulph.-VERAT.
— **Dry.**—Acon.-Arn.-Ars.-BELL.-BRY.-CALC.-CHAM.-CHIN.-Merc.-Nux.-PHOS.-Puls.-Rhus.-SULPH.
— **Flaccid.**—CALC.-CHIN.-Sulph.-VERAT.
— **Heal (difficult to).**—Calc.-CHAM.-HEP.-Merc.-Rhus.-Sulph.
— **Inflammation of the.**—Acon.-BELL.-CANTH.-Cham.-MERC.-Puls.-RHUS.-Sulph.
— **Itching of the.**—Bry.-Calc.-MERC.-Nux.-PULS.-RHUS.-SPONG.-SULPH.-Verat.
— **Painful.**—ARS.-Bell.-CALC.-MERC.-NUX.-Rhus.-SULPH.-VERAT.
— **Pains, Biting, in the.**—Bry.-Calc.-PULS.
— —— **Pricking.**—BRY.-Merc.-Puls.-RHUS.-Sulph.
— —— **Shooting.**—Acon.-Ars.-Bry.-PULS.
— —— **Tearing.**—Bell.-BRY.-Nux.
— **Peeling off of the.**—Bell.-Merc.-PHOS.-Verat.
— **Red.**—Acon.-Arn.-BELL.-Merc.-Nux.-Puls.-RHUS.
— **Rough.**—CALC.
— **Sensibility of the.**—Calc.-CHIN.-Verat.
— **Spots, Black, in the.**—ARS.-LACH.-Rhus.
— —— **Blue.**—ARN.-ARS.-BRY.-Rhus.
— —— **Brown.**—Bry.-MERC.-Phos.-SULPH.
— —— **Hepatic.**—Merc.-Sulph.
— —— **Purple.**—ARS.-BRY.-RHUS.
— —— **Scarlet.**—Ars.-BELL.-Bry.-MERC.-Sulph.

MEDICAL INDEX. 123

Skin, Spots, Whitish, in the.—ARS.-Phos.-Sulph.
—— —— **Yellowish.**—Arn.-PHOS.-SULPH.
—— **Sunburnt.**—BELL.
—— **Unhealthy.**—CALC.-Cham.-HEP.-Merc.-SULPH.
—— **Yellow.**—Acon.-Bell.-Bry.-Cham.-Chin.-MERC.-NUX.-Sulph.
Sleep, Agitated.—Acon.-ARS.-BELL.-Bry.-Calc.-CHAM.-CHIN.-Merc.-Nux.-PHOS.-PULS.-RHUS.-SULPH.
—— **Anxious.**—ACON.-Ars.-Bell.
—— **Comatose (stupor).**—BELL.-Bry.-Phos.-Puls.-Verat.
—— **Cries (with).**—BELL.-Bry.-Calc.-CHAM.-Merc.
—— **Delirium (with).**—Acon.-Arn.-Ars.-BELL.-Bry.-Cham.-NUX.-Puls.-Sulph.-Verat.
—— **Moans (with).**—Ars.-BELL.-Calc.-Cham.-Ipec.-Merc.-NUX.-Puls.
—— **Refreshing (not).**—BRY.-Calc.-Chin.-Phos.-SULPH.
—— **Starts (with).**—Acon.-ARS.-BELL.-Bry.-Calc.-CHAM.-NUX.-Phos.-PULS.-SULPH.
—— **Talking in the.**—Bell.-Calc.-Cham.-Merc.-NUX.-Phos.-PULS.-Rhus.-SULPH.
—— **Waking with fright.**—Ars.-BELL.-Calc.-CHAM.-Merc.-PULS.-SULPH.
*****Sleeplessness** (In general).—Acon.-ARS.-BELL.-BRY.-CALC.-CHAM.-Chin.-COFF.-MERC.-Nux.-Phos.-PULS.-Rhus.-Sulph.

The principal uses in the treatment of—
*****Sleeplessness.**
Acon.—Feverishness: Anxiety, &c.
Ars.—With uneasiness and tossing about; with moaning, &c.

Sleeplessness, Drowsiness (with).—Ars.-BELL.-Bry.-Calc.-Cham.-Chin.-Nux.-Phos.-PULS.

——————— **Flow of Ideas** (from a).—Calc.-Chin.-Nux.-PULS.-SULPH.

Sleep-walking.—Bry.-Phos.-Sulph.

*****Smallpox** (In general).—Acon.-Ars.-Bell.-Bry.-MERC.-Puls.-RHUS.-Sulph.

——————— **Commencement (at).**—ACON.-Bell.-BRY.-RHUS.

The principal uses in the treatment of—
Sleeplessness, continued.

Bell.—A strong desire to sleep without being able, &c.
Cham.—If complaints of the bowels and flatulency are the cause, &c.
Coff.—From over excitement. The effect of long watching, &c.
Merc.—Excessive restlessness, anxiety and malaise, &c.
Nux.—From excessive thinking, reading, &c.
Puls.—From eating too much supper, &c.

*****Smallpox.**
Acon.—Violent fever.
Ars.—If the eruption assumes a malignant aspect. In the suppurative stage if the diarrhœa is very violent, &c.
Bell.—If head symptoms are present. Delirium. Sore throat. Inflammation of the eyes and brain, &c.
Bry.—Pains in the back with a bruised feeling, nausea, headache, &c.
Merc.—Salivation. Inflammation of the eyes, nose, and mouth. Catarrh with cough and hoarseness. Diarrhœa, &c.
Puls.—If there is a disposition in the pustules to become confluent, accompanied with nausea and vomiting, &c.
Rhus.—During the eruptive stage if there are acute pains in the back and loins, &c.
Sulph.—When the eruption is drying up, &c.

Smallpox, Eruptive Stage (during the).—Bry.-
    Merc.-Rhus.-SULPH.
——————— **Malignant.**—ARS.-Bell.-CARB.-Rhus.
——————— **Suppurative Stage.**—MERC.-Sulph.
Smell, Feeble.—Bell.-CALC.-Phos.-PULS.
—— **Loss of.**—Bell.-CALC.-PHOS.-Puls.
—— ——————— **Catarrhal.**—Nux.-PULS.
Sneezing.—Ars.-CARB.-CIN.-Merc.-Nux.-Puls.-RHUS.
*****Sore Throat** (In general).—Acon.-BELL.-Cham.-
    MERC.-Nux.-Puls.-Sulph.

The principal uses in the treatment of—
*****Sore Throat.**
    Acon.—Pricking in the throat. Violent fever, &c.
    Ars.—Burning in the throat. Inability to swallow as from paralysis of the parts. Great dryness, &c.
    Bell.—In most cases. Shooting in the throat. Contraction and spasmodic constriction of the fauces. Pain as of excoriation. Complete inability to swallow even the least liquid, &c.
    Carb.—Scraping, burning pain. If from abuse of mercury, &c.
    Cham.—Swelling of the glands under the jaws. Tickling in the larynx. Especially in the case of children, or from a chill, &c.
    Lach.—In most cases where *Bell.* and *Merc.* seem indicated, but are not sufficient. Constant desire to swallow, with spasms in the throat, or sensation as if a lump was sticking there. Danger of suffocation, &c.
    Merc.—Often at the commencement. Violent shootings extending to the ears. Inflammatory redness of the parts. Salivation. Worse at night, or in the open air, &c.
    Nux.—Pain during empty swallowing. Sensation of swelling with stitches and pressure. Small, fetid ulcers, &c.
    Puls.—Sensation of swelling. Accumulation of tenacious mucus. Worse towards evening, &c.
    Sulph.—Dryness. Soreness. Shooting pains, &c.
See Throat, Rawness in the, &c. Catarrhal Sore Throat, Swallowing, Difficulty of, &c.

Sore Throat, Catarrhal.—BELL.-CHAM.-MERC.-Nux.-Puls.
——— ——— **Chronic.**—Calc.-CARB.-Sulph.
——— ——— **Malignant** (Putrid).—ARS.-LACH.
——— ——— **Mercurial.**—Bell.-HEP.
*****Spasms** (In general).—Acon.-Ars.-BELL.-Bry.-Cham.-Ipec.-Merc.-NUX.-Sulph.-Verat.
——— **Cries, with.**—BELL.
——— **Eyes, Eyelids, or Face convulsed, with.**—Bell.-Cham.
——— **Face puffed, with.**—BELL.-Cham.
——— **Pupils dilated, with.**—BELL.
——— **Vomitings, with.**—Nux.

The principal uses in the treatment of—
*****Spasms.**
Acon.—In young plethoric people who lead a sedentary life, &c.
Ars.—Epileptic spasms with burning in the stomach, spine, and abdomen, &c.
Bell.—Convulsive motion of the mouth. Congestion to the head with giddiness. Dilated pupils. Excited again by the least touch or contradiction. Complete loss of consciousness. Deep and comatose sleep with smiling and distortion of features. Sudden starting from sleep with a cry, &c.
Cham.—Involuntary moving of the head. Redness of one cheek. Especially in children. If caused by anger, &c.
Ipec.—Asthmatic sufferings. Loathing of food. Spasmodic bending backwards, &c.
Merc.—Spasms caused by worms with distension and hardness of the abdomen, &c.
Nux.—Feeling of rigidity in the limbs and as though they would go to sleep, &c.
Sulph.—In chronic cases. From repelled chronic eruptions, &c.
Verat.—Great distress and despondency, &c.

Speech, Stammering.—BELL.-Merc.-Sulph.-Verat.
Spine, Curvature of the.—CALC.-Puls.-Rhus.-Sulph.
Sprains or Strains.—ARN.-Bry.-Puls.-RHUS.
*St. Vitus' Dance.—BELL.-Cham.-NUX.
Stomach, Acidity of the.—Ars.-Calc.-CARB.-Cham.-NUX.-PHOS.-Puls.-SULPH.
——— Anguish in the Pit of the.—ARS.-Verat.
——— Burning in the.—ARS.-Bry.-CARB.-PHOS.-Sulph.
——— ——— in the Pit of the.—ARS.-Bry.-NUX.-Phos.-Verat.
——— Coldness in the.—ARS.-Phos.
——— Distension of the.—Ars.
——— ——— Pit of the.—Calc.-CHAM.
——— Fulness in the (sensation of).—CHIN.-PHOS.
——— Heat in the.—ARS.
†——— Inflammation of the.—ACON.-Ars.-Bell.-BRY.-IPEC.-NUX.-PHOS.-PULS.-Verat.

The principal uses in the treatment of—
*St. Vitus' Dance.
Bell.—Twitching in the flexor muscles. The paroxysms preceded by a creeping and feeling of numbness, &c.
Nux.—With a sensation of numbness and as if gone to sleep in the affected parts after the paroxysms, &c.
†Stomach, Inflammation of the.
Acon.—At the commencement. Violent inflammatory fever, &c.
Ars.—Sudden prostration. Burning internal heat and pains in the stomach and abdomen with general coldness and anguish. Excessive pain with rapid failure of strength. If caused by eating ice, &c.

Stomach, Neuralgic pains in the.—Arn.-ARS.-BRY.-Cham.-Merc.-NUX.-Phos.-PULS.-Rhus.

——— **Oppression in the.**—Cham.-CHIN.-Rhus.

——— **Painful Sensibility, Pressure, to.**—Ars.-Bry.-NUX.-Puls.

——— ——— ——— **Touch, to the.**—ARS.-Bry.-MERC.-NUX.-PHOS.

——— **Pains, Aching, in the.**—Merc.-Nux.-Puls.

——— ——— **Contractive.**—Arn.-BELL.-Bry.-Chin.-Merc.-NUX.-PHOS.-Puls.-Sulph.

——— ——— **Oppressive.**—Ars.-Cham.

——— ——— **Pressive.**—BELL.-Calc.-Merc.-Puls.-Rhus.

——— ——— **Spasmodic.**—ARS.-Bell.-Bry.-Calc.-Chin.-PHOS.

——— ——— **Stitching, in the Pit of the.**—Arn.-Chin.-Phos.

——— ——— **Tearing.**—Ars.-NUX.

The principal uses in the treatment of—
Stomach, Inflammation of the, continued.
Bell.—Cerebral symptoms. Loss of consciousness, &c.
Bry.—If caused by taking cold drinks when heated, &c.
Ipec.—If the vomiting predominates, &c.
Nux.—When caused by abuse of spirituous liquors. Burning in the region of the pit of the stomach. Violent vomiting, &c.
Phos.—Cutting burning with pressure. Burning heat in the stomach. Prostration of strength, &c.
Puls.—If caused by gastric derangement or by a chill, &c.
Verat.—Great coldness of the extremities. Prostration, &c.

Stomach, Pains, Violent, in the.—ARS.-Phos.
———— Pressure in the.—ARS.-Bell.-BRY.-Calc.-CHAM.-Chin.-HEP.-NUX.-PHOS.-Rhus.-Sulph.
———— ———— in the Pit of the.—Acon.-ARS.-Bell.-Cham.-MERC.-Puls.-RHUS.-VERAT.
———— Sensibility (Painful) of the.—Ars.-Bry.-Merc.-NUX.-PHOS.-Sulph.
*———— Spasms in the.—BELL.-Bry.-Calc.-CARB.-CHAM.-NUX.-PULS.-Sulph.
———— Throbbing in the.—Nux.-Puls.
———— Weight as from a Stone in the.—Acon.-Arn.-ARS.-MERC.-NUX.

The principal uses in the treatment of—
*Stomach, Spasms in the.

Bell.—If the pain is so violent that the patient loses his consciousness and swoons away, &c.

Bry.—Pressure as from a stone. Sensation of swelling. Increase of the pains by motion, with stitches in the region of the stomach on making a false step, &c.

Calc.—After a meal, frequently with vomiting of food. Spasmodic pains. Constipation, &c.

Carb.—Painful burning pressure with great distress. Frequent flatulence. Constipation. Especially after flatulent food, &c.

Cham.—Pressure as from a stone or as if the heart was squeezed. At night with great distress and restlessness, &c.

Nux.—In most cases at the commencement. Contractive, pressing, and spasmodic pains, or as if the stomach was clutched. After a meal. Constipation. Piles, &c.

Puls.—If the pains are shooting or spasmodic. Vomiting of food. No thirst. Worse in the evening, &c.

Sulph.—Pressive pain as from a stone. Acidity. Heartburn. Regurgitation of food. After a meal, &c.
See Pains in the Stomach.

Straining during Stool (difficult evacuation).—Ars.-Bell.-Ipec.-MERC.-Nux.-Phos.-Puls.-Rhus.-SULPH.

——————— **without Evacuation.**—Acon.-Ars.-Bell.-Ipec.-MERC.-NUX.-Puls.-RHUS.-SULPH.

Stye on the Eyelid.—PULS.

*****Sunstroke.**—ACON.-BELL.-Bry.

†**Suppuration** (In general).—Ars.-Bell.-CALC.-HEP.-MERC.-PHOS.-PULS.-Rhus.-Sulph.

Swallowing, Difficulty of (In general).—ARS.-BELL.-Bry.-LACH.-MERC.-RHUS.

——————— ——— **Constriction of the Throat, with.**—BELL.-Lach.-RHUS.

——————— ——— **Drinks escape through the Nostrils.**—Bell.-Lach.-MERC.

——————— ——— Excoriation in the Throat (with sensation as of).—BELL.-Bry.-LACH.-NUX.

The principal uses in the treatment of—
*****Sunstroke.**

Acon.—Symptoms of inflammatory fever, &c.

Bell.—Loss of consciousness. Violent stupefying pain in the head. Stupor, &c.

Bry.—The head feels too full, want of appetite, thirst, fever, trembling, nausea, or vomiting, &c.

†**Suppuration.**

Calc.—In the case of ulcers, discharge scanty.

Hep.—Shooting, burning, and throbbing pains in the suppurating part. To promote suppuration in the case of boils, abscesses, &c. In the case of ulcers, discharge bloody or fetid, &c.

Merc.—Pulsative shooting pains. Suppurations of a bad nature. In the case of ulcers, discharge bloody, thin, or corroding, &c.

Puls.—In the case of ulcers, discharge profuse, or yellow, &c.

Swallowing, Difficulty of, Frequent desire to swallow, with.—BELL.-Lach.-MERC.
——— ——— Painful.—ARS.-BELL.-LACH.-MERC.-Nux.-Puls.-Rhus.
——— ——— Paralytic weakness of the throat, from.—Ars.-Bell.-Lach.-Puls.-Verat.
——— ——— Shooting Pains in the throat, with.—BELL.-Bry.-Puls.-Rhus.-Sulph.

Taste, Acrid.—Ars.-Nux.-Puls.-Sulph.
——— Bitter.—Acon.-Arn.-Ars.-BRY.-Calc.-CHAM.-Chin.-MERC.-NUX.-PULS.-Sulph.-VERAT.
——— Greasy.—PULS.
——— Insipid.—Bell.-BRY.-Chin.-Ipec.-Phos.-Puls.-Sulph.
——— Loss of.—Bell.-Calc.-Merc.-Phos.-PULS.
——— Metallic.—Calc.-Nux.-Rhus.
——— Offensive.—Bry.-Calc.-Merc.-Nux.-PULS.
——— Putrid.—Acon.-ARN.-Ars.-Bell.-BRY.-Cham.-Chin.-Merc.-Nux.-Phos.-PULS.-Rhus.-Sulph.
——— Salt.—ARS.-Chin.-MERC.-Phos.-Puls.-Rhus.-Sulph.
——— Sour.—Ars.-CALC.-Cham.-Chin.-Merc.-NUX.-PHOS.-PULS.-Rhus.-SULPH.
——— Sweetish.—Bry.-Chin.-Merc.-Nux.-Phos.-PULS.-Rhus.-Sulph.

Teeth, Loose.—MERC.-Nux.-Sulph.
——— Pains, Boring, in the.—Nux.-Phos.
——— ——— Digging.—Nux.-Puls.
——— ——— Drawing.—Bell.-Bry.-Cham.-Phos.-Puls.-SULPH.

Teeth, Pains, Dull, in the.—CHIN.
— — **Gnawing.**—Cham.-Phos.-Puls.
— — **Insupportable.**—Cham.-Coff.-Merc.
— — **Jerking.**—Bry.-NUX.-Phos.-PULS.-RHUS.
— — **Pulsative.**—Acon.-Cham.-CHIN.-Merc.-Phos.-Puls.-SULPH.
— — **Semilateral.**—CHAM.-MERC.-PULS.-Rhus.
— — **Shooting.**—Cham.-Phos.-PULS.-RHUS.-Sulph.
— — **Stinging.**—MERC.-NUX.
— — **Tearing.**—Ars.-Bell.-Bry.-Cham.-Chin.-MERC.-Nux.-PHOS.-PULS.-RHUS.-Sulph.
***Teething, Constipation, with.**—Bry.-Nux.
— — **Diarrhœa, with.**—CHAM.-Ipec.-MERC.-Sulph.
— — **Fever, with.**—ACON.-CHAM.-COFF.
— — **Restlessness, with.**—Acon.-Cham.-COFF.
— — **Sleeplessness, with.**—BELL.-Cham.-COFF.
— — **Slow.**—Calc.
— — **Spasms, with.**—Bell.-Cham.
†**Tetters, Herpes** (In general).—ARS.-Bry.-CALC.-Merc.-RHUS.-SULPH.

The principal uses in the treatment of—
***Teething.**—*See Infants, Diseases of.*
†**Tetters, Herpes.**
Ars.—Tetters having a red unhealthy appearance with blisters and burning, &c.
Bry.—Red or whitish herpes, &c.
Calc.—Herpes which quickly re-appear. Branlike, &c.
Merc.—With burning when touched. Dry. Itching. Pricking. Red. Scabby. Suppurating, &c.

MEDICAL INDEX. 133

Tetters, Burning.—ARS.-MERC.-Rhus.-Sulph.
——— Corroding.—Calc.-Rhus.
——— Moist.—RHUS.
——— Scurfy.—CALC.-Merc.-Rhus.-SULPH.
——— Spreading.—Ars.-Calc.-Rhus.-Sulph.
——— Suppurating.—MERC.-RHUS.
Thighs, Pains as if Bruised, in the.—Acon.-Merc.-Nux.
——— ——— Drawing.—Cham.-Rhus.
——— ——— Shooting.—Calc.-Merc.-Nux.
——— ——— Tearing.—Cham.-Chin.-Rhus.
——— Rigidity of the.—Rhus.
——— Weakness of the.—Chin.-Merc.-Nux.
Thirst.—ACON.-ARS.-Bell.-BRY.-Calc.-CHAM.-CHIN.-MERC.-Nux.-Puls.-Rhus.-SULPH.-Verat.
——— Absence of.—Ars.-Chin.-Ipec.-PULS.
Throat, Burning in the.—Acon.-ARS.-BELL.-CARB.-Cham.-Merc.-PHOS.
——— Choking (sensation of)—Acon.-BELL.-RHUS.
——— Constriction in the.—Ars.-BELL.-Merc.-Sulph.-Verat.
——— Dryness in the.—ARS.-BELL.-BRY.-MERC.-PHOS.
——— Pains, Shooting, in the.—Acon.-BELL.-BRY.-MERC.-PULS.-Rhus.-Sulph.
——— Plug (Sensation as of a) in the.—BELL.-Cham.-LACH.-MERC.-NUX.-Sulph.

The principal uses in the treatment of—
Tetters, Herpes, continued.
Rhus.—When alternating with pains in the chest and dysenteric stools. Burning itching, &c.
Sulph.—Itching in the evening. Burning. Pricking. Spreading, &c. *See Eruptions.*

Throat, Rawness in the.—BELL.-CARB.-LACH.-MERC.-Nux.-PHOS.-PULS.-Sulph.

——— **Roughness in the.**—Acon.-Ars.-Bell.-CARB.-HEP.-PHOS.-Puls.-SULPH.

——— **Spasms in the.**—BELL.-Calc.-LACH.

——— **Swelling of the.**—Ars.-BELL.-MERC.-Nux.-Puls.-Sulph.

——— **Ulcers in the.**—Bell.-LACH.-MERC.

***Thrush** (Sore Mouth).—MERC.-Nux.-Sulph.

——— **in Children.**—Cham.-MERC.-SULPH.

†**Tic Doloreux.**—ACON.-Arn.-ARS.-BELL.-Bry.-Calc.-Cham.-Chin.-HEP.-Merc.-NUX.-PHOS.-Puls.-Rhus.-Sulph.-Verat.

The principal uses in the treatment of—
***Thrush.**
Merc.—In ordinary cases.
Nux.—Acidity. Regurgitation, &c.
Sulph.—In tedious cases. With burning pain, &c.

†**Tic Doloreux.**
Acon.—Violent pains with restlessness. Fever. Heat, &c.
Ars.—Burning, pricking pains. Pain so severe as to drive to despair. Periodical. Great prostration, &c.
Bell.—Pains in the nerves under the eyes. Tearing and shooting pains in the bones of the face and in the jaws. Inflammatory. Heat and redness of the face. Worse by rubbing the part affected, &c.
Hep.—If the pains in the cheek bones become worse by touching the parts and extend to the ears and temples, &c.
Nux.—Tearing pains extending to the ears with swelling of the cheeks. Redness of the face or cheek. Rheumatic nervous faceache. Aggravation by mental labour, or wine, or after dinner, &c.
Phos.—Tension of the skin of the face, with tearing pains especially on the left side. Pains extending from the jaw to the root of the nose, or into the ear. Inflammatory rheumatic faceache, &c.

See *Face, Pains in the. Neuralgia. Pains in general.*

MEDICAL INDEX. 135

Toes, Gout in the.—Arn.-SULPH.
Tongue, Burning in the.—Acon.-Bell.
———— Burnt (sensation).—MERC.
———— Coated.—Acon.-Arn.-Ars.-BELL.-BRY.-Cham.-CHIN.-Ipec.-MERC.-Nux.-PULS.-Rhus.-Sulph.
———— ———— Slimy.—Bell.-Merc.-Phos.-Puls.-Sulph.
———— ———— Thick.—Bell.-MERC.-Puls.
———— ———— Whitish.—Arn.-MERC.-NUX.-Phos.-PULS.-Sulph.
———— ———— Yellowish.—Chin.-Ipec.-Nux.-Puls.
———— Coldness of the.—Ars.-VERAT.
———— Colour, Black.—Ars.
———— Dryness of the.—ARS.-BELL.-BRY.-CHAM.-MERC.-Nux.-Phos.-Rhus.-Sulph.-Verat.
*———— Inflammation of the.—ACON.-Arn.-Ars.-BELL.-MERC.
———— Soreness of the.—MERC.-NUX.
———— Swelling of the.—Ars.-BELL.-MERC.
———— Torpor in the.—Bell.-Merc.
———— Ulceration of the.—Merc.-NUX.

The principal uses in the treatment of—
*Tongue, Inflammation of the.
Acon.—Itching. Burning of the tongue, &c.
Arn.—When caused by mechanical injuries, &c.
Ars.—When the parts threaten to become gangrenous, &c.
Bell.—Heat, dryness, swelling and inflammation, &c.
Merc.—Swelling and inflammation with profuse secretion of saliva. Thrush, &c.

*Tonsils, Inflammation of the.—BELL.-Calc.-MERC.

—————— **Suppuration of the.**—Bell.-Merc.

—————— **Swelling of the.**—BELL.-LACH.-MERC.-Nux.-Sulph.

†Toothache (In general).—BELL.-BRY.-CHAM.-CHIN.-MERC.-NUX.-Phos.-PULS.-Rhus.-SULPH.

The principal uses in the treatment of—
*Tonsils, Inflammation of the.
Bell.—Shootings and pain as of excoriation extending to the ears. Sensation as if they were of large size, &c.
Calc.—With contractive sensation in the throat during swallowing, &c.
Merc.—Shooting pain with swelling. Tendency to suppurate. Salivation, &c.
†Toothache.
Acon.—Feverishness. If the pains are difficult to describe. The patient is beside himself, &c.
Bell.—Beating in the head. Hot face. Great thirst. Worse in the evening and especially at night, or in the open air or by contact of food. In inflammatory and congestive toothache, &c.
Bry.—Looseness of the teeth. Sensation of elongation. Pains with desire to lie down, &c.
Cham.—Beating and shooting pains. Pains which seem intolerable, especially at night, in bed, driving one to despair with hot swelling of the cheeks. Pains with heat and redness especially of one cheek. Semilateral pains in the whole side of the head. Worse from warmth, &c.
Chin.—At night or after the least contact. After debilitating losses, &c.
Merc.—Tearing shooting pains in hollow teeth or in the roots of the teeth. Pains in the whole side of the head and face, or extending to the ears and head. Salivation. Worse at night in bed, &c.
Nux.—Sore pains or jerking drawing. Swelling and sensitiveness of the gums, with beating as of an ulcer.

MEDICAL INDEX. 137

Toothache, Children (in).—ACON.-CHAM.-MERC.
——— **Cold or Chill (from a).**—Acon.-CHAM.-MERC.-Puls.
——— **Cold (aggravated by).**—Calc.-Merc.-Sulph.
——— **Cold Water (aggravated by).**—Bry.-Calc.-Cham.-Nux.-Sulph.
——— **Cold Air (relieved by).**—Nux.-Rhus.
——— ——— **Water (relieved by).**—Bry.
——— **Congestive.**—Acon.-Bell.-Chin.-Puls.
——— **Damp Air (from).**—Calc.-Merc.-Puls.-RHUS.-Sulph.
——— **Decayed Teeth (in).**—BELL.-Calc.-Cham.-MERC.-Nux.Phos.-Puls.-Rhus.-Sulph.
——— **Eating, after.**—Cham.-Nux.
——— **Heat (aggravated by).**—Bry.-Calc.-Cham.-Merc.-Nux.-Puls.
——— ——— **(relieved by).**—Ars.
——— **Nervous.**—ACON.-BELL.-Cham.-NUX.
——— **Pains extending into the Ears, with.**—Ars.-Merc.-Puls.

The principal uses in the treatment of—
Toothache, continued.
Worse at night, or early after waking, or in the open air. In persons who indulge in wine or coffee, or who lead a sedentary life, &c.

Puls.—Pains which extend to the face, head, eye, and ear, with pale face. Worse in the evening or after midnight. Relief by cold water or by cool, fresh air, &c.

Rhus.—Tearing, jerking, or shooting pains. Creeping in the teeth. Worse at night, &c.

Sulph.—Tearing, jerking, and beating pains in hollow teeth. Congestion of blood to the head. Worse in the evening or at night in bed, or by applying cold water, &c.

See Teeth, *Pains in the. Nervous Toothache, &c.*

K

Toothache, Pains extending into the Face, with.—Merc.-Nux.-Puls.-Rhus.-Sulph.

———— ———— **Gums.**—Bell.-Merc.

———— **Rheumatic.**—Bell.-Bry.-CHAM.-Merc.-Nux.-PULS.-SULPH.

———— **Swelling (with) of the Face.**—Cham.-Merc.-Nux.-Puls.

———— ———— **Glands under the Jaw.**—Cham.-Merc.-Nux.

———— ———— **Gums.**—Merc.-Nux.

———— **Touch (aggravated by).**—Bell.-Puls.

———— **Warmth of the Bed, worse from.**—Cham.-Merc.-Phos.-Puls.

Tumors (In general).—Arn.-ARS.-BELL.-Bry.-Cham.-Chin.-MERC.-PHOS.-PULS.-RHUS.-SULPH.

———— **Burning.**—Acon.-Arn.-ARS.-Bell.-BRY.-Merc.-PHOS.-PULS.-Rhus.-SULPH.

———— **Dropsical.**—ARS.-BRY.-CHIN.-Merc.-PULS.-Rhus.-SULPH.

———— **Hard.**—Arn.-BRY.-Cham.-PHOS.-PULS.-Rhus.-Sulph.

———— **Inflammatory.**—Acon.-Arn.-Ars.-BELL.-BRY.-Cham.-MERC.-Phos.-PULS.-Rhus.-Sulph.

———— **Itching.**—Merc.-Puls.-RHUS.-Sulph.

———— **Pricking.**—BRY.-PULS.-Rhus.-Sulph.

———— **Spongy.**—Ars.-Bell.-LACH.-PHOS.-Sulph.

***Typhus Fever.**—Arn.-BELL.-BRY.-Chin.-Merc.-Nux.-Phos.-RHUS.

The principal uses in the treatment of—
***Typhus Fever.**
Arn.—Coma with delirium and grasping at flocks. Involuntary evacuations, &c.

Ulcerations.—Ars.-Bell.-Calc.-HEP.-MERC.-Phos.-PULS.-Sulph.

———— **Chronic.**—CALC.-HEP.-Merc.-PHOS.-Sulph.

*****Ulcers** (In general).—ARS.-Bell.-Calc.-LACH.-MERC.-Phos.-PULS.-Rhus.-SULPH.

The principal uses in the treatment of—
Typhus Fever, continued.

Bell.—Redness and burning heat of face. Dilated pupils. Intolerance of light. Unsteady or furious look. Starting during sleep or on waking. Grasping at flocks. Violent headache in forehead. Loathing of food. Scanty red urine. Raging delirium, &c.

Bry.—Constant heat all over the body. Aversion to food. Red, brown, or bright yellow urine. Oppressive, stupefying headache. Great weakness and giddiness on raising one's self. Delirium day and night. Grasping at flocks. Stitches in the chest or side, &c.

Chin.—Loss of appetite and earthy taste of food. Diarrhœa day and night, yellow stools or of undigested food. Constant stupor or unrefreshing sleep, &c.

Merc.—Pressing headache in the forehead. Great sensitiveness and painfulness of the pit of the stomach, region of the liver, and about the navel. Green-yellow diarrhœic stools. Copious, debilitating, and clammy sweats, &c.

Nux.—Drowsiness as if intoxicated, with loss of consciousness. Headache with giddiness. Painful pressure and tension in the region of the stomach, &c.

Phos.—With symptoms of congestion of the lungs, oppression of breathing, &c.

Rhus.—Loquacious delirium with desire to escape. Redness of the face and cheeks. Blood coloured diarrhœic stools. Great prostration and weakness. Dark coloured urine, &c

*****Ulcers.**

Ars.—Scrofulous ulcers. With raised and hard edges, surrounded by a red and shining crown. With the bottoms like lard. With burning and shooting pains, when the parts affected become cold, &c.

Ulcers, Bleeding.—ARS.-Merc.-PHOS.-Puls.-Sulph.

———— **Burning.**—ARS.-Bell.-CARB.-MERC.-Puls.-RHUS.-Sulph.

———— **Cancerous.**—ARS.-Bell.-HEP.-Sulph.

———— **Deep.**—Ars.-Bell.-CALC.-PULS.-Sulph.

———— **Fetid.**—Ars.-Calc.-Chin.-HEP.-Merc.-SULPH.

———— **Gangrenous.**—ARS.-Bell.-Chin.-LACH.

———— **Hard.**—ARS.-Bell.-Merc.-PULS.

———— **Inflamed.**—ACON.-ARS.-Bry.-HEP.-MERC.-PULS.

———— **Painful.**—ARN.-Ars.-Bry.-Chin.-HEP.-Merc.-Nux.-Phos.-Puls.-Verat.

———— **Painless.**—Ars.-Bell.-Merc.-Phos.-Puls.

———— **Proud Flesh (with).**—ARS.-Cham.-Sulph.

———— **Swollen.**—Ars.-BELL.-Bry.-MERC.-PULS.-Rhus.-SULPH.

Urethra (canal of the bladder), **Burning in the.**—ARS.-CALC.-Merc.-Nux.-Phos.-SULPH.

The principal uses in the treatment of—
Ulcers, continued.

Bell.—With burning and drawing pains, and secretion of a purulent and bloody matter, &c.

Calc.—Every injury tends to ulceration. Swelling and ulceration of bones, &c.

Lach.—Ulcers surrounded by pimples. Superficial ulcers, foul at the bottom, &c.

Merc.—Readily bleeding, superficial, or secreting a fetid watery and corrosive pus, &c.

Puls.—Readily bleeding with smarting, burning, stinging or with itching all round, and hard, shining redness, &c.

Sulph.—With unhealthy skin and elevated margins surrounded by itching pimples. With red and bluish areola. With sharp lancinating pains, bleeding readily and secreting a fetid or thick yellow pus, &c.

Urethra (canal of the bladder), **Discharge of Mucus from.**—Merc.-Nux.-Puls.

——— **Pains, Cutting, in the.**—Canth.-Lach.-Merc.

——— ——— **Shooting.**—Canth.-Lach.-Merc.-SULPH.

Urination, Desire, Frequent.—Acon.-Bell.-Bry.-MERC.-Nux.-Puls.-RHUS.-Sulph.

——— ——— **Ineffectual.**—Acon.-Arn.-Ars.-CANTH.-NUX.-Puls.-Sulph.

——— ——— **Urgent.**—Acon.-Arn.-Bell.-BRY.-Merc.-Nux.-PULS.-Rhus.-SULPH.

——— **Drops (discharge in).**—Arn.-Bell.-CANTH.-Nux.-Puls.-SULPH.

——— **Frequent.**—Bry.-Calc.-MERC.-NUX.-RHUS.-SULPH.

——— **Involuntary.**—Acon.-Ars.-Bell.-Merc.-PULS.-RHUS.-SULPH.

——— ——— **at Night.**—Ars.-BELL.-CIN.-Merc.-PULS.-RHUS.-SULPH.

——— **Painful.**—Ars.-CANTH.-Merc.-NUX.-Rhus.-Sulph.

——— **Scanty.**—Acon.-Arn.-Ars.-Bell.-Bry.-CANTH.-Chin.-Nux.-Phos.-Puls.-Sulph.-Verat.

——— **Straining, with.**—Arn.-CANTH.-Merc.-NUX.-PULS.

——— **Suppressed.**—Acon.-Arn.-Ars.-CANTH.-NUX.-Puls.-Rhus.-Sulph.

Urinary Sediment, Flocculent.—CANTH.-Cham

——— ——— **Gravelly.**—Calc.-Nux.-Phos.

——— ——— **Reddish.**—Acon.-Arn.-Phos.-PULS.

Urinary Sediment, Whitish.—Calc.-PHOS.-RHUS.-Sulph.
Urine, Bloody.—Arn.-Ars.-Calc.-CANTH.-Ipec.-Merc.-Nux.-Phos.-PULS.-Sulph.
——— **Burning.**—Acon.-ARS.-CANTH.-MERC.
——— **Dark.**—ACON.-Arn.-BELL.-BRY.-Calc.-Ipec.-MERC.-Puls.-Rhus.-Sulph.-Verat.
——— **Purulent.**—CANTH.
——— **Turbid.**—Chin.-CIN.-MERC.-Rhus,
Uvula, Elongation of the.—Merc.
——— **Inflammation of the.**—Bell.-Merc.-NUX.-Puls.
——— **Swelling of the.**—Bell.-Merc.-NUX.

Veins, Distended.—Arn.-BELL.-Calc.-CHIN.-Nux.-Phos.-Puls.-Sulph.
——— **Pulsation in the.**—Ars.-BELL.-Calc.-Nux.-Puls.
*——— **Varicose.**—ARN.-Ars.-PULS.-Sulph.
Voice, Croaking.—ACON.-LACH.
——— **Deep.**—Chin.-DROS.
——— **Feeble.**—Bell.-CANTH.-Chin.-HEP.-Verat.
——— **Hollow.**—DROS.-SPONG.-VERAT.
——— **Loss of.**—BELL.-MERC.-PHOS.-Sulph.-Verat.
——— **Rough.**—Carb.-Lach.-Phos.-Spong.-Sulph.

The principal uses in the treatment of—
***Veins, Varicose.**
Arn.—Frequently useful in alternation with *Puls.*
Ars.—Burning pains.
Puls.—Great pain, swelling, and inflammation. Of a livid hue.
Sulph.—If partial relief only is obtained.

Vomiting (In general).—ARS.-Bell.-BRY.-Cham.-Calc.-Chin.-IPEC.-Merc.-NUX.-PULS.-Sulph.-VERAT.

——— **Bilious.**—Acon.-ARS.-BRY.-CHAM.-Chin.-IPEC.-MERC.-NUX.-PHOS.-PULS.-VERAT.

——— **Blackish.**—ARS.-Chin.-Ipec.-NUX.-Phos.-VERAT.

——— **Blood** (of).—Acon.-ARN.-Ars.-Bry.-Chin.-IPEC.-Nux.-PHOS.-Puls.-Sulph.-Verat.

——— **Colic** (with).—ARS.-IPEC.-Puls.-VERAT.

——— **Diarrhœa** (with).—Ars.-IPEC.-VERAT.

——— **Drinking** (after).—Acon.-Arn.-ARS.-Bry.-Ipec.-Nux.-Puls.-VERAT.

The principal uses in the treatment of—
Vomiting.

Arn.—Vomiting of coagulated blood of a dark colour. Cramp-like pains in the pit of the stomach, &c.

Ars.—Black vomiting. With violent internal burning in the stomach. Great weakness. Chronic vomiting, &c.

Bry.—Of food, bitter water or of bile. Inclination to vomit, especially after eating food which one relishes, &c.

Chin.—Useful after very severe attacks, &c.

Ipec.—Vomiting after eating or drinking ever so little, &c.

Nux.—Early in the morning and after eating. In sedentary habits, or after wines or spirituous liquors. From weakness of the stomach. Periodical attacks, &c.

Puls.—From overloading the stomach, fat, rich food, &c.

Sulph.—Chronic vomiting, &c.

Verat.—Coldness of the extremities. Great prostration. Great sensibility of the stomach and burning pains. Before, during, or immediately after an evacuation of the bowels, &c.

See Vomiting, Bilious, &c.

Vomiting, Food (of).—ARS.-BRY.-Calc.-Ipec.-LACH.-NUX.-Phos.-PULS.-Sulph.-VERAT.
——— **Frothy.**—VERAT.
——— **Greenish.**—Acon.-ARS.-IPEC.-PULS.-VERAT.
——— **Mucus (of).**—Acon.-Ars.-Bell.-Cham.-Calc.-Chin.-IPEC.-Merc.-Nux.-PULS.-Sulph.-Verat.
——— **Sour.**—Ars.-CALC.-Cham.-Chin.-Ipec.-NUX.-PHOS.-Puls.-SULPH.
——— **Violent.**—ARS.-Merc.-NUX.-VERAT.
——— **Watery.**—Ars.-Bell.-Bry.-IPEC.-Nux.-Sulph.-VERAT.
——— **Weakness, with.**—ARS.-Ipec.-Phos.-VERAT.

Warmth (Sufferings aggravated by) In general.—Acon.-Bry.-Cham.-Merc.-PULS.-Sulph.-Verat.
——— ——— **of the Bed.**—CHAM.-DROS.-MERC.-Phos.-Puls.-Rhus.-SULPH.-Verat.
——— (Sufferings relieved by).—ARS.-HEP.-NUX.-RHUS.
——— ——— **of the Bed.**—Ars.-Bry.-Nux.-Rhus.
Warts.—Bell.-CALC.-SULPH.
*****Waterbrash.**—CALC.-Ipec.-NUX.-Phos.-PULS.-SULPH.

The principal uses in the treatment of—
*****Waterbrash.**
Calc.—Sour eructations with a burning sensation, &c.
Nux.—Cramp-like pain and weight in the stomach. After meals. With painful sensitiveness of the pit of the stomach, &c.
Puls.—After fat, fruit, pastry, &c.
Sulph.—Regurgitation of food or drink with acid taste. Acid risings, &c.

Weakness (In general).—Acon.-Arn.-ARS.-CALC.-CARB.-CHIN.-Merc.-NUX.-PHOS.-RHUS.-Puls.-Sulph.-VERAT.

———— **Acute Diseases, after.**—CHIN.-PHOS.-Verat.

———— **Children, in.**—CALC.-Sulph.

———— **Exertion (after any Physical).**—Calc.-Nux.-Verat.

———— **Extreme Prostration.**—ARS.-Chin.-NUX.-PHOS.-Rhus.-VERAT.

———— **Hysterical.**—NUX.-Phos.

———— **Long-continued.**—Ars.-Chin.-VERAT.

———— **Loss of Humors, from.**—Ars.-Calc.-CHIN.-Nux.-Phos.-Puls.-Sulph.

———— **Nervous.**—Bell.-Calc.-Chin.-NUX.-PHOS.-Puls.-Sulph.-Verat.

———— **Old People, in.**—Chin.-Phos.

———— **Paralytic (sensation of).**—CHAM.-CHIN.-PULS.-RHUS.-Verat.

———— **Sudden.**—ARS.-CARB.-Ipec.-LACH.-Merc.-NUX.-PHOS.-VERAT.

———— **Watching, after.**—NUX. Puls.

Wens.—CALC.-Phos.

***Whitlow.**—HEP.-Merc.-Sulph.

†**Worms** (In general).—ACON.-Calc.-CIN.-MERC.-Nux.-SULPH.

The principal uses in the treatment of—
***Whitlow.**
Hep.—Tendency to suppurate. Painful to the touch,&c.
Merc.—To commence the treatment.
Sulph.—To prevent a return or sometimes at the commencement to prevent a further developement, &c.
           See Abscess.
†**Worms.**
Acon.—Fever with colic. Tendency to vomit. Feverish agitation at night, &c.

Worms, Round.—Acon.-Cham.-CIN.-Merc.-SULPH.
———— **Tape.**—Ars.-CALC.-Merc.-Nux.-PULS.-SULPH.
———— **Thread.**—Acon.-CALC.-Chin.-CIN.-Merc.-Nux.-SULPH.
Worm Fever.—ACON.-Chin.-MERC.
Wounds (In general).—ARN.-Phos.-Puls.-Rhus.
———— **Bleeding Profusely.**—Arn.-LACH.-PHOS.
———— **Gangrenous.**—ARS.-CHIN.-LACH.
———— **Inflamed.**—CHAM.-Merc.-Puls.-Rhus.-Sulph.
———— **Joints Injured.**—Arn.-Bry.-Phos.-RHUS.
———— **Opening again after healing.**—PHOS.
———— **Suppurating.**—Cham.-Chin.-HEP.-MERC.-PULS.-Sulph.
Wrists, Pains, Drawing, in the.—CARB.-Sulph.
———— ———— **Sprain, as from a.**—Arn.-CALC.
———— ———— **Tearing.**—Acon.-CARB.
———— **Rigidity of the.**—Merc.-Puls.

The principal uses in the treatment of—
Worms, continued.
Calc.—In feeble debilitated constitutions. Chronic derangement of the digestive organs. To eradicate a tendency to worms, &c.
Cin.—Fever with colic. Hardness of the abdomen. Discharge of pin worms. Pale bloated face with livid circles round the eyes, &c.
Merc.—Straining and small slimy evacuations. Colic. Worm diarrhœa, &c.
Nux.—Worm symptoms with derangemement of the digestive organs, constipation, and irritability, &c.
Sulph.—In most stages of the disease. In chronic cases. Disposition to have worms, &c.

PART II.

SECTION 1.

The Characteristic Properties and Uses

Of the sixteen principal Homœopathic Medicines; being the most important symptoms for which each is curative.

Under this division of the Work will be found a large number of separate symptoms arranged under the heading of each medicine. Each one symptom or every symptom may be cured by that medicine under which it or they may be found placed; provided all that the patient is suffering from, whether it be little or much, is found recorded under the same medicine. It is not expected for a patient to have all the symptoms mentioned under a medicine or section of a medicine, but all the patient's symptoms or the greater part of them must be found recorded under one medicine. See Preface and Introduction; also for Dose, &c.

1.—ACONITUM NAPELLUS.—ACON.*

General Symptoms.—Congestions, especially of the chest, heart, and head, arising from plethora. Acute local and especially congestive inflammations, with

---

* NOTE.—† Is particularly useful in fevers generally; acute inflammations; active congestions; inflammatory fevers; pleurisy; pneumonia; hæmorrhages; croup; &c.

† This list is not intended to include all the diseases for which the medicine is applicable, but to give an idea of its range of action.

ACONITUM NAPELLUS.

violent fever. Neuralgia, rheumatism, and gout, with stinging pains; or with a lame and numb feeling in the affected parts, violent intolerable pains, and great nervousness. Shooting pains, or pains confined to a small spot. Pains as if bruised. Painful sensitiveness to contact, either of the whole body or of the affected part. Intolerable pains, especially at night, which seem insufferable. Great irritation of the nervous system. Attacks of pain, with thirst and redness of the cheeks. Ailments caused by fright and chagrin. Attacks of fainting, especially when rising from a recumbent posture; also attended with paleness of face or congestion of blood to the head. Ailments arising from a cold, especially from a dry sharp wind. Uneasiness, as if from suppressed perspiration, or in consequence of a chill. Feeling of bruising and weight in all the limbs. Great debility.

Skin.—Skin dry and burning. Yellow colour of the skin. Eruption like flea-bites. Erysipelatous inflammations with violent fever. Red hot shining swellings.

Sleep.—Sleeplessness, with anxiety; restlessness and continual tossing about. Startings in sleep. Anxious dreams with nightmare. Nightly delirium. Inability to lie on the side.

Fever.—General dry heat with thirst, short breathing, quick pulse, redness of the face or cheeks, disposition to uncover one's-self and chilliness when uncovered. Burning heat, especially in the head and face, with redness of the cheeks, and shivering over the entire body. Intermittent fever commencing with evening-chilliness,

ACONITUM NAPELLUS.

followed by continuous heat. A good deal of thirst during the heat. Pulse hard, frequent, and quick. Inflammatory fevers with great irritation of the nervous system.

Moral Symptoms.—Anguish with apprehensive and trembling state of mind and bitter wailing. A strong tendency to be angry, to be frightened, and to quarrel. Alternate paroxysms of laughter and tears. Anxiety respecting one's malady and despair of a cure. Apprehensions of death, predicting beforehand the day one is to die. Sensitive and irritable mood. Delirium; especially at night. Weakness of memory.

Head.—Giddiness particularly on raising the head, or with reeling and sensation of intoxication; loss of consciousness; dimness of sight and nausea. Beating and shooting in the head. Fulness and heaviness in the forehead, as from a weight which with the entire brain would press through the forehead. Crampy sensation in the forehead or above the root of the nose with sensation as though one would lose one's senses, worse during a walk in the open air. On going into a warm room, the forehead feels as if it were compressed. Headache as though the brain were moved or raised, worse during motion or when drinking or talking. Congestion of the head with heat and redness of the face.

Eyes.—Eyes red and inflamed, with deep redness of the vessels, and intolerable pains. Profuse lachrymation and with intense pain. Dilated pupils. Intense dread of the light. Heat and burning in the eyes, with pressive and shooting pains, especially on moving the balls. Red, hard swelling of the eyelids.

Ears.—Humming or roaring in the ears. Extreme sensitiveness and intolerance of noises.

Nose.—Bleeding from the nose; especially in plethoric persons.

Face.—Bloated, very red face; redness of the cheeks, also only of one cheek; alternate redness and paleness. When rising from a recumbent posture, the face which is generally very red, turns pale as in death. Sweat on the forehead. Bluish face with blackish lips. Semi-lateral faceache with swelling of the lower jaw. Lips black and dry.

Teeth.—Toothache (especially from cold) in a raw air, with throbbing pains in one side of the face. Rheumatic pains in the face and teeth; also congestive, especially in young plethoric persons who lead a sedentary life.

Mouth.—Sensation of dryness, and dryness of the mouth and tongue. Inflammation of the tongue. Tremulous stammering speech.

Throat.—Burning and stinging in the throat, with difficulty of swallowing. Acute inflammation of the throat, palate, and tonsils, with violent fever, and dark redness of the parts. Stinging choking in the throat, when swallowing or talking.

Appetite and Taste.—Taste bitter; or foul, flat, fishy; or as of spoiled eggs. Loss of appetite; or loathing of food. Burning unquenchable thirst.

Gastric Symptoms.—Hiccough. Vomiting of blood; mucus; or green bile.

Stomach.—Pressure as from a load or stone in the

stomach and pit of the stomach. Tightness, pressure, fulness and weight in the region under the false ribs. Pressure in the region of the liver, with oppression of breathing. Acute inflammation of the liver with violent fever and painful sensitiveness. Jaundice. Violent pains after eating and drinking.

Abdomen.—The abdomen is painfully sensitive to the touch. Distended abdomen, with inflammation, and paroxysms of anguish. The abdomen is distended and swollen as in dropsy. Inflammation of strangulated hernia (rupture) with bilious vomiting. Cutting colicky pains, with tension and pressure.

Stool, &c.—Frequent scanty and loose stools with straining. Watery diarrhœa. Bleeding piles. White stools with red urine.

Urinary Organs.—Retention or suppression of urine, with pressure in the bladder, or stitches in the region of the kidneys. Incontinence of urine. Painful anxious urging to urinate. Scanty, deep red, hot urine, without sediment.

Menstruation, &c.—Increased and profuse menses, especially in plethoric females. Suppressed menses in plethoric young women leading a sedentary life. Fear of death and restlessness during pregnancy. Milk fever with delirium.

Windpipe, Cough, &c.—Short dry cough, excited by titillation in the larynx, with constant inclination to cough, or occurring at night, returning every half hour. Cough during the fever heat. Spasmodic, rough, croaking cough, sometimes with danger of suffocation and constriction of the windpipe. Cough with thick white, bloody or mucous expectoration. Influenza with inflammatory symptoms, pleurisy, rheumatic pains, and sore throat. Inflammation of the windpipe and bronchia. Spitting of blood.

Chest, Respiration, &c.—Shortness of breath, especially when sleeping. The breathing is anxious, laboured, sobbing; or quick and superficial; or loud strong and noisy, with open mouth and asthma. Paroxysms of suffocation, with anxiety. Stinging and single stitches in the chest and sides of the chest, especially when drawing breath and coughing. Palpitation of the heart, with oppressive anxiety, and general increase of heat of the body. Stitches in the region of the heart.

Back.—Pains in the small of the back as if bruised and lamed by blows. Painful stiffness of the nape of the neck.

Extremities.—The hip joint and thigh feel as if lamed and bruised. Unsteadiness of the knees. Tearing pain in the knees. The arms feel as if lamed and bruised by blows.

2.—Arnica Montana.—Arn.*

Characteristic Peculiarities.—The pains are

---

* NOTE.—Is particularly useful in rheumatic and gouty affections; affections in consequence of mechanical injuries; bastard pleurisy, &c. See foot note, page 147.

aggravated by talking, moving about, blowing one's nose, and even by every sound.

General Symptoms.—Chronic rheumatism with tensive tearing pains. Stinging and tingling; or else laming pains as if bruised, especially in the limbs and joints during motion. Pains as if sprained, contused, or hurt. Rheumatic and gouty pains, with inflammatory swelling of the affected part. Ailments arising from a shock, fall, contusion, strains by lifting, sprains, luxations. Wounds, bed-sores, bites or stings of insects, or wounds inflicted by the teeth. Hæmorrhages from wounds or mechanical injuries. Bodily fatigue. Rushes of blood with congestion of the head, burning of the upper, and coldness of the lower parts of the body. Fainting, after injuries. Tremulous uneasiness and languor. General sinking of strength.

Skin.—Small boils. Sore excoriation. Hot, hard, red swelling of the affected parts. Frostbites.

Sleep.—Anxious frightful dreams. Starting and moaning during sleep.

Fever.—A good deal of thirst and drinking during the yawning stage previous to fever, afterwards thirst, but little drinking during the hot stage. Fever early in the morning, first chilliness, then heat. Typhoid fever, with loss of consciousness, without delirium.

Moral Symptoms.—Hypochondriac anxiety.

Head.—Giddiness when raising one's head and moving it; or when walking. Giddiness with nausea. Delirium. Loss of consciousness. Jerking, tearing, and stitching in the head. Spasmodic contractive feeling in the forehead, above the eyes as if the brain were pressed together. Pressing headache especially in the forehead, generally with heat in the brain, especially when walking, reflecting, or after eating. Rush of blood to the head, with burning heat in the head, the body being cool or naturally warm. Headache caused by a shock, or some other mechanical cause. Concussion of the brain.

Eyes.—Ophthalmia from mechanical causes. Redness of the whites. Profuse discharge of burning tears. Excoriating pain in the eyes. The eyes are half closed; or protruded. Dim eyes without lustre.

Ears.—Pains, as if the ears were bruised or contused.

Nose.—Inflammation and swelling of the nose. Bleeding of the nose.

Face.—Face pale and sunken; or yellow and bloated. Redness and burning of one cheek only, the body being cool. Inflammatory faceache. Hot, red, shining, hard swelling of the cheek.

Teeth.—Toothache, with hard rigid swelling of the cheeks; or as if the teeth were sprained and loose.

Mouth.—Spitting of blood. Dry or white coated tongue. Swollen lips. Chapped lips. Biting sensation in the tongue.

Appetite and Taste.—Taste putrid; or slimy; or bitter. Loss of appetite and aversion to food.

Gastric Symptoms.—Bitter or putrid eructations; or violent and empty. Empty retching, with pressure in the pit of the stomach, as from a lump. Vomiting of coagulated blood, coming on again after eating or drinking. Nausea

Stomach.—Pinching, spasmodic griping in the stomach. Pressure in the stomach as from a stone. Stitches in the pit of the stomach, with pressure extending to the back, and constriction of the chest.

Abdomen.—Hard distension of the abdomen with cutting sore pain, lessened by emission of flatulence. Stitches under the false ribs, arresting the breathing. Dull stitches in the abdomen when walking.

Stool.—Undigested. Constipation. Involuntary discharges of stool, while asleep. Frequent scanty discharges of mucus.

Urine.—Retention of urine, with pressing in the bladder. Urging, the urine dropping out involuntarily. Straining of the bladder. Brown urine with brick red sediment. Bloody urine. Incontinence of urine at night.

Menstruation, &c.—Uterine hæmorrhage. The afterpains are extremely painful and last too long.

Windpipe, Cough, &c.—Dry, short, and hacking cough, as from a titillation in the windpipe, every morning after rising. Cough in children after crying. Bloody cough, with difficulty of breathing, rush of blood, palpitation, and periodical heat which favours the expectoration of a bright frothy blood with lumps of coagulated blood and mucus. Nightly cough during sleep.

Chest, Respiration, &c.—Oppressed breathing. Difficult, anxious, sniffling breathing; or short, panting respiration. Fetid breath. Stitches in the chest, with stoppage of breath and cough, aggravated by every motion. Soreness and excoriation of the nipples. Pain in the chest as if from a bruise or sprain. Stitches at the heart with fainting.

Back.—Pain in the back and small of the back, as if lamed and bruised with blows.

Extremities.—Pain in the arm as if lamed and bruised, with tingling in the arm. Pain as if sprained in the arm and wrist joints. Pain in the hands as if bruised, with want of power. The legs and feet feel as if bruised by blows. Painful weakness in the joints. Erysipelatous inflammation and swelling of the feet, with heat and drawing, stinging pains. Hot, red, shining swelling of the toes. Varicose veins; also during pregnancy.

3.—Arsenicum Album.—Ars.*

Characteristic Peculiarities.—The pains are felt at night while sleeping. The pains seem intolerable, drive one to despair and frenzy. The pains appear periodically, and are particularly apt to recur every day or every fourth day. The paroxysms of pain are frequently accompanied with secondary complaints, such as, shuddering; coldness; anxiety; excessive failing of strength and inability to remain up. The pains are aggravated by other peoples' talking, or by lying on the affected part; the pains abate by external warmth, or when standing or moving the body.

---

* Note.—Is particulary useful in diseases of an intermittent type; dropsical complaints; scrofulous affections; skin diseases; asthmatic sufferings; cholera and severe diarrhœas; cancer; epilepsy; paralysis, &c. See foot note, page 147.

ARSENICUM ALBUM. 157

General Symptoms.—Burning pains in internal and external parts. Dropsical swellings. Scrofulous complaints. Excessive prostration; general rapid sinking of strength. Emaciation. Consumption. Atrophy of children. Fainting fits. Spasms. Convulsions. Epilepsy. Trembling of the limbs; also in drunkards. Asiatic cholera. Complaints arising from cold and wet. Gouty and rheumatic pains, drawing and lacerating, particularly in the limbs, with inability to lie on the affected part, and diminution of the pains when moving it.

Skin.—Dry parchment-like; or else blue and cold skin. Burning and burning itching. Itch-like pimples. Rash, or miliary eruptions, especially white. Nettlerash. Pustules. Red pustules, changing to crusty, burning, and spreading ulcers. Black pocks, as if gangrenous. Ulcers with raised callous edges; with red shining halo; with fetid watery discharge or proud flesh. Cancerous or gangrenous ulcers. Ulcers with thin bloody pus; or extremely painful with stinging or burning. Blood blisters cover the whole body. Carbuncle. Chilblains. Suppurating herpes with burning pains. Varicose veins.

Sleep.—Sleeplessness, with uneasiness and tossing about. Starting of the limbs when on the point of falling asleep. Only half asleep, constantly disturbed with moaning and grating of the teeth. Frightful dreams. Nightly restlessness, with great anguish about the heart.

Fever.—General coldness, with loss of pulse and clammy cold sweat. Chilliness and shuddering without thirst; particularly after drinking. Attacks of fever preceded by giddiness and great debility, attended with humming in the ears or followed by aching pain in the forehead. Nightly burning heat all over with burning in all the veins, without thirst or sweat. Quotidian, tertian, and quartan fevers, with indistinct chilliness and heat, with great restlessness and thirst; or else without thirst during the chilliness and heat. Cold clammy sweats. Nightly sweats. Pulse irregular; or rapid, weak, small.

Moral Symptoms.—Excessive anxiety and restlessness, driving one to and fro in the day time and out of bed at night. Dread of being alone. Excessive fear of death. Vexed mood. Religious melancholy. Delirium.

Head.—Giddiness with reeling; or as if one would fall. Beating pain in the forehead, with inclination to vomit. Aching, stupefying pain, with heaviness. Periodical headache. Swelling of the head and face. Scaldhead. Burning pustules on the head. The hairy scalp is painful, when touched.

Eyes.—Inflammation of the eyes, with violent burning pain. Scrofulous inflammation. Inflammation of the inner surface of the eyelids, with inability to open the eyes. Lachrymation. Nightly agglutination. Violent swelling of the lids; also inflammatory. Acrid corrosive tears. Wild staring look. Excessive intolerance of light. Spasmodic closing of the lids.

Ears.—Humming in the ears, with hard hearing, as if the ears were stopped.

Nose.—Profuse fluent cold in the head; discharge of an acrid burning water; also with sneezing.

Face.—Sunken countenance. Sunken face with

ARSENICUM ALBUM.   159

sunken eyes which are surrounded by blue margins, and with pointed nose. Pale; death-coloured face. Yellow, livid, or bluish face. Bloated, puffed, red face. Distorted features. Cadaverous face. Swelling of the face, especially below the eyelids. Drawing, or burning faceache. Scabbing ulcers; cancer of the face. Eruption about the mouth. Bluish, blackish, or dry lips. Swelling of the glands of the lower jaw, with pain as from contusion.

Teeth.—Drawing pressure in the teeth. Spasmodic grinding of the teeth.

Mouth.—Tongue bluish; or coated white; or brown; or blackish; also dry and cracked. Swelling and gangrene of the tongue. Fetor from the mouth. Scurvy of the gums. Great dryness of mouth, often accompanied with violent thirst. Hurried speech.

Throat.—Sore throat when swallowing, as from an internal swelling; burning pain. Gangrenous sore throat. Impeded swallowing, as if the parts were paralysed. Accumulation of greyish or greenish mucus.

Appetite and Taste.—Bitter taste in mouth, particularly after eating and drinking; also putrid or sour taste. Violent, burning, unquenchable, suffocative thirst, obliging to drink frequently, but little at a time; or else complete absence of thirst. Loss of appetite. Derangement of the stomach in consequence of ices, acids, fruits, &c.

Gastric Symptoms.—Frequent hiccough and empty eructations. Nausea; obliging one to lie down. Waterbrash. Vomiting;—after every meal, and after drinking;

chronic vomiting of every thing one eats or drinks; vomiting of yellow green mucus or bile; of brownish or blackish substances; also of blood. Vomiting;—with diarrhœa; with violent colic; internal burning heat and thirst; of water; or attended with great weakness.

Stomach.—Excessive pains in the stomach, and pit of the stomach. Great painfulness to the touch. Pressure at the stomach; with weight as of a stone. Colic after food. Spasmodic pains. Heat or burning pains in the stomach, and pit of the stomach, with pain and oppression. Distension of the stomach.

Abdomen.—Excessive colic, with violent anguish in the abdomen. Distended, hard abdomen; also painful cutting colic; or spasmodic pains. Violent burning pains in the whole abdomen. Coldness and chilliness in the abdomen. Periodical colic. Swelling of the abdomen. Dropsy.

Stool, &c.—Diarrhœa;—after eating; violent with frequent discharges; with straining; with colic; with vomiting; or with great weakness. Involuntary discharge of stool. Evacuations;—burning; bilious; undigested; mucous; putrid; watery; or bloody. Burning, swollen, or painful piles.

Urinary Organs.—Suppression of urine. Difficult painful urination. Bloody or burning urine.

Menstruation, &c.—Profuse menstruation. Leucorrhœa; also corrosive. Menstruation with various pains; also suppressed. Premature menstruation.

Windpipe, Cough, &c.—Feeling of dryness and burning in the larynx. Dry cough; short and hacking with soreness, as from excoriation in the chest. Cough; as if occasioned by the smoke of sulphur, with sense of suffocation; or after drinking; or as caused by a titillation in the windpipe. Cough in the evening when in bed. Expectoration difficult; scanty and frothy; or consisting of tenacious mucus, which is lodged in the chest. Expectoration consisting of a blood-streaked mucus. Periodical coughing.

Chest, Respiration, &c.—Anxious and oppressive shortness of breath. Oppression, laboured breathing, when going up hill or when walking rapidly. Arrest of breathing and suffocative oppression, sometimes with weakness and excessive debility; or at night. Suffocative paroxysms in the evening after going to bed. Constriction of the chest; with anguish; burning; or feeling as if excoriated and raw. Palpitation of the heart, violent, excessive, with great anguish, especially at night. Shootings in the breast and breast-bone.

Extremities.—Drawing and lacerating in the arms, particularly at night. Ulcers on the lower limbs. Ulcerated spreading blisters on the tips of the feet. Swelling of the feet; hot, shining, with burning red spots. Trembling of the limbs. Pains in the knees as if bruised.

4.—BELLADONNA.—Bell.*

Characteristic Peculiarities.— Belladonna is

---

* NOTE.—Is particularly useful in nervous affections; rheumatic and gouty inflammations; scarlatina; erysipelas; convulsions; congestion to the head and chest; inflamma-

particularly suited to complaints of plethoric individuals disposed to inflammation; or for complaints of lymphatic scrofulous individuals liable to glandular swellings.

General Symptoms.—Rheumatic pains, aching and tearing especially in the limbs. Spasms, startings, and convulsions of the limbs;—after a fit of chagrin; renewed by the least contact; with screams and loss of consciousness; with delirium; with extension of the limbs; or violent distortion of the muscles. Paroxysms of stiffness and immobility of all the limbs or of single limbs only. Epileptic spasms; hysteric spasms; St. Vitus' dance, especially in girls. Trembling of the limbs; weariness. Great general debility. Lameness and paralysis; paralysis of one side of the body. Liability to take cold, with great sensitiveness to cold air. Atrophy and wasting of scrofulous subjects. Bad effects from taking cold; from fright, chagrin, or mortification; or from abuse of mercury. Rheumatic and gouty complaints, with inflammation and swelling. Pressure, burning, stinging, or tingling in the limbs. Congestion of blood to various parts. Inflammation of internal organs, with disposition to suppurate. Scrofulous and ricketty complaints. Fainting fits, sometimes resembling lethargy. Plethora.

Skin.—Uniform, smooth, shining, scarlet redness of

---

tory and nervous fevers; mental alienation with madness and fury; nervous and congestive headaches; neuralgia; inflammation of the eyes; inflammation and falling of the womb; sore throat; toothache; inflammation of the brain, &c. See foot note, page 147.

BELLADONNA.

the skin, with dryness, heat, itching, burning, and bloatedness of the parts, especially the face, neck, chest, abdomen, and hands. Erysipelatous inflammation with swelling. Red, hot swelling of affected parts. Vesicular erysipelas (when fever is violent). Scarlet rash over the whole body; eruption resembling measles; purple rash; natural small pox when the brain is affected. Vesicular eruptions, with scurf, whitish border and swelling. Glandular swellings, painful or suppurating. Scrofulous and mercurial ulcers, also cancerous. Jaundice.

Sleep.—Drowsiness. Somnolence; stupor; lethargy; deep sleep with snoring. Sleeplessness; even with drowsiness; sleeplessness from anguish at night; restless; frequent waking with difficulty of getting asleep again; starting as if in a fright. During sleep;—tossing about; screaming; moaning; starts. Anxious, frightful dreams.

Fever.—Alternations of chilliness and heat.—Chilliness and coldness of single parts (of the limbs) with burning heat of other parts (of the head). Heat;—violent burning; internal or external; dry; principally of the head and face. During the hot stage; delirium, redness, and puffiness of the face, and great thirst.* Inflammatory fever; catarrhal; rheumatic; milk; puerperal, and typhoid fevers, with furious delirium and loss of consciousness. Throbbing of the veins.

Moral Symptoms.—Great anguish about the heart, and restlessness. Crying and howling of children, as from rage. Tremulous despondency. Loss of courage. Great

---

* In Eruptive fevers, &c., with head symptoms.

BELLADONNA.

irritability and excitability of the senses. Delirium. Frenzy; with attempts at violence. Raging mania.

Head.—Loss of consciousness, and stupefaction. Absence of thought and consciousness. Feeling of intoxication, and reeling. Giddiness; with falling and without consciousness. Congestion of blood to the head; with heat, and distension, and throbbing. Headache; especially in the forehead. Aching in the forehead; during motion it increases so much as to cause the eyes to be closed. Headache; as though the brain were being pressed out. Stupefying headache, mostly in the forehead with loss of consciousness or with sensation as though the head would split. Periodical nervous headache. Feeling of throbbing in the brain. Stitches and tearing in the head. Fulness and heaviness of the head. Convulsive shaking and bending backwards of the head. Boring of the head into the pillow. Swashing in the head, as if full of water. The headache is aggravated by moving the eyes, by motion, contact, or by a draught of air.

Eyes.—Pains in the orbits. Feeling of burning dryness in both eyes. Inflammation of the eyes; with redness and swelling and eversion of the lids, also of new born infants; of gouty or scrofulous persons, after catching cold. Violent aching pains in the eyes, from without, inwards. Itching and burning of the lids. Heaviness of the lids. Heat in the eyes. Wild, wandering looks. The eyes are dim, faint, without lustre, or else glistening red, sparkling. Half opened, protruded, staring eyes. Dilated pupils. Burning tears. Dimness of sight. Partial blindness; one cannot read

BELLADONNA.

anything printed. Spasms of the eyes. Squinting. Intolerance of light. Agglutination of the eyelids. Nocturnal blindness, commencing at twilight. Halo seen around the candle light. Weakness of the sight from doing fine work.

Ears.—Earache, with boring and screwing in the ears. Tearing and stitches in the glands beneath the ears. Lacerating from above, downwards in the external and internal ear. Tingling in the ears. Humming and murmuring. Roaring in the ears. Hardness of hearing owing to having taken cold. Acute inflammation. Inflammatory swelling of the salivary glands beneath the ears; also shooting pain.

Nose.—Inflammatory swelling and redness of the internal and external nose. Bleeding at the nose. Diminished or increased smell. Ulceration in the nostrils. Cold in the head, with cough. Fluent cold, with smell as of herring brine. Putrid smell from nose. Pain as if bruised, when touching the nose. Nocturnal stitches in the nose.

Face.—Red face, with burning heat. Bluish-red, bloated face. Pale sunken face, with distorted features, expressive of anguish. Scarlet red spots in the face. Swelling of the cheeks, with heat. Faceache, with violent cutting pains. Erysipelas of the face. Eruptions at the corners of the mouth, painful when touched. Paleness of the face, sometimes suddenly alternating with red. Dark red face. Glowing redness of the face, with violent inexpressible headache. Swelling of the cheeks, with burning pains; also of one side of the face. Lips dark red. Swelling of the lips. The mouth is half open or else spasmodically closed in consequence of lock-jaw. Convulsive movements of the face and mouth, which is drawn obliquely to the ear. Stitching and tightness in the joints of the jaw. Inflammation and swelling of the glands under the jaws, and of the neck. Tearing in the jaws.

Teeth.—Lock-jaw. Grinding of the teeth, with foam at the mouth. Dull drawing in the upper and right row of the teeth, the whole night. Digging toothache. The teeth feel elongated. Rheumatic toothache; particularly in females, especially when pregnant. Lacerating toothache; worse in the evening. Toothache; with red hot face, and throbbing in the head. Throbbing in the teeth of pregnant women. Difficult dentition.

Mouth.—Red, inflammatory swelling of the inner mouth and soft palate. The tongue is painful, especially to the touch; it is red, hot, and dry, with red edges and white in the middle. Cracked tongue; white coated with salivation. Feeling in the tip of the tongue as if it had a blister upon it, painfully burning when touched. The small eminences on the tongue are bright red, inflamed, and swollen. Tremor of the tongue. Stammering; and paralytic weakness of the organs of speech. Nasal voice. A good deal of tenacious mucus in the mouth. Profuse salivation. Tongue coated white, yellow, brown, or with strong mucus on it. Inflammatory swelling of the tongue. Great dryness in the mouth and throat, with or without thirst. Hæmorrhage from the mouth and nose.

Throat.—Rawness and soreness of the palate. Great

dryness and burning in the throat. Inflammation of the throat, and back part of the mouth. Sore throat; shooting pain as from an internal swelling. Internal swelling of the throat. Soreness when swallowing or spitting. Sensation as of a lump, which cannot be removed. Violent lancinating pains in the throat when swallowing or breathing. Inflammation of the tonsils; also swelling and suppuration. Redness and swelling of the uvula, or soft palate. Impeded deglutition, or entire inability to swallow even liquids, which return by the nose. Painful contraction and narrowing of the upper part of the throat. When swallowing, one experiences a sensation in the throat, as though the parts were too narrow, contracted, as if nothing would go down. Aversion to every kind of liquid.

Appetite and Taste.—Loss of taste. Insipid taste in the mouth. Disgusting taste; the tongue being clean. Putrid taste. Aversion to food. Complete loss of appetite. Absence of thirst. Violent, burning, suffocative, unquenchable thirst, with inability to swallow the least drop, or with great aversion to drinks.

Gastric Symptoms.—Bitter, frequent eructations; with want of appetite and giddiness. Half-suppressed incomplete eructations. Repeated attacks of violent hiccough. Eructation resembling hiccough; a sort of spasmodic eructation. Nausea; with loathing of food. Vomiting of bile and mucus; or water. Unsuccessful inclination to vomit; empty retching.

Stomach.—Hard and painful pressure, especially after a meal. Painful pressure in the pit of the stomach, felt only when walking. Spasms of the stomach, resembling cramps.

Abdomen.—Continual colic. Pressure in the abdomen as from a stone. Distended, but neither hard nor painful abdomen. Cramplike constrictive pain in the lowermost intestines. Constriction of the abdomen around the navel, as if a ball or lump would form. Colic as if a spot in the abdomen were seized with the nails; a griping. Contractive dragging in the region of the navel, especially about noon and in the afternoon. Pinching colic; flatulent colic lessened by stooping forward and by pressing on the part. Pain in the abdomen as if raw and sore. Painfulness of the abdomen to contact. Pressure in the abdomen, as from a stone (in the evening), with pains in the loins.

Stool.—Diarrhœic stool, followed by frequent urging, little or no stool being passed. Straining with diarrhœic stool in small quantity, followed immediately by increased straining. Straining and colic. Constipation. Papescent stool mixed with mucus. Contractive pain in the rectum. Violent itching and constrictive sensation in the anus. Involuntary discharge of stool.

Urinary Organs.—Suppression of stool and urine. Difficult urination. Retention of urine, which comes off only drop by drop. Frequent desire to urinate, but in small quantities. Yellow, turbid urine. Scanty, turbid, dark, or else flaming red urine. Frequent and copious emission of urine. Involuntary emission of urine; also when standing. Inability to retain the urine.

Menstruation, &c.—Violent pressing as though

BELLADONNA. 169

the internal parts would fall out. Congestion of blood to the uterus. False spasmodic labour-pains. Stitches in the parts. Uterine hæmorrhage; or flooding of bright red blood, or with discharge of lumps of fetid blood, with pressing to the parts. Moral derangement, toothache, spasms, and colic of pregnant females. Hæmorrhage after confinement, or after miscarriage. Convulsions of lying-in women; milk fever; deficiency of milk, or too great a flow; puerperal fever, particularly after a violent emotion, or after suppression of the milk. Erysipelatous inflammation of the breasts, particularly from weaning. Swelling and induration of the breasts. Ophthalmia, spasms, sleeplessness, and crying of new born infants; troubles from teething.

Windpipe, Cough, &c.—Great painfulness of the upper part of the windpipe, with danger of suffocation when touching or turning the throat; when coughing, talking, or taking breath. Spasmodic constriction of the throat. Hoarseness. Noise and rattling in the bronchia. The voice is rough, hoarse; weak and whizzing. Loss of voice. Violent cough about noon, with discharge of a large quantity of tenacious mucus. Nocturnal cough, mostly dry, with tearing in the chest, or with cold in the head and stitches in the breast bone. Dry cough, day and night, with tickling in the throat, or with headache and redness of the face. Dry and short cough. Coughing fit, with subsequent heat: with asthma, from rush of blood to the chest. Violent dry cough, as if a foreign body had got into the throat. Dry spasmodic cough with retching, especially after midnight. Paroxysms of hooping cough.

Hollow cough. The cough is preceded by weeping; or pain in the stomach and inclination to vomit. Expectoration of bloody mucus. The slightest movement at night renews the cough.

Chest, Respiration, &c.—Oppression of the chest. Laboured irregular breathing, at times hurried, at times slow. Difficult respiration. Small, frequent, hurried, anxious, and short inspirations. Pressure in the chest, affecting the heart. Danger of suffocation when swallowing, or when turning or touching the neck. Stitches in the chest, with desire to cough, or particularly when coughing or yawning. Rush of blood to the chest. Violent palpitation of the heart, reverberating in the head. Tremor of the heart, with anguish and an aching pain.

Back.—Stiffness of the nape of the neck. Painful swelling and stiffness of the neck, and nape of the neck. Painful swelling of the glands of the neck and under the arm. Perceptible throbbings of the vessels of the neck.

Extremities.—Lacerating, with pressure in the shoulder, darting suddenly along the arm, particularly painful at night. Lameness and pressure of the arms, with weakness. Swelling; also scarlet redness of arms and hands. Painful jerking; spasms and convulsions of the arms and hands. Laming and drawing pressure and tearing in the arms. Hip-gout, with burning, stinging, most violent at night and by contact. Stiffness of the hip joint. Heaviness and lameness of the legs and feet.

5.—BRYONIA ALBA.—Bry.*

Characteristic Peculiarities.—The symptoms are aggravated at night, after eating and on motion.

General Symptoms.—Rheumatic and gouty tension, drawing, tearing, and stitching, mostly in the limbs especially when moving the parts, with intolerance of contact. Laming and bruised feeling in the extremities. Gouty, red, shining, swelling of single parts, with stinging when moving them. Sweat on the affected part during rest, and trembling of the part when the pains abate. Pains as if bruised, or as from ulceration, or as if the flesh were detached from the bones. Swelling and induration of the glands. Ailments arising from chagrin, and other conditions, when attended with chilliness and coldness of the body. Hysteric spasms.

Skin.—Yellow colour of the skin, jaundice. Erysipelas of the joints. Rash, especially of lying-in women and their infants. White miliary eruption. Ailments from suppression of measles or scarlet eruptions.

Sleep.—Sleeplessness; especially before midnight, owing to heat and anxiety, especially on the chest. Somnambulism. Comatose sleep, broken by delirium.

Fever.—Chilliness and coldness of the body, also in bed. Shaking chill, frequently with heat in the head,

---

* NOTE.—Is particularly useful in rheumatic and gouty affections; rheumatic fevers; inflammatory fevers with gastric, nervous, or bilious symptoms; gastric or dyspeptic ailments; constipation; in inflammatory affections of the chest; pleurisy; inflammation of the lungs; milk fever; &c., &c. See foot note, page 147.

red face and thirst. General dry heat, external and internal, generally with intense desire for cold drinks. Profuse night and morning sweats. Febrile symptoms preceding the eruption of smallpox and miliary fever; secondary affections remaining after measles and scarlatina.

Moral Symptoms.—Apprehensive; uneasiness and dread on account of the future. Irritable; vexed; vehement. Delirious talk, especially at night.

Head.—Giddiness on stooping. Giddiness, especially when rising from a seat, or from a recumbent position. Headache after every meal. Great fulness and heaviness of the head, with digging pressure in the direction of the forehead. Headache, when stooping, as though all the contents of the head would issue from the forehead. Stitches in the head or only through one side of the head. Pain in both temples, pressing from within, outwards. Congestion of blood to the head, heat in the head. Throbbing headache, aggravated by motion. The headache is worse when moving about, especially when moving the eyes. Burning in the forehead.

Eyes.—Pressure in the eyes, as if full of sand. Burning in the eyes. Inflammation of the eyes and lids, especially in the case of new-born infants, and gouty persons. Dry burning itching tetters on the lids. Dread of light.

Ears.—Humming in the ears. Intolerance of noise. Feeling of stoppage in the ears.

Nose.—Swelling of the nose, with violent ulcerative pain when touched. Inflamed and· ulcerated nostrils.

BRYONIA ALBA. 173

Bleeding of the nose; also during suppression of the menses. Dry cold in the head.

Face.—Pale, yellow, or livid colour. Red burning, hot face. Bloatedness of the face; swelling of the face. Lips swollen and cracked. Dry lips.

Teeth.—Darting or flashing pain in the teeth. Toothache on introducing anything warm into the mouth. Looseness, and sensation as if elongated.

Mouth.—Dryness of the mouth, with great thirst. Tongue coated; white or yellow. Dry tongue.

Throat.—Great dryness in the throat. Stinging in the throat, when swallowing or touching it.

Appetite and Taste.—Loss of appetite. Flat, insipid, or putrid taste. Every thing tastes bitter. Violent thirst. Aversion to food. Desire for unusual things. Loss of taste.

Gastric Symptoms.—Frequent empty eructations, mostly bitter. Regurgitation of food; also after every meal. Nausea; also on waking in the morning. Empty retching, with waterbrash. Vomiting; after drinking; of food; or bitter vomiting. Vomiting of blood. Inclination to vomit, especially after eating food which one relishes.

Stomach.—Pressure; (particularly after eating,) as of a stone. Stitching in the stomach when lying on the side, also in the pit of the stomach, when making a false step. Burning in the stomach during motion.

Abdomen.—Pains in the liver, mostly stinging or tensive and burning, especially when touching the part, coughing, or drawing breath. Cutting and stitching in the abdomen; pinching every time after eating or drinking. Distension of the abdomen, especially after eating. Dropsy.

Stool, &c.—Constipation. Chronic constipation. Large sized stool which is passed with difficulty. Hard tough stool, with protrusion of the rectum. Diarrhœa, with previous colic; or from cold; or of undigested matter.

Urinary Organs.—Urine scanty, red, brown, and hot. Almost irresistible desire to urinate.

Menstruation.—Flooding of dark blood, with pain in the small of the back, and headache. Puerperal fever, particularly when the breasts are swollen with milk. Milk fever, with rheumatic pains in the breast. Excessive flow of milk. Inflammation of the breasts, with suppression of the flow of milk.

Windpipe, Cough, &c.—Hoarseness with inclination to sweat. Cough, mostly dry, caused by titillation in the throat; or spasmodic and suffocating, after eating and drinking; or with vomiting of the food. Cough, with stitches in the sides of the chest, or with headache as if the head would fly to pieces. Cough, with yellowish expectoration or with expectoration of pure blood, or blood-streaked mucus.

Chest, Respiration, &c.—Breathing difficult; sobbing; or short, quick and anxious. Paroxysms of asthma, at night, with stitching pains in the abdomen. Stitches in the chest and sides of the chest, especially when coughing or drawing a long breath, obliging one to sit up, or lie on the back, aggravated by motion.

Heat and burning pain in the chest. Palpitation of the heart; frequently violent, and with oppression of the chest.

Back.—Pain in the small of the back, like a painful stiffness, not allowing one to stand erect. Rheumatic stiffness and tension in the nape of the neck and neck.

Extremities.—Tearing in the shoulder joints and upper arms, with tension and stitching, and shining red swelling of the parts. Swelling of the arm round the elbow. Pain at the wrist, as if strained. Swelling of the hands. Tensive, painful stiffness of the knees. Rheumatic, shining red swelling. Swelling of the legs, down to the feet. Gouty swelling of the feet, with redness, heat, and tensive pain. Pain in the feet, as if sprained on walking. Tightness in the calves.

6.—CALCAREA CARBONICA.—Calc.*

General Symptoms.—Crampy feeling in single parts, and contraction especially of the fingers and toes. Gouty complaints, and tearing in the limbs, with liability to relapsing during a slight change of weather. The pains are excited, and aggravated by washing or working in cold water. Numbness of single parts. Swelling and curvature of bones. Epileptic spasms. Difficult walking of children. Atrophy, with glandular swelling of scrofulous

---

* NOTE.—Is particularly useful in scrofulous and rickety diseases; curvature of the spine; difficult teething of infants; eruptive diseases; consumption; ulcers, &c. See foot note, page 147.

subjects. Corpulency of young men. Want of strength especially in the morning ; or arising from loss of animal fluids. Fatigue from speaking, or moderate walking. Emaciation. Liable to take cold; sensitive to cold air. Nervous excitement. The upper arms and thighs feel as if lamed and bruised.

Skin.—Chronic eruptions. Freckles. Nettlerash, generally passing off in the cool air. Rough, dry skin as if covered with rash. Scaly skin. Humid, scurfy eruptions or tetters with burning pain, or they are clustered like grapes. Fistula. Unwholesome readily ulcerated skin; even small wounds suppurate and do not heal. Boils. Warts. Corns. Chaps. Carious ulcers. Gouty nodosities. Varicose veins.

Sleep.—Drowsiness in the day time, and weariness. Difficulty of falling asleep, on account of many thoughts thronging the mind. Nocturnal tightness of breathing, with heat, apprehensive anxiety, restlessness. Frightful dreams the whole night. Anxious dreams. Wandering of the mind and fancy with cries, talking and starting during sleep and anxiety even after waking.

Fever.—Frequent flushes of heat with anguish, and throbbing at the heart. Tertian evening fever, first heat in the face, then chilliness. Intermittent fever particularly after abuse of quinine. Hectic fever, with alternate chills and heat. A good deal of sweat during moderate exercise, and at night in bed.

Moral Symptoms.—Low spirited, and melancholy. Anxiety, anguish. Apprehension. Despairing mood, with fear of disease and misery; with foreboding of sad events. Tendency to start. Vexed mood, obstinacy. Indifference.

Head.—Giddiness; when ascending an eminence. Dizziness before breakfast, with trembling. Headache from taking cold. Semilateral headache with inclination to vomit. Stupifying or throbbing headache, aggravated by mental efforts. Boring in the forehead, as if the head would burst. Heaviness in the head; congestion. Icy coldness in and about the head. Scurf on the hairy scalp. The hair falls out, also in the case of lying-in women. Fleshy and suppurating tumours on the scalp.

Eyes.—Pressure in the eyes. Stitches; and itching in the eyes. Inflammation, caused by a cold, or by foreign bodies penetrating into the eyes, or in the case of new born infants or scrofulous persons. Swelling and redness of the eyelids; they become agglutinated every night. Smarting, burning, and cutting in the eyes and lids; especially when reading by candle light. Slight twitching in the upper eyelids. Dilated pupils. Dimness of sight. Longsightedness. Light dazzles the eyes.

Ears.—Pulsations; and heat in the ears. Discharge of pus. Hard hearing. Ringing, buzzing, or singing in the ears. Cracking in the ears, when chewing.

Nose.—Inflammation, with redness and swelling. Sore, ulcerated nostrils. Bleeding at the nose. Very bad smell from the nose. Dryness of the nose at night. Dullness of smell. Stoppage of the nose. Troublesome dryness of the nose. Dry cold in the head.

Face.—Pale, thin face. Itching, and eruption on the face. Eruptions on the lips, and about the mouth.

Chapped lips. Swelling of the upper lip. Tearing pains in the facial bones. Ulcerated corners of the mouth. Painful swelling of the glands under the jaws.

Teeth.—Toothache; caused by a draught; or by cold; or excited again by cold or warm things, mostly of a gnawing character. Swelling; or bleeding of the gums. Difficult dentition. Painful sensibility of the gums.

Mouth.—Dry tongue, at night or early on waking.

Throat.—Swelling of the tonsils, with contractive sensation in the throat, during swallowing. Swelling and inflammation of the palate; the uvula is dark, red, and covered with little blisters. Great dryness of the mouth and tongue, with a sense of roughness. Hawking of phlegm, early in the morning.

Taste and Appetite.—Sour taste. Great thirst. Bitter or metallic taste, with complete loss of appetite. Canine hunger. Ravenous appetite, the stomach being weak. Aversion to meat, and warm food. Desire for wine and dainties. Hunger soon after eating.

Gastric Symptoms.—Eructations; bitter or sour, or tasting of food. Heartburn after any kind of food. Sour vomiting, particularly in children, Waterbrash. Dyspepsia.

Stomach.—Aching or crampy pains after eating; or with vomiting of food. Pressure at the stomach. Aching in the stomach after fasting.

Abdomen.—Tension in the region under the ribs. Cannot bear tight clothes around the abdomen. Pressure in the abdomen, from the pit of the stomach downwards. *Frequent* severe spasms, especially in the evening and at

CALCAREA CARBONICA.

night, with coldness of the thighs. Enlargement and hardness of the abdomen. Coldness in the abdomen. Swollen, hard, mesenteric glands of children. Cutting or aching colic. Incarceration of flatulence.

Stool, &c.—Constipation; also increasing from day to day. Hard undigested stool. Diarrhœa, particularly of children, having a sour smell; or of scrofulous individuals; during teething; or frothy; or involuntary. Swelling and protrusion of piles. Thread worms.

Urinary Organs.—Excessive urination; also at night. Burning during urination.

Menstruation, &c.—Itching of the parts. The menses are too profuse and too early. Uterine hæmorrhage, tendency to miscarry. Leucorrhœa before the menses. Itching, burning leucorrhœa, or like milk and passing off while urinating. Toothache, congestion to the head, &c., during the menses. Deficiency of milk or too great a flow, in lying-in females. Muscular weakness in infants.

Windpipe, Cough, &c.—Chronic or frequent painless hoarseness. Accumulation of mucus in chest. Dry hacking cough in the evening, or at night. Cough with yellow fetid expectoration, or with expectoration of thick mucus, mostly at night or early in the morning. Bloody cough.

Chest, Respiration, &c.—Stoppage of breathing, when stooping. Stitching in the chest during motion. Palpitation of the heart; also at night, or after eating. Sensitiveness and soreness of the chest, when drawing breath. Pressure on the chest. Burning in the chest.

Back.—Pains in the small of the back, back and nape of the neck, after straining the parts, or pains as if sprained. Stiffness of the nape of the neck. Painful swelling of the glands of the neck.

Extremities.—Pains in the wrists, as if sprained. Laming weakness of the arms. Drawing or tearing pains in the arms, mostly at night. Cramp in the hands at night. Crampy feeling and pain in the arms, hands, and fingers. Sweaty hands. Deadness of the hands, especially when grasping anything. Deadness of the fingers. Swelling of the hands. Drawing and shootings in the hip. Heaviness and weariness of the legs. Crampy feeling in the legs. Stitches in the knees, also swelling. Crampy feeling in the bends of the knees, calves, soles, and toes, especially when extending the limbs. Ulcers on the legs. Red spots on the legs. Burning of the soles of the feet. Sweaty feet. Varicose veins. Corns. Numbness and deadness of the feet at night.

7.—CHAMOMILLA.—Cham.*

General Symptoms.—Rheumatic, drawing tearing pains, with laming, numb feeling in the affected part, worse at night. Pains which appear intolerable, drive

---

* NOTE.—Is particularly useful in diseases where there is too much excitement of the nervous system; convulsions, especially of children; diseases of infants; bilious affections; colics; very painful rheumatic and neuralgic affections; troubles during dentition; uterine hæmorrhages; diarrhœa; &c. See foot note, page 147.

CHAMOMILLA.

one to despair. Ailments* caused by chagrin, by coffee, or by a cold. Spasms of internal and external organs; convulsions, especially in children during dentition, or in lying-in or pregnant women. Catalepsy. Epilepsy. The whole nervous system is very irritable and sensitive. Great intolerance of pain. The limbs are stiff, as if paralysed. Very sensitive to open air, especially to wind. Fainting fits. Sudden prostration as soon as the pain commences.

Skin.—Rash; especially of children. Thick clusters of red pimples on a red spot on the skin, itching especially in the night. Soreness of children. The skin becomes unhealthy, and every injury ulcerates.

Sleep.—Nocturnal sleeplessness with paroxysms of anguish. Talking, crying, screaming, starting, or tossing about during sleep. Coma.

Fever.—Shuddering of single parts, with or without external coldness. Internal heat with shuddering. Burning heat with smarting, sour sweat. Fever with nightly aggravation; inclination to vomit; colic; and diarrhœa. Feverish heat and redness of the cheeks, with tossing about, moaning, and delirium, eyes open. Constant alternation of shuddering and coldness on single parts, with heat of other parts. Fevers with violent delirium.

Moral Symptoms.—Excessive anguish; also with palpitation of the heart. Excessive restlessness, anxious

---

* In asthma, from mental emotions; jaundice, and headache from anger.

tossing about; with lacerating pains in the abdomen. Vexed and whining mood with crying. Crying of new born infants. Inclination to be quarrelsome and angry.

Head.—Giddiness and dimsightedness after lying down, with flushes of heat. Oppressive heaviness in the head. Semilateral drawing and tearing in the head. Stitching headache, from suppression of sweat, or after a cold.

Eyes.—Inflammation of the eyes and margins of the lids, with aching pains, especially after a cold, in new born infants, or gouty persons. Agglutination of the lids at night, with redness and swelling. Hæmorrhage from the eyes. Twitching of the eyes and lids, spasmodic closing of the lids. Distortion of the eyes. Sparks before the eyes.

Ears.—Earache, with shooting and tearing, or drawing and tension. Inflammatory swelling of the salivary glands beneath the ear. Humming in the ears. Discharge from the ears.

Nose.—Bleeding.

Face.—Redness and burning heat of the face, particularly of the cheeks, sometimes of only one cheek, with coldness or paleness of the other. Frequent change of colour. Bloatedness of the face ; also swelling with hardness, blueness, and throbbing in the cheek. Convulsive movements and twitchings of the facial muscles and lips. Erysipelas of the face, after toothache.

Teeth.—Toothache after taking cold, with drawing *jerks in the jaws.* Toothache after eating and drinking,

CHAMOMILLA.

especially after warm drinks. Digging and gnawing in decayed teeth; intolerable toothache. The pains are often only on one side; are worse at night in bed; or with swelling of the cheeks. Difficult dentition in children, with diarrhœa, fever, or convulsions.

Mouth.—Dry mouth and tongue. Froth at the mouth. Fetid odour of the mouth. Red cracked tongue, or it is covered with a thick white, or yellow coat. Convulsive movements of the tongue.

Throat.—Sore throat, with swelling of the glands under the jaws, or ear; or caused by a cold. Pain as from a plug, when swallowing. Deep redness of the throat.

Appetite and Taste.—Bitter or foul taste.

Gastric Symptoms.—Sour eructations. Vomiting of food. Sour or bilious vomiting.

Stomach.—Incarceration of flatulence with pressure upwards. Aching pains in the pit of the stomach, as from a stone, after every meal, with stoppage of breath. Spasms of the stomach; particularly in persons addicted to coffee.

Abdomen.—Burning in the pit of the stomach. Anxious tension and fulness in the pit of the stomach. Flatulent colic with distension of the abdomen, also of children. Very painful colic; tearing colic. Compressive pain in the abdomen. Spasms in the abdomen. Darting in the abdomen, particularly when coughing, sneezing, or touching the part; also painful sensitiveness to contact, as if the parts were ulcerated.

Stool, &c.—Diarrhœa, generally watery, green, or like *stirred*-up eggs. Hot, fetid, diarrhœic stools.

Nocturnal diarrhœa, or diarrhœa consisting of white mucus with colic. Undigested stools. Diarrhœa during dentition; from cold; or from anger.

Menstruation, &c.—Uterine flooding. Frequent discharge of coagulated blood, with tearing pains in the veins of the legs, and violent labour pains. Pressure, like labour pains. Cutting colic, and pressure in the thighs, previous to the menses. Soreness of the breasts. Painful after-pains. Sleeplessness, colic, diarrhœa, crying, soreness, and restlessness of children.

Windpipe, Cough, &c.—Hoarseness with tenacious mucus. Catarrhal hoarseness of the windpipe. Hoarseness and cough, from rattling mucus; the place from which the mucus has been detached, feels sore. Cough especially after a cold; or in children; or after measles. Dry cough excited by tickling in the throat; at night; or with expectoration of a tenacious bitter substance, early in the morning.

Chest, Respiration, &c.—Oppression of the chest, as from flatulence. Asthma as in suffocative catarrh, in the region of the pit of the throat, with constant desire to cough. Sudden stoppage of breath in children. Shooting in the chest whilst drawing breath.

Extremities.—Nocturnal pains in the arms, with paralytic weakness. Cramp in the legs. Twitching of the fingers. Paralytic and drawing pain in the hips, chiefly at night.

8.—CHINA OFFICINALIS.—Chin.*

Characteristic Peculiarities.—Pains, which are aggravated by contact, or at night.

General Symptoms.—Stretching, drawing, or jerking, and tearing, mostly in the extremities, with lameness and weakness of the affected parts. Inertia. Lassitude and languor, mental and physical. General tremulous debility, with disposition to sweat during exercise or sleep. Painful weariness of the extremities, with sensation as if lamed or bruised. Weakness † from loss of animal fluids (blood, &c.), or after severe and exhausting illness. The limbs go to sleep when lying on them. Excessive sensitiveness of the whole nervous system. Emaciation, particularly of children. Dropsy of single parts, and of the whole body. Ailments ‡ arising from abuse of mercury.

Skin.—Skin flaccid and dry. Yellow colour of the skin, jaundice. Gouty and rheumatic, hard swellings. General dropsy, particularly after excessive depletions. Humid gangrene.

Sleep.—Sleeplessness, or falling asleep late, from abundance of ideas. Unrefreshing sleep. Sleeplessness with headache or great hunger. Frightful, heavy,

---

* NOTE.—Is particularly useful in debility and diseases arising from loss of blood and humours; dropsy; ague; hæmorrhages arising from debility; uterine and pulmonary hæmorrhages; gastric and bilious affections; diarrhœa; &c. See foot note, page 147.

† In Fainting.   ‡ In Jaundice.

anxious dreams; also confused, absurd dreams, waking only half conscious.

Fever.—Heat for several hours in the evening, without previous chilliness, with burning thirst, and succeeded by sweat. Fever with thirst during the chill, and vomiting after the attack. Marsh intermittent fever, also with pains in the region of the liver, vomiting of bile and great anguish. During the chilly stage, headache, congestion of the head, paleness of the face; during the hot stage, dryness of the mouth and lips, with burning headache, and violent desire for cold drinks. Acute fevers with profuse sweats. Copious sweats. Exhausting night sweats. Hectic fever, particularly after great loss of animal fluids.

Moral Symptoms.—Excessive nervousness, with lowness of spirits and intolerance of noise. Indifference and apathy. Anguish.

Head.—Giddiness on raising the head. Headache from suppressed cold. Heaviness, with reeling sensation. Headache, particularly at night, with sleeplessness. Pressure, as if the head would burst. Soreness of the brain, or as if bruised, aggravated by thinking or talking. Jerking, tearing in the head, or tearing with pressure. Rush of blood to the head, with heat and fulness. Aggravation of the headache, by contact or movement. Great sensitiveness of the scalp. Profuse sweat in the hair, especially when walking in the open air.

Eyes.—Inflammation; worse at night; also in scrofu*lous* individuals. The pupils are very much dilated and *insensible*. Dimness and weakness of the sight. Sparks,

CHINA OFFICINALIS. 187

motes, and darkness before the eyes. Pains like pressure in the eyes. Yellowness of the whites.

Ears.—Ringing or humming in the ears.

Nose.—Frequent bleeding; also early in the morning. Hæmorrhage from the nose and mouth.

Face.—Faceache; also nervous or rheumatic. Pale, sickly or dark yellow face. Sunken face with hollow eyes, surrounded with blue margins, and pointed nose. Bloated. Heat and redness of the face. Lips dry and chapped; or blackish.

Teeth.—Throbbing toothache. The toothache is relieved by pressure upon the tooth; and appears principally at night and after eating. Distressing dull pain in hollow teeth.

Mouth.—Cracked, black, or yellow coated tongue. Spitting or vomiting of blood.

Appetite and Taste.—Flat, watery, or bitter taste. Food insipid. Aversion to every kind of nourishment, with feeling of fulness. Indifference to food. Yearning for dainties. Desire to drink frequently, but only little at a time. Canine hunger; also at night. Voracity. Loss of appetite. A good deal of thirst. After eating, drowsiness, oppressive fulness of the stomach and abdomen, general malaise and languor.

Gastric Symptoms.—Dyspepsia. Empty eructations; also bitter and tasting of food; particularly after a meal. Heartburn. Inclination to vomit. Vomiting. Sour vomiting:

Stomach.—Oppression of the stomach, as if too full. *Spasmodic pains.*

Abdomen.—Shooting in the region of the liver; also pain when touching the part. Swelling of the liver. Colic with thirst. Hard pressure and fulness; after every meal. Pinching in the abdomen, bending double affords relief. Doughy, dropsical swelling of the abdomen. Considerable distension of the abdomen. Incarceration of flatulence; also accumulation of flatulence. Flatulent colic. Fetid flatulence.

Stool, &c.—Difficult passage of soft stool, as from inactivity of the bowels. Diarrhœa; loose, yellow, watery; mucous; undigested; or white. Various kinds of diarrhœas, particularly after a meal; at night; from eating fruit; or after measles, also when involuntary. Tingling and discharge of pin worms.

Urinary Organs.—Dark coloured urine, with brick dust sediment.

Menstruation, &c.—Profuse menses. Uterine flooding, with discharge of clots of black blood. Threatening miscarriage. Useful for weakly persons, who have lost much blood. Bloody leucorrhœa.

Windpipe, Cough, &c.—Cough, with expectoration of blood-streaked mucus; or with difficult expectoration of clear, tenacious mucus. Nocturnal suffocative cough, with pains in the chest and shoulder blades, causing one to cry out. Violent, spasmodic cough with retching. Violent cough, immediately after eating, excited by laughter. Cough with purulent expectoration. Pressure at the chest when coughing, with sore pain in the throat. Hæmorrhage of the lungs.

Chest, Respiration, &c.—The breathing is tight,

oppressed and painful; or short and hurried. Suffocative fits. Difficult respiration, one has to have the head raised. Stitching in the chest and sides of the chest, also when coughing or drawing breath. Violent rush of blood to the chest and palpitation of the heart.

Back.—Pressure as from a stone between the shoulder blades.

Extremities.—Gouty swelling of the foot, hot, with pain on contact.

9.—IPECACUANHA.—Ipec.*

General Symptoms.—Attacks of illness, with loathing of food and sudden prostration. Hæmorrhages of bright-red blood from various organs. Spasms and convulsions with distortion of the features, redness and bloating of the face and twitching of the facial muscles, especially of children and hysteric females. Cholera. Apoplexy. Ill effects of pork and pastry. Catalepsy.

Skin.—Rash; also if suppressed.

Fever.—Thirst only during the chilliness. Intermittent fever, also after an abuse of bark, especially when the chilliness is but slight, with many gastric ailments. Heat all over, with alternate coldness and paleness of the face, and cold sweat on the forehead.

Head.—Headache, as if the brain and skull were bruised, penetrating through all the bones down to the

---

* NOTE.—Is particularly useful in derangement of the stomach and bowels; ague; asthmatic sufferings; hæmorrhages; &c. See foot note, page 147.

root of the tongue with nausea. Semilateral headache, with nausea and vomiting. Aching pain, especially in the forehead.

Nose.—Cold in the head, with stoppage of the nose.

Face.—Pale, bloated, or livid, yellowish face. Convulsive movements of the facial muscles. Rash in the face. Red skin round the mouth.

Appetite and Taste.—Bitter taste. Sweet taste. Aversion to every kind of food. Desire for dainties.

Gastric Symptoms.—Nausea, as if proceeding from the stomach, with empty eructations and much saliva. Empty retching. Vomiting of food; or thin bile; or jelly-like mucus. Vomiting with diarrhœa. Spitting or vomiting of blood. Waterbrash.

Stomach.—Violent distress in the stomach and pit of the stomach. Sensation of emptiness and relaxation of the stomach.

Abdomen.—Flatulent colic with frequent loose stools. Griping sensation in the abdomen, as if one were grasping with the hands, aggravated by motion. Sore feeling in the abdomen.

Stool, &c.—Stool green as grass. Diarrhœa; stools having the appearance of being fermented. Bloody stools. Pitch-like stool. Diarrhœa with nausea, colic, vomiting.

Urinary Organs.—Bloody urine.

Menstruation, &c.—Uterine flooding, the blood being bright red. Miscarriage. Nausea and vomiting of pregnancy.

Windpipe, Cough, &c.—Rattling noise in the bronchia, when drawing breath. Suffocative cough;

IPECACUANHA.

also with rigidity of the body and blue face. Dry cough produced by titillation in the upper part of the larynx. Dry, racking, spasmodic cough, with suffocative arrest of breathing. Whooping cough, with bleeding at the nose and mouth, and vomiting of food. Cough especially at night, with loathing and vomiting. Bloody cough; or spitting of blood from the least effort.

Chest, Respiration, &c.—Anxious and hurried breathing. Paroxysms of shortness of breath, also with panting. Asthma. Spasmodic tightness of the chest, with contraction of the throat and panting breathing. Mucous rattling in the chest when drawing breath. Sighing breathing. Oppression of the chest and shortness of breath, as from inhaling dust. Hæmorrhage from the lungs. Difficulty of breathing from the least exercise. Fits, and feeling of suffocation.

Extremities.—Convulsive twitchings of the legs and feet.

10.—MERCURIUS SOLUBILIS.—Merc.*

Characteristic Peculiarities.—The symptoms are generally worse at night. The pains are rendered intolerable by the warmth of the bed.

General Symptoms.—Rheumatic, gouty, drawing,

---

* NOTE.—Is particularly useful in scrofula; eruptive diseases; jaundice; inflammatory fevers; dysentery; thrush; sore throat; inflammation of the liver; catarrhal affections with hoarseness; cold in the head; bilious and gastric affections; swollen glands; mumps; small pox; &c. See foot note, page 147.

stitching, and tearing pains, especially at night, or with copious sweats which do not afford any relief. Gouty, shining, red swellings. Influenza. Scrofulous complaints. Swelling and inflammation of bones, with nocturnal pains. Inflammation of internal organs, terminating in exudition and suppuration. Rheumatic-catarrhal inflammations, with disposition to sweat. Languor. Sinking, with an indescribable malaise of body and soul, obliging to lie down. Hæmorrhage from internal organs. The whole body is painful as if bruised, with painfulness of all the bones. All the bones ache. Rush of blood to the chest, head, and abdomen. Apoplexy arising from effusion or congestion. Excessive emaciation. Nervous excitement.

Skin.—Itching. Nightly itching, aggravated by the warmth of the bed. Itching eruptions, with burning after scratching. Pustular eruptions. Herpetic spots and suppurating pustules, which sometimes run into each other; forming at times dry and scaly spots, at times discharging an acrid humour. Itch-like eruptions. Dry, rash-like, readily-bleeding itch. Malignant scarlatina, particularly with violent inflammation of the throat; also small pox in the suppurative stage. Herpes, with burning when touched. Erysipelatous inflammations. Spreading ulcers. Readily-bleeding ulcers. Carious ulcers. Caries and abscesses in the joints. Healthy and malignant suppurations. Glandular swellings, particularly when not inflamed, or with intense, shining redness, and beating and stinging. Suppuration of glands. Jaundice. Skin dingy, yellow, rough, and dry.

Sleep.—Somnolence; very drowsy in the day time. Uneasy superficial sleep with frequent waking. Wakeful until three in the morning. Falls asleep late. Excessive restlessness, and malaise, with sleeplessness.

Fever.—Paroxysms of fever, especially at night. Hectic fever, especially of children. Mucous fever, with prostration. Inflammatory fevers with disposition to perspire. Profuse night sweats. Violent thirst.

Moral Symptoms.—Great restlessness. Anguish. Indifference. Inability to think. Obstinate, impatient.

Head.—Headache as if the head would fly to pieces, with fulness in the brain. Stitches through the whole head. Tearing, burning headache. Tearing headache only on one side, or stinging down to the teeth with stitches in the ear. Lacerating pains in the outer parts of the head, particularly the bones. Catarrhal and rheumatic headache. Rush of blood to the head, with heat. Giddiness. Itching, dry, or humid eruptions. The hair falls off. Tenderness of the scalp. Sweat upon the head.

Eyes.—Pressure in the eyes, as from sand. Stitches in the eyes. Cutting under the lid, as from a sharp body. Itching; and heat in the eyes. Burning, smarting, chiefly in the open air. Inflammation of both eyes; especially of a rheumatic or scrofulous nature with redness of the whites. Lachrymation of both eyes, in the morning. The lids are closed as if by force and opened again with difficulty. Considerable redness and swelling of the lids. Ulcers and scurfs on the margins. Nightly agglutination of the lids. Dimness of sight.

Black points before one's eyes. Complete vanishing of sight for a few minutes. Pustules and ulcers on the cornea. Dread of the light and the glare of the fire.

Ears.—Tearing; or shooting pain in the ears. Soreness and excoriation of the inner ear. Purulent discharge in the ears. Hardness of hearing; or with stoppage; or buzzing in the ears. Swelling of the glands under the ear; also inflammatory. Inflammation of the outer and inner ear.

Nose.—Swelling of the bones. Bleeding from the nose. Cold in the head with much sneezing. Profuse, excoriating, watery cold in the head.

Face.—Complexion pale, livid, or jaundiced. Red face. Feverish heat and redness of the cheeks. Swelling of the cheeks; with toothache. Lacerating pain in the face. Yellow scurf in the face, continued itching and bleeding after scratching. Dry, cracked, or ulcerated lips. Cracks and chaps in the corners of the mouth; also ulcers. Swelling of the glands under the jaws; also inflammatory with stinging and throbbing.

Teeth.—Toothache; aggravated by cold or warm things; by eating; at night; or becoming intolerable in bed at night. Toothache caused by a chill. Tearing toothache, affecting the whole side of the face. Lacerating in decayed teeth, with painful swelling of the cheek. Violent stitches in the teeth. The teeth are loose and fall out. The gums recede from the teeth; they are sore and swollen. Ulcerated gums. Spongy, readily bleeding gums.

Mouth.—*Fetid* smell from the mouth. Inflammatory

MERCURIUS SOLUBILIS.

swelling of the inner mouth. Thrush. Ulcers and sores in the mouth. Accumulation of tenacious saliva. Tongue coated as with fur. Inflammatory hard swelling of the tongue; or with ulcerated edges. Fetid salivation. Complete loss of speech and voice.

Throat.—Sore throat; sensation as if something had lodged in the throat. Difficult swallowing. Rawness and dryness of the throat; also burning, as if a hot vapour were rising from the abdomen. Shooting pains in the throat when swallowing; also in the tonsils. Liquids return by the nose. Elongation and swelling of the uvula; also inflammation. Ulceration of the tonsils, with sharp stinging pains in the fauces when swallowing. Ulcers in the throat. Suppuration of the tonsils. Inflammatory swelling of the tonsils. The soreness of the throat frequently extends to the ears and adjacent glands.

Appetite and Taste.—Bitter; putrid; salt; sweet or slimy taste. Violent burning thirst for cold drinks. Canine hunger. Complete loss of appetite. Aversion to food. Very weak digestion with constant hunger.

Gastric Symptoms.—Constant risings of air. Nausea, or inclination to vomit. Bitter, bilious vomiting.

Stomach.—The region of the stomach is very painful, particularly to the touch. Pressure at the stomach. The food weighs like a stone in the pit of the stomach.

Abdomen.—Sensitiveness in the region of the liver. Acute inflammation of the liver, with stinging pain. Distension of the abdomen. Colic as from a cold. Colic *occasioned* by the cool evening air, with diarrhœa.

Excessive colic. Excessive pain, not passing off till one lies down. The abdomen is painful to contact or pressure. Complete jaundice.

Stool, &c.—Desire for stool every moment, with straining, without being able to accomplish anything. Constipation. Hard, tenacious, or lumpy stool. Discharges of bloody mucus accompanied with colic and straining. Tenacious; sour smelling; green bilious; bloody, or excoriating stools. Slimy diarrhœa. Dysenteric stools; or with violent urging, succeeded by violent straining. Diarrhœa, caused by cold evening air, with cutting colic. Burning pain at the anus during stool. Discharge of thread and round worms.

Urinary Organs.—The urine is very turbid even while being voided, and deposits a sediment. Sudden urging to urinate. Excessive urinating. Dark red, or sour smelling urine; or mixed with flocks and pus. Discharge of blood. Burning, when urinating.

Menstruation, &c.—Profuse menses, with anxiety and colic. Suppression of the menses. Before the menses, dry heat, with congestion to the head. Purulent, corrosive leucorrhœa. Hard swelling of the breasts, with soreness, or suppuration and ulceration. Bad milk which the infant refuses to take.

Windpipe, Cough, &c.—Catarrh with chilliness. Catarrh, with cough, cold in the head, hoarseness, and sore throat. Constant hoarseness and loss of voice. Dry cough; racking; especially at night. Fatiguing, short, dry cough. Cough with expectoration. Dry, spasmodic cough with retching.

MERCURIUS SOLUBILIS.   197

Chest, Respiration, &c.—Shortness of breath when going up stairs, or when walking. Palpitation of the heart.

Back.—Swelling of the glands of the neck, also with painful closing of the jaws, or with inflammation.

Extremities.—Lacerating in the shoulder joints, arms, and wrists; especially at night and when moving the part. Scaly, burning tetters on the arms. Itch-like eruption on the hands. Chaps on the fingers, which look sore and bleeding. Contraction of the fingers. Lacerating in the hip joint, intolerable at night. Tearing and stitching in the lower limbs, at night and during motion, with sensation of coldness. Tetters on the thighs and legs.

11.—Nux Vomica.—Nux.*

Characteristic Peculiarities.—Many of the symptoms are aggravated or excited by coffee, wine, smoking, watching, and mental exertions. Many of the symptoms appear early in the morning, or after dinner. The pains which arise within doors are relieved by going out, and vice-versa.

---

* NOTE.—Is particularly useful in bilious affections; derangement of the stomach and bowels; ague; gastric and bilious fevers; nervous debility; paralytic and spasmodic affections; hysterical and hypochondriacal affections; catarrhal, congestive, nervous, and gastric headaches; apoplexy; rupture; constipation; piles; profuse and painful menstruation; sufferings of the urinary organs with difficulty of urinating; cold in the head; &c. See foot note, page 147.

NUX VOMICA.

General Symptoms.—Ailments arising from abuse of coffee, wine, or spirits. Complaints arising from a cold, anger,* mental exertions; from a sedentary life generally, and from watching. Periodical and intermittent ailments. Rheumatic and gouty tearing and drawing, or tension and stiffness in the limbs. Rheumatic † affections, particularly of the large muscles of the back, loins, and chest. Scrofulous atrophy of infants. Congestion of blood to the head, chest, or abdomen. Pains in all the joints, also as if bruised, particularly during motion. Bruised pain in the limbs. Numbness of the affected parts. Paralysis, particularly of the lower limbs. Trembling of the lower limbs; also stiffness. Trembling of drunkards. Convulsions and spasms; epileptic spasms, bending the head backwards. St. Vitus' dance, particularly of boys, with sensation of numbness. Fainting fits; also after a walk in the open air. Great prostration, with heaviness and trembling of the limbs, especially early, or after a walk in the open air. Sudden failing of strength. Great nervous weakness, with excessive irritation of all the organs of sense. Dread of motion. Excessive sensitiveness to the open air. Great liability to take cold. Emaciation, especially of children. Hysterical and hypochondriacal affections.

Skin.—Boils. Jaundice. Blue spots. Chilblains with burning itching.

Sleep.—Excessive drowsiness in the day time; also after eating. Falls asleep late, owing to ideas crowding

---

* In Jaundice and Headache.   † In Sciatica.

NUX VOMICA. 199

upon the mind. Violent starting on going to sleep. Delirious, frightful visions at night. Weeping and talking during sleep.

Fever.—Chilliness, evening or night, or after drinking or exercise. Chilliness with heat in the head, or with drawing in the limbs, attended with pain in the back. Coldness of the whole body, with blue skin, particularly on the hands, and blue nails. Coldness at night, not even yielding to the warmth of the bed. The fever is attended with yawning, stretching, gastric symptoms, and headache. The chill is attended with pain in the small of the back. During the heat, giddiness, headache, red face, vomiting, red urine, and pain in the chest.

Moral Symptoms.—Anxiety. Hypochondriac mood. Excessive sensitiveness to external impressions. Nervous excitement. Disposed to quarrel and get vexed. Grief and melancholy. Irascible, irritable. Indolence. Anguish and restlessness. Incapability of thinking correctly. Insanity. Mental derangement occasioned by excessive study, or in the case of drunkards (delirium tremens). Loss of consciousness.

Head.—Confusion of the head, as after intoxication. Stupefaction. Intoxication and cloudiness. Giddiness of various kinds; chronic; with obscuration of sight; with loss of consciousness; with sensation as if turning round, or with staggering in walking. Fainting sort of giddiness. Apoplexy, with loss of consciousness, and paralysis of limbs. Headache, after eating; increased by motion, or stooping forward; from taking wine or coffee; aggravated by reflection; from mental exertions; or from leading a sedentary life. Congestive headache. Semi-lateral headache, as if from pressing a nail into the brain. Headache, with nausea and vomiting. Heaviness in the head. Headache, when reflecting, as if the skull would fly to pieces. Headache, as if the brain would be smashed. Tensive, crampy feeling, or drawing, tearing, or jerking in the head. Pressure; distensive sensation; or lacerating pains in the forehead. Congestion of blood to the head; with violent pains in the forehead; giddiness; or fainting. Soreness of the scalp when touched.

Eyes.—Burning and smarting. Pressure in the eyes. Itching. Inflammation of the eyes of scrofulous persons and new born infants; also after a cold. Bleeding from the eyes. Red, swollen, agglutinated lids. Intolerance of light, especially early in the morning. Twitching of the lids.

Ears.—Shooting, or tearing in the ears. Humming or roaring.

Nose.—Stoppage of the nose and dry cold in the head; also of infants at the breast. Dry cold in the evening, fluent in the day time. Stopped nose with acrid discharge.

Face.—Sickly, pale, sallow complexion. Red, bloated face. Swelling and redness of the face. Redness and heat of the cheeks. Yellow appearance round the nose and mouth. Tearing pains in the face; with swelling on one side. Dry lips. Painful peeling off of the lips.

Teeth.—Continuous painful soreness of the teeth, aggravated by fatiguing the head, and by reflection.

Toothache; when walking in the open air; after food; or caused by a cold. Dull tearing in the teeth and jaws, extending through the facial bones to the head, excited by cold drinks, abated by warmth. Lacerating toothache; brought on again by cold water. Drawing, boring, and stinging in decayed teeth. Looseness of the teeth. Putrid, bleeding swelling of the gums.

Mouth.—Putrid smell from the mouth. Inflammatory swelling, particularly of the palate and gums. Fetid ulcers in the mouth and throat. White tongue, coated with mucus; or dry and cracked. Stammering with heavy tongue. Painful blisters on the tongue.

Throat.—Sore throat, with sensation of swelling; or as though a plug was in the throat. Feeling of excoriation. Swelling of the uvula; also inflammatory. Swelling of the tonsils.

Appetite and Taste.—Bitter; sour; or foul taste. Thirst, with aversion to water. Hunger, with aversion to food. Aversion to all food. Hypochondriac malaise after dinner, with drowsiness. Heat in the head when eating. The food has no taste.

Gastric Symptoms.—Frequent hiccough; also violent. Bitter, foul, sour, eructations. Nausea, and inclination to vomit, especially early in the morning, or after a meal. Heartburn. Waterbrash. Vomiting of food, or sour-smelling mucus. Vomiting of blood. Vomiting, and nausea of pregnant women. Regurgitation of food. Violent vomiting.

Stomach.—The region of the stomach is very sensitive to pressure. Pressure in the stomach, as from a stone; especially after eating. Tension in, and across the stomach. Cramp-like pains or spasms in the stomach; with pressure. Griping, lacerating pains; particularly after a meal. Throbbing in the stomach. Burning in the pit of the stomach.

Abdomen.—Beating, tensive pressure, and shooting in the region of the liver; aggravated by motion or contact. Colic; of pregnancy; after a meal; as from a cold; with cramp-like pains; or contractive colic. Weight; also distension after a moderate meal. The clothes feel tight. Hysterical abdominal spasms. Pinching; or cutting in the abdomen, with desire to vomit and eructations. The bowels feel as if bruised. Pain in the abdomen, as if raw; also at every step. Sanguineous congestion and heaviness in the abdomen. Flatulence; also incarcerated. Flatulent colic. Rupture; also of infants.

Stool.—Constipation; also of infants. Chronic and obstinate costiveness; or, as if from inactivity of the bowels; from sedentary habits; or of pregnancy. Ineffectual urging to stool; or large hard stool, frequently streaked with blood. Frequent, small, mucous stools, with straining. Watery diarrhœa. Discharge of blood. Painful piles.

Urinary Organs.—Painful, ineffectual desire to urinate. Nightly urging to urinate, ending in discharge of blood, and burning. Frequent inclination and urging. Burning in neck of the bladder and urethra when passing water. Painful desire; with discharge of drop by drop, **and burning.**

Menstruation, &c.—Congestion of blood to the parts, with pressing weight and heat. Menses profuse; too early, and last too long. Excessive violent labour-pains. During the menses, spasms and headache. Contractive, uterine spasms. Leucorrhœa, also fetid, yellow.

Windpipe, Cough, &c.—Catarrhal hoarseness, with scraping in the throat and tenacious phlegm. Feeling of choking. Cough; which is excited or aggravated by exercise; reading; thinking; after a meal; or with titillation, worse early in the morning. Racking cough, with headache, or with pain in the stomach as if bruised. Dry cough, with rattling of mucus. Spasmodic cough with retching. Dry cough from midnight to day-break.

Chest, Respiration, &c.—Difficulty of breathing. Dry spasmodic asthma. Anxious oppression of the chest. Asthmatic, constrictive sensation, when walking or going up stairs. Oppression, as from a load. Rush of blood to the chest. Palpitation of the heart; also with nausea or vomiting.

Back.—Pain in the back and small of the back, as if bruised. Tearing in the back, also in paroxysms.

Extremities.—Drawing in the arms, with numbness and immobility. Chilblains. Frequent dartings from the feet to the hips. Shootings, jerking and sprained feeling in the hips. Numbness and paralysis of the lower limbs. Unsteadiness of the lower limbs and giving way of the knees, with trembling weakness. Gouty inflammation and swelling of the knees, also with nodosities. Cramp in the calves at night. Itching burning in the toes as if frozen.

12.—PHOSPHORUS.—Phos.*

General Symptoms.—Tearing and shooting in the limbs, after every cold, especially at night in bed. Chronic rheumatism and attacks of gout of years' standing. Hysteric and hypochondriac affections. Sensitiveness to cool weather. The limbs feel bruised. Heaviness of the mind and body. General sudden excessive weakness; also hysterical. Trembling of the limbs especially during work. Languor with great nervous weakness. Weakness from loss of animal fluids. Paralysis. Emaciation. Hæmorrhage from different organs, lungs, gums, varicose veins, &c. Burning pains. Congestions of blood. Pains setting in, when the weather changes.

Skin.—Lymphatic abscesses, full of fistulous ulcers, with callous edges, bad pus and hectic fever. Yellow or brown spots upon the skin. Small boils. Profuse bleeding of small wounds. Chilblains. Corns. Affections of the glands after contusion. Scaly dry herpes.

Sleep.—Frequent yawning. Falls asleep late, sleepless or frequent waking, with uneasiness and anxiety. Unrefreshing sleep, or sensation as if one had not slept enough. Anxious, frightful dreams.

---

* NOTE.—Is particularly useful in catarrhal affections; consumption; rheumatic and gouty ailments; physical and nervous weakness; chronic diarrhœa; bleeding from different organs; &c. See foot note, page 147.

PHOSPHORUS.

Fever.—Chilly feeling in the evening. Flying heat. Heat at night. Hectic fever, with dry heat towards evening. Clammy night sweat. Morning sweat.

Moral Symptoms.—Great lowness of spirits. Anxious and irritable when alone. Irritability. Somnambulism. Sensitiveness of the senses, and tendency to start.

Head.—Giddiness; also chronic; or with vanishing of ideas. Dull, stupefying headache. Morning headache. Heaviness. Rush of blood to the head. Great falling out of the hair. Scabs on the head. A number of scales on the hairy scalp.

Eyes.—Inflammation; with heat and pressure as from sand. Determination of blood to the eyes. Scrofulous ophthalmia. Agglutination of the eyelids in the morning when waking; with secretion of gum during the day. Lachrymation; in the open air. Dread of light. Short-sightedness. Frequent attacks of sudden blindness in the day time, and sensation as of a grey cover before the eyes. Burning in the eyes. Difficulty of opening the lids.

Ears.—Beating, throbbing in the ear. Heat and redness. Dragging pains in the ear. Humming. Hard hearing, chiefly for the human voice.

Nose.—Stoppage and troublesome dryness of the nose. Constant discharge of a green yellow mucus. Dry cold in the head. Loss of smell. Nose bleeding. Blood is blown from the nose. Nose, red and swollen. Great sensitivenes to odours.

Face.—Face pale; sunken; with sunken eyes surrounded by blue margins. Puffing and swelling round the eyes. Tension of the skin of the face, frequently only on one side. Tearing pain in the facial bones, as if every part would be torn out. Lacerating in the jaws, in the evening, when lying. The pains in the face return again after the least cold, when talking, eating, or by contact. Dry lips. Freckles.

Teeth.—Tearing or shooting toothache, especially in the open air; or from taking the least cold, with salivation.

Mouth.—Soreness of the inner mouth. Dry tongue. White mucus on the tongue. Flow of saliva. Spitting of blood.

Throat.—Dry throat, day and night. Smarting, scraping, and burning in the throat. Hawking up of mucus, in the morning.

Appetite and Taste.—Sour taste. Canine hunger.

Gastric Symptoms.—Frequent eructations, generally empty, especially after eating, or sour and tasting of food. Sour regurgitation of food. Heartburn. Waterbrash, after eating anything sour. Nausea. Vomiting with pains in the stomach and great weakness. Vomiting of food; bile; sour matter, or blood.

Stomach.—The region of the stomach is painful when touched; also painfulness when walking. Fulness; pressure after a meal; or cramps in the stomach. Heat and burning in the stomach and pit of the stomach. Griping in paroxysms; also with arrest of breathing. Inflammation of the stomach.

Abdomen.—Distension, especially after dinner.

Colic; pinching, and tearing in the abdomen, especially early in bed. Heat and burning. Relaxed feeling in the abdomen. Incarceration of flatulence. Flatulent colic, deep in abdomen. Large yellow spots and boils on the abdomen.

Stool, &c.—Chronic diarrhœa. Pappy; mucous; or bloody stools. Exhausting diarrhœa of consumptive individuals. Alternate diarrhœa and constipation of old people. Undigested or involuntary stools. Itching and stinging in the anus. Protruded, readily-bleeding piles.

Urinary Organs.—Involuntary emission. Urine with white flocks; or yellow; or brick dust sediment. Burning, between the acts of urinating.

Menstruation, &c.—Menses too early and scanty; or too early, too profuse, and too long. During the menses, violent pain in the back, great languor, and fever. Smarting leucorrhœa. Erysipelas of the breasts, with burning and stinging. Abscesses of the breasts.

Windpipe, Cough, &c.—Hoarseness and roughness; also chronic. Loss of voice. Cough, caused by a tickling in the chest; or with rawness and hoarseness on the chest; or with stinging in the throat; or of a dry racking character, as if the skull would fly to pieces, caused by cold air, drinking or loud reading. Cough, with saltish purulent expectoration, especially morning and evening; or with expectoration of blood, or tenacious mucus, with soreness of the chest. Mucous consumption. Catarrh, with fever and cough.

Chest, Respiration, &c.—Difficulty of breathing of various kinds; morning and evening, or when moving about. Oppression; heaviness; fulness; or tightness of the chest. Stitching in the chest, especially of the left side; also chronic. Sore and burning pains in the chest. Palpitation of the heart; when sitting; or during an emotion. Rush of blood to the chest. Yellow spots on the chest.

Back.—Stiffness of the nape of the neck. Swelling of the glands of the neck, and armpits.

Extremities.—Rheumatic pains in the right shoulder. Burning in the arms and hands. Tremor of the hands and arms. Numb-hands; especially the tips of the fingers. Swelling of the hands; also of the feet. Gouty stiffness of the knee, with lameness of the legs. Pain in the soles of the feet, as if ulcerated. Icy cold feet. Drawing and tearing in the knee, down to the feet.

13.—PULSATILLA.—Puls.*

Characteristic Peculiarities.—The pains come on again, and are worse while sitting; after a long exercise; or, when rising from a seat; or generally during rest. The pains abate when sitting up after having been lying

---

* NOTE.—Is particularly useful in diseases of females, or persons subject to diarrhœa, catarrh, &c; derangement of the stomach from rich food; rheumatic and gouty affections; flying gout; measles; headaches from indigestion; earache; rheumatic and nervous toothaches; gastric and bilious affections; diarrhœas both mucous and bilious; many sufferings caused by the suppression or irregularity of the menses; leucorrhœa; difficult or painful menstruations; nervous affections; &c. See foot note, page 147.

PULSATILLA.

down, or when turning to the side after lying on the back; also by moving about or walking, by external pressure and in the open air.

General Symptoms.—Jerking, tearing or drawing pains in the muscles of the extremities, with aggravation of the pains at night, or in the evening in bed. Rheumatic and gouty affections; also with swelling. Wandering gout; also in rheumatism. Wandering pains, which rapidly shift from one part to another; with swelling and redness of the joints. Pains as if bruised or ulcerated internally, when touching the parts. Semi-lateral ailments. Ailments arising from the use of pork, fat pastry, or other fat. Bad effects arising from fright, or mortification. Attacks of pain with chilliness, asthma, and paleness of the face. Heaviness of the limbs. Excessive debility. Anxious feeling of trembling. Fainting fits, with great paleness of the face. Epileptic convulsions, with violent tossing of the limbs, followed by relaxation, disposition to vomit, and eructations. Emaciation. Hysteria. Inflammation of internal parts, with disposition to suppurate.

Skin.—Biting itching, here and there. Measles and their secondary ailments, or bad consequences from suppression of measles. Eruptions caused by eating fat things. Chicken pox. Frozen, inflamed parts. Chaps. Suppurating wounds. Varicose veins. Readily-bleeding ulcers, with smarting, burning, stinging, or with itching all around, and hard shining redness.

Sleep.—Yawning. Drowsiness in the day time. *Feverish somnolence.* Sleeplessness; with extreme restlessness; or from ideas crowding upon the mind. Liability to start; talking, weeping, and crying out. Frequent waking. Sleep full of dreams. Anxious, frightful dreams.

Fever.—Coldness, with paleness and sweat over the whole body. Chilliness without thirst. Constant internal chilliness. Dry heat of the whole body at night, with anguish, headache, sweat in the face, and chilliness when taking off the cover of the bed. Aggravation of the fever in the evening or afternoon. The fever generally, is characterised by headache, painful oppression of the chest, moist cough, bitterness of the mouth, and diarrhœa. Copious morning sweat, or at night.

Moral Symptoms.—Gloomy and melancholy. Anguish in the region of the heart, sometimes increasing to a desire for suicide. Anxiety. Peevishness. Hypochondriac peevishness. Silent mood. Disgusted at every thing. Timidity. Fear of death.

Head.—Delirium. Loss of consciousness. The head is affected by mental labour. Confusion of the head, with pains as after intoxication or watching. Giddiness; as if intoxicated; or with inclination to vomit; or whilst stooping. Feeling of emptiness in the head. Headache caused by overloading the stomach; or by eating fat; or from a cold. Semilateral headache; also with nausea and vomiting. Tearing in one side of the head, also in the ear and teeth. Heaviness of the head. Headache, as if the brain would burst, or when moving the eyes. Beating; jerking; lacerating pains; or feelings as though *the head was* in a vice. The headache is generally worse

PULSATILLA.

in the evening. Sweat on the hairy scalp. Humming in the head.

Eyes.—Pressure in the eyes; also as from sand. Inflammation of the eyes and eyelids. Swelling and redness of the lids. Styes on the lids. Dryness of the eyes and lids. Lachrymation in the open air; in the cold air, in wind. Frequent obscuration of sight. Dimness of sight, as through mist. Fiery circles before the eyes. Tearing and shooting pains in the eyes.

Ears.—Jerking tearing pain in the ears. Shooting in the ears. Inflammation of the outer and inner ear, with heat, redness, and swelling. Purulent discharge from the ears. Roaring in the ears. Deafness, as if the ears were stopped; especially after suppression of measles.

Nose.—Ulceration of the external wing of the nose. Bleeding of the nose. Catarrh, with loss of smell and taste; or with discharge of a yellow, green, fetid mucus from the nose.

Face.—Complexion pale or yellowish. Erysipelas of the face, with stinging and peeling off of the skin. Puffed, blue red face. Alternate redness and paleness of the face.

Teeth.—Toothache with earache. Drawing, jerking toothache, as if the nerve was put upon the stretch, and then let loose again; with shootings in the gums. Throbbing pains or digging in hollow teeth; with drawing, extending to the eye. Toothache; worse at night; or in bed, and in a warm room; or coming on *every time one eats* ; or takes any thing warm into one's mouth. The pains abate in the cool air. Toothache of pregnancy. Semilateral toothache.

Mouth.—Flow of sweetish saliva. Tongue coated yellow, and covered with tenacious mucus. Gums are painful, as if sore. Dry mouth.

Throat.—Throat, as if raw. Sore throat when swallowing, as if swollen. Stinging sore throat, with pressure and tension, when swallowing. Inflammation, with dark varicose distension of the vessels. Dryness, and tenacious phlegm in the throat.

Appetite and Taste.—Putrid; or flat; or bilious; or bitter; or sweetish taste. Loss of appetite. Absence of thirst, or violent thirst with moist tongue. Aversion to food. Hunger. Derangement of the stomach, by fat or pastry. The taste of all kinds of food is diminished.

Gastric Symptoms.—Eructations; tasting and smelling of food. Waterbrash. Bitter, bilious, eructations. Hiccough; especially after drinking. Inclination to vomit. Vomiting; of food; or of mucus; or of bilious matter; or chronic, after eating. Vomiting of blood.

Stomach.—Spasms after eating; or early in the morning, terminating in vomiting. Pressure in the pit of the stomach, after every meal, with vomiting of food. Perceptible pulsation in the pit of the stomach. Pain on pressure.

Abdomen.—Abdominal spasms; also of pregnant women. Cutting colic, especially in the evening; also *with diarrhœa*. Oppressive flatulent colic; especially of

PULSATILLA. 213

hysteric females. Flatulence. Painful sensitiveness of the abdomen to the touch.

Stool, &c.—Constipation. Frequent urging to stool as if diarrhœa would set in. Frequent soft or diarrhœic stools, consisting of mucus, sometimes mixed with blood, and generally preceded by cutting colic. Watery diarrhœa. Diarrhœa with cutting in the abdomen. Slimy diarrhœa. Diarrhœa after measles, or at night. Nightly watery, or green, bilious diarrhœa preceded by shifting flatulence. Painful, protruding piles with smarting and soreness.

Urinary Organs.—Frequent desire to urinate with drawing in the abdomen; particularly in pregnant females. Straining. Inability to retain the urine. Difficult emission, with discharge of the urine drop by drop. Wetting the bed. Increased, watery, colourless, or scanty, red-brown urine. Jelly-like sediment. Voiding of blood, with burning.

Menstruation, &c.—Uterine spasms, resembling labour-pains. Suppression of the menses; also with nausea and vomiting. Too early menses. Delay of the menses; also in the case of the first menses. During the menses, colic, pressure in the stomach and small of the back, nausea, and chilliness. Uterine hæmorrhage. The blood is thick and black. False, spasmodic, or too feeble labour-pains. Leucorrhœa; thin acrid; or milky. The after-pains are too long, or too violent. Ailments from weaning. Swelling of the breasts. Vanishing of the milk of nursing females, or excessive flow.

Windpipe, Cough, &c.—Hoarseness; and rough

ness of the throat. Catarrhal huskiness, with cough and expectoration of tenacious mucus. Scraping and dryness in the throat. Dry night cough, going off when sitting up in bed. Continuous cough in the evening after lying down. Violent cough, with difficult expectoration, and painful shooting in the chest and sides. Cough with expectoration of yellow mucus; or bitter; or greenish expectoration. Spitting of blood. Cough, with expectoration of pieces of dark, coagulated blood. During the cough, sensation as if the stomach would turn to vomiting. Stitches in the side.

Chest, Respiration, &c.—Anxious, also spasmodic difficulty of breathing; as if the throat was constricted; mostly in the evening, and at night, when lying down. Stoppage of breath, as if caused by the vapour of sulphur. Suffocative paroxysms at night. Pain in the chest, as if ulcerated internally. Spasmodic, contractive tightness in the chest, especially when drawing breath. Tearing, cutting, and stitching in the chest. Frequent violent paroxysms of palpitation of the heart; frequently with anguish and obscuration of sight. Heaviness, pressure, and burning in the region of the heart.

Back.—Pain in the back, and small of the back, as if from stooping long; or as if weary. Stitching in the small of the back. Rheumatic drawing and tension in the loins; and also in the nape of the neck with difficulty of moving about.

Extremities.—Drawing, jerking, and tearing pains in the shoulder joints and arms. Feeling of tension as *if sprained in* the elbow, wrist and finger joints.

Oppressive heaviness in the arms, from the shoulder to the fingers, with numb feeling. Drawing and tension in the thighs and legs, especially in the calves. Inflammatory swelling of the knees, with shooting pains. Red, hot swelling of the legs and feet, with tensive burning pain. Drawing heaviness and weariness of the legs; with trembling. Varicose veins of the legs. Swelling of the feet, and soles of the feet.

14.—Rhus Toxicodendron.—Rhus.*

Characteristic Peculiarities.—The pains come on or are worse during rest; on entering a room, from the open air; or in cold weather.

General Symptoms.—Rheumatic and gouty tension, drawing and tearing in the limbs; worse during rest; with a feeling of numbness and insensibility in the affected part, after moving it. The greatest rigidity and pain is experienced on first moving the joints, after rest; and on waking up in the morning. Laming stiffness in the limbs, especially when first moving a part. Creeping pains here and there. Red shining swellings, with stinging soreness when touched. Bruised pains in single parts; or sensations as if the flesh had been

---

* NOTE.—Is particularly useful in rheumatism and gout; vesicular erysipelas; paralysis; eruptions, especially itching; rheumatic and typhus fevers; sufferings caused by a strain; dislocation, or other mechanical injury, especially with sufferings of the joints and their membranes, &c. See foot note, page 147.

detached from the bones by blows. Pains as if sprained. Bad consequences from spraining or straining parts. Semilateral complaints. The parts on which one is lying, go to sleep. Complete paralysis. Paralysis of the lower limbs; also semilateral; with tingling in the affected parts. Twitchings of the limbs and muscles. Great languor of the whole body. Languor, with constant disposition to be sitting or lying, Great debility. Great sensitiveness to the open air. Affections of the ligaments, tendons, and membranes connected with the joints. Scrofulous and rickety affections.

Skin.—Small burning vesicles, with redness of skin on the whole body, except on the hairy scalp, hands, and feet. Burning, itching eruptions. Scabbing, itching, burning vesicles. Eruptions, alternating with pains in the chest, and dysenteric stools. Nettlerash and other eruptions; especially vesicular; forming scurfs, with burning itching. Vesicular erysipelas. Shingles. Confluent vesicles; most of them containing a milky or watery fluid. Black pustules, with inflammation and itching, rapidly spreading over the whole body. Warts. Glandular swellings. Ulcers, as if gangrenous from small vesicles, attended with violent fever. Chaps.

Sleep.—Violent and spasmodic yawning. Somnolence; with snoring, muttering, and grasping at flocks. Sleeplessness before midnight. Restless sleep. Frightful dreams.

Fever.—Evening fever, with diarrhœa. Chilliness and coldness, generally towards evening, mostly setting *in attended* with pain, or some other secondary ailments.

Evening fever; first chilliness; afterwards heat and thirst; attended with or succeeded by colic and diarrhœa. Double tertian fever; first chilliness with thirst, followed by warmth all over; with chilliness during the least motion, afterwards sweat. During the chilliness, pains in the limbs; and during the fever, twitchings. Night and morning sweats.

Moral Symptoms.—Sadness and anxiety. Mental derangement. Delirium. Languor of the mind; is unable to hold an idea.

Head.—Giddiness as if one would fall, especially when rising from bed. Headache immediately after a meal. Headache obliging one to lie down, coming on again after the least chagrin, and the least exercise in the open air. Pain, as if the brain were torn, worse when moving the eyes. Shooting headache, day and night, extending to the ears, root of the nose, and cheeks, with painfulness of the teeth. Swelling of the head. Painful tingling in the head. Dry herpes on the hairy scalp. Scaldhead with a thick crust, eating away the hair; or with greenish pus and violent nightly itching. Periodical scaldhead, occurring every year. Small soft tumours on the hairy scalp.

Eyes.—Pains in the eyes when moving or turning the eye-balls. Inflammation of the eyes and lids, with redness and nightly agglutination. Lachrymation. Swelling of the lids. Intolerance of light of scrofulous persons.

Ears.—Inflammatory swelling of the salivary glands beneath the ears; also after scarlatina.

Nose.—Bleeding, at night. Dryness and stoppage of the nose. Frequent, almost spasmodic sneezing.

Face.—Pale face. Red face with heat. Erysipelas and swelling of the face, with tight, aching, stinging and burning tingling. Vesicular erysipelas, the vesicles being filled with yellow water. Chronic suppurating eruptions on the face. Herpetic crusty eruptions round the nose and mouth, with itching, and burning. Pimples round the mouth and chin. Milk crust with thick crusts and secretion of a fetid bloody matter. The lips are dry and parched, covered with a reddish, brown crust.

Teeth.—Toothache; as if sore, or tearing, stinging, jerking, and creeping, frequently at night, or worse in the open air, and abating by the application of warmth.

Mouth.—Dry mouth, with thirst. The tongue is not coated, but very dry. Nightly discharge of yellowish or bloody saliva.

Throat.—Sore throat as if swollen, with pressure and stinging. Dryness of the throat, with thirst.

Appetite and Taste.—Bitter taste. Complete loss of appetite.

Stomach.—Pressure at the pit of the stomach, as if swollen. Oppression in the stomach, towards evening. Pain in the stomach as if a stone was lying in it, especially after dinner. Violent throbbing below the pit of the stomach. Ulcerative pain in the pit of the stomach, or sensation as if something would be torn off, especially when stooping and making a wrong step.

Abdomen.—Distension, especially after a meal, with

colic. Contractive abdominal spasms obliging one to walk bent. Nightly colic.

Stool, &c.—Constant straining at stool, with nausea and lacerating. Alternate constipation and diarrhœa. Stools mixed with blood. Watery or slimy gelatinous stool. Nightly diarrhœa, with colic, passing off after stool. Involuntary stool; especially at night during sleep.

Urinary Organs.—Frequent urging to urinate, with increased discharge. Inability to retain the urine, especially during rest, when the urine passes off involuntarily. Retention of urine. Bloody urine with discharge of drop by drop, with straining.

Menstruation, &c.—Menses too soon and profuse. Uterine hæmorrhage with coagulated blood and labour-like pains. Increase or suppression of milk, in the case of nursing females.

Windpipe, Cough, &c.—Cough with expectoration of bright red blood, and qualmish feeling in the chest.

Chest, Respiration, &c.—Tightness of breath. Oppression. Anxious oppression, as if unable to draw breath. Stitches in the chest and sides of the chest, especially when sitting bent, talking, or taking a long breath. Weak and tremulous feeling about the heart.

Back.—Pain in the small of the back as if bruised; it is relieved by lying on a hard couch. Pain as if sprained in the back and shoulders; also in the nape of the neck. Rheumatic stiffness in the neck and nape of the neck, with pain on moving those parts.

Extremities.—Tearing and burning in the shoulders,

with lameness of the arms, particularly during cold weather, rest, and in bed. Erysipelas of the arms; also of the feet; with swelling. Coldness, immobility, and insensibility of the arm. Warts on the fingers. Pains as if bruised, or sprained, in the joints. Paralysis of the legs and feet. Hip-gout, with painfulness of the joint when rising from a seat, or going up stairs. Heaviness of the lower limbs.

15.—SULPHUR.—Sulph.*

General Symptoms.—Drawing, tearing pains in the limbs, and especially the joints, with stiffness. Pains in the limbs with weakness and numbness in the parts, with shootings and rigidity. Pains as if sprained. Gouty and rheumatic complaints; with or without swelling. Ailments from abuse of metals; especially mercury. Scrofulous and rickety complaints. Inflammation and swelling of the bones. Cracking in the joints; chiefly the knees and elbows. Frequent, spasmodic jerking in the whole body. Talking fatigues and excites the pains. Hysteria and hypochondria. Fainting fits

---

* NOTE.—Is particularly useful in chronic diseases in general; constitutional disorders; skin diseases; dropsical affections; gout and rheumatism, also chronic; chronic nervous affections; chronic giddiness and headache; chronic dyspepsia; chronic constipation and diarrhœa; piles; scrofulous and rickety affections; consumption; chronic cough and catarrhal affections; thrush; dysentery; &c. *See foot note, page* 147.

and spasms; also hysteric. Trembling sensation in the arms and lower limbs. Palpitation in the muscles. Pains which are felt, or are worse, at night. Unsteady gait, and tremor of the hands. Inclination to catch cold. Paralysis. Emaciation; also of children. Scrofulous emaciation. Dropsy. Epilepsy, with stiffness. Periodical ailments. Sensitiveness to the open air and winds.

Skin.—Itching of the skin, worse at night in bed. Eruptions on the skin. Chronic eruptions with burning itching. Small pox, particularly during the suppurative stage. Erysipelatous inflammations with throbbing and stinging. Rash, with soreness of the skin. Itch. Nettlerash with fever. Yellow or liver coloured spots. Dry, scaly eruptions. Chilblains which itch in the warmth. Excoriation; also of children. Herpes. Chaps. Warts. Unhealthy skin. Boils. Fistulous ulcers. Ulcers, with raised swollen edges; readily-bleeding; surrounded with pimples; or with tearing stinging pains and discharging a fetid pus. Corns. Inflammation, swelling, suppuration, and induration of glands. Red, hot, gouty, and rheumatic swellings.

Sleep.—Irresistible drowsiness in the day time. Difficulty of falling asleep. Wakeful the whole night. Light, and unrefreshing sleep. Loud talking while asleep. Raving, restless dreams. Starting during sleep and fear on waking. Jerking and starting of the limbs during sleep. Vivid dreams.

Fever.—Chilliness; a great deal of chilliness at night. Dry heat in the morning when in bed. Frequent flushes of heat. Evening heat. Profuse sweat during slight exercise. Copious morning sweat, setting in after waking. Night sweat, when waking.

Moral Symptoms.—Despondency. Melancholy. Great disposition to weep. Irritable and taciturn. Weak memory. Tendency to start, with fearfulness. Great inclination to philosophical and religious speculations. Monomania. Delirium with picking the clothes.

Head.—Giddiness, when walking in the open air; or when sitting; or early in the morning with bleeding of the nose. Dulness of the head with difficulty of thinking. Headache with nausea. Violent headache at night, disturbing rest. Violent pressure in the forehead. Pressure in the temples and tightness in the brain, when reflecting or doing some other mental labour. Headache every day, as though the head would burst. Drawing and tearing through the head. Periodical headache, every week, with lacerating sensation and stupefaction. Shooting headache, especially in the forehead. Beating in the head. Rush of blood to the head. Throbbing headache, mostly with heat, caused by a rush of blood to the head. Humming in the head. Feeling of coldness about the head. Scaldhead, dry, or fetid, and humid, with thick pus, yellow crust, and itching. The roots of the hair are painful when touched. Falling off of the hair; also of lying-in females.

Eyes.—Pressure in the eyes and lids, with stinging and rubbing as if sand was in them. Itching, smarting, and burning in the eyes and lids. Redness and feeling of heat in the eyes. Inflammation of the eyes and lids, *especially in* scrofulous subjects, or after a cold, or of new-born infants. Swelling of the lids. Ulceration of the margins of the lids. Dryness of the eyes, or profuse lachrymation. Nocturnal agglutination. Specks, or ulcers on the cornea. The lids are closed as by a cramp, early in the morning. Mistiness of sight. Short-sightedness. Intolerance of light.

Ears.—Drawing and shooting in the ears. Purulent discharge from the ears. Dull hearing. Humming or whizzing in the ears.

Nose.—Inflammation; also swelling of the nose. Freckles. Bleeding of the nose. Chronic stoppage; also of one nostril. Dryness of the nose. Dry cold of the head. Profuse catarrhal discharge of burning water; or bloody mucus.

Face.—Pale and sickly complexion; or with sunken eyes surrounded with blue margins. Redness and heat of the face. Swelling of the cheeks with pricking pain. Erysipelas of the face; also with swelling. Chronic eruption in the face. Milk crust. Freckles and pimples. Lips dry, rough, and cracked. Swelling of the lips. Swelling of the glands under the jaws.

Teeth.—Toothache; coming on in the open air, or in a draught. Tearing and drawing in the teeth; aggravated by warm substances. Jerks and shootings in the teeth; also in decayed teeth, extending up into the teeth. Toothache in the evening, and at night. Painful feeling of looseness of the teeth; also of elongation, or dulness. Swelling of the gums with throbbing pains.

Mouth.—*Blisters* in the mouth, with soreness.

Thrush. Dry tongue in the morning. Cracked or brown parched tongue. White-coated tongue. Bad smell from the mouth; also particularly after eating.

Throat.—Sore throat; or pressure in the throat as from a lump. Painful feeling of contraction in the throat, when swallowing. Dryness of the throat.

Taste and Appetite.—Sweetish, foul taste; or else bitter, or sour taste, especially early in the morning, on waking. Too much appetite. Canine hunger. Complete loss of appetite. Aversion to meat. Constant thirst. After eating, oppression across the chest, pressure at the stomach, fulness in the abdomen, chilliness and nervousness.

Gastric Symptoms.—Eructations, generally empty, or tasting of food; or after eating. Sour eructations, and much troublesome acidity in the stomach. Sour regurgitations; also of food and drink. Heartburn. Hiccough. Nausea, every morning; or after eating; or with desire to vomit. Waterbrash; early in the morning, or after a meal. Vomiting of food, especially early in the morning, and in the evening. Sour vomiting.

Stomach.—The region of the stomach is very sensitive to contact. Pressure at the stomach, also after eating. Swelling of the pit of the stomach. Contractive pains; also immediately after eating.

Abdomen.—Pressure, tension, and shooting in the region of the liver. Swelling and hardness of the liver. Pressure under the last ribs; also with eructations. Colic immediately after eating, or after drinking. Pain-*ful sensitiveness* in the abdomen, as if all the parts in it

SULPHUR.

were raw and sore. Pain as if something would be torn out. Weight in the abdomen, as from a lump; less when sitting bent. Spasmodically contractive colic. Crampy colic; from piles; from flatulence, relieved by sitting bent; with cutting or pinching; or with diarrhœa. Congestion of blood in the abdomen. Shooting colic, especially in the left side, when walking, or drawing a long breath. Rumbling, as if empty. Incarceration of flatulence. Painfulness of the abdomen, when touching it. Painful swelling of the glands of the groin. Rupture.

Stool, &c.—Constipation; also chronic, or of infants. Hard, lumpy, insufficient stool. Frequent unsuccessful desire for stool. Pressure on the rectum, as if it would protrude, with pressing on the bladder. Diarrhœa, after cold; chronic; of pregnant females; with colic and distension; or of children, consisting of green, bloody mucus, with moaning and crying. Mucous diarrhœa. Passage of undigested food, with stool. Passage of thread, or round worms with stool. Tape worms. Itching, stinging, and burning in the anus and rectum, also during stool. Piles; also humid and bleeding.

Urinary Organs.—Violent desire to urinate; also at night. Frequent urination; also at night. Wetting the bed. Fetid urine. Hæmorrhage from the urethra. Burning during urination. Painful desire, with discharge of drops of bloody urine, requiring great efforts.

Menstruation, &c.—Troublesome itching of the parts. Pressure to the parts. Congestion. Suppressed menses, or too scanty. Menses too soon and profuse. *The menses* are preceded by headache, or bleeding of the nose. Burning and painful leucorrhœa, causing soreness. Disposition to miscarry. Rawness and itching of the female breasts; also induration and inflammation. Chapping of the female breasts.

Windpipe, Cough, &c.—Hoarseness; and roughness in the throat, with a good deal of mucus on the chest. Loss of voice. Creeping in the larynx; talking excites coughing. Catarrh, with fluent cold in the head; chilliness and rawness of the chest, and cough. Violent desire to cough, after a meal; the chest becomes spasmodically constricted, with retching almost to vomiting. Dry cough, with hoarseness, dryness in the throat, and cold in the head with watery discharge. Loose cough, with soreness and pressure in the chest, and expectoration of thick mucus; also with rattling in the windpipe and hoarseness. Coughing up greenish lumps, having a sweetish taste. Headache, when coughing, as if bruised or torn; also vomiting. Expectoration of bloody pus.

Chest, Respiration, &c.—Rattling in the chest, relieved by expectoration. Nightly suffocative fit. Tightness and oppression. Weakness in the chest, when talking. Pressure; also heavy feeling in the chest. Shootings in the chest, extending to the back. Shootings in the breast-bone. Pains in the chest, chiefly in the left side. Pains as if the chest would fly to pieces, when coughing, or drawing a deep breath. Burning in the chest, rising to the face. Palpitation of the heart; also without any apparent cause.

Back.—Rheumatic tearing, drawing, and tension, in the back and nape of the neck, with stiffness. Pain

SULPHUR. 227

in the small of the back, when rising from a seat. Stiffness in the back, as after a cold. Curvature of the spine.

Extremities.—Drawing pain in the shoulder joint, and in the arm. Lacerating in the shoulders, and shoulder joints, especially at night. Drawing and tearing in the arms and hands. Swelling of the arms. Weakness of the arms and hands. Swelling of the hands; also trembling. Fissures and chaps on the hands, especially in the joints. Deadness of the fingers, in the morning. Thick, red chilblains on the fingers. Whitlows, twice in succession. Heaviness of the legs, and tightness in the knees and thighs. Excessive heaviness of the limbs when walking, almost as if paralysed. Weakness in the legs. Pain in the knees, as if stiff. Rigidity in the bends of the knees. Dropsy of the knee joints. Swelling of the knees; also inflammatory, thick, shining, with curvature and stiffness. Varicose veins. Swelling of the feet. Erysipelas of the leg. Chilblains. Cold feet. Large, shining swelling of the toes. Corns with aching and stinging pains. Cramp in the calves of the legs, and soles of the feet. Crawling sensation at the ends of the toes. Cold sweat on the feet.

16.—VERATRUM ALBUM.—Verat.*

General Symptoms.—Paralytic pain in the limbs,

---

* NOTE.—Is particularly useful in cholera; Asiatic cholera; cramps and spasms; madness; great weakness and convulsions; rupture; hooping cough, &c. See foot note, page 147.

as after excessive fatigue. Pains in the limbs, which do not bear the warmth of the bed, and cease entirely when walking about. Relaxation of the muscles. Trembling of the limbs. Spasmodic paroxysms and convulsive movements of the limbs. Cholera; also Asiatic cholera. General prostration, as if paralysed. Excessive weakness. Fainting fits after the least exertion. General emaciation.

Skin.—Flaccid skin. Dry, itch-like eruptions; with nightly itching. Blue skin during cholera.

Sleep.—Coma. Nightly sleeplessness, with great anguish. Anxious dreams.

Fever.—Coldness all over; with cold, clammy, sweat; especially on the forehead, Intermittent fever, with external coldness only. Chilliness, with much thirst, afterwards constant heat and thirst. Cold sweat all over. Pulse collapses, or is almost extinct. Liability to sweating in the day-time, when performing the least exercise. During the heat, constant coma, or delirium, with red face.

Moral Symptoms.—Anxiety. Tendency to start with fear. Excessive anguish and oppression. Rage. Madness. Religious madness. Delirium.

Head.—Headache; or semilateral headache, with nausea, vomiting, and pale face. Paroxysms of pain in various parts of the brain; partly as if bruised, partly pressure. Beating headache. Chilliness on the top of the head, as if ice were lying there. Cold sweat on the forehead.

Eyes.—Blindness at night.

Face.—Face pale, cold, sunken, as of a dead person;

VERATRUM ALBUM.

also with pointed nose, and sunken cheeks. Bluish face. Dark red, hot face. Extreme redness and heat of face. Yellow face. One cheek is red, the other pale. Alternate redness and paleness; redness in a recumbent posture, paleness when rising up. Cold sweat on the face. Lips dry, blackish, and cracked.

Teeth.—Locking of the jaws. Toothache with headache, and red, swollen face. Great weakness with the toothache. Beating toothache. Looseness of the teeth.

Mouth.—Froth at the mouth. Dry, blackish, cracked tongue. Yellow-coated tongue. Speechlessness.

Throat.—Scraping or roughness in the throat.

Appetite and Taste.—Desire for fruits; or acids. Diminished taste. Bilious, bitter taste. Canine hunger Unquenchable thirst; particularly for cold drinks.

Gastric Symptoms.—Vomiting and diarrhœa after taking the least food or drink. When eating, nausea with hunger, and pressure at the stomach. Violent empty eructations; also after eating. Bitter eructations. Constant flow of saliva from the mouth, like waterbrash. Violent nausea, with desire to vomit. Violent vomiting, with constant nausea, prostration, and need of lying down. Vomiting of food. Sour or bitter vomiting. Vomiting of black bile and blood. Constant vomiting, with diarrhœa, and pressure at the pit of the stomach. The vomiting is renewed by the least motion, or by swallowing the least quantity of liquid.

Stomach.—Painfulness of the pit of the stomach. Violent pressure in the pit of the stomach. Burning in the pit of the stomach; also great feeling of anguish.

Abdomen.—The abdomen is very painful to contact. Pains in the abdomen, as if cut with knives. Colic; also after a cold. Colicky abdominal spasms. Flatulent colic, affecting the bowels, and the whole abdomen. Distension of the abdomen; also with hardness. Rupture, especially in children. Burning in the abdomen, as from a live coal.

Stool, &c.—Constipation; also chronic; or in the case of children. Costiveness, owing to the hardness and size of the stool. Violent diarrhœa; also painful, with cutting colic. Unperceived discharge of thin stool, during the emission of flatulence. Extreme weakness during stool. Greenish or brown-blackish stools.

Urinary Organs.—Involuntary emission of urine.

Menstruation, &c.—Diarrhœa, nausea, and chilliness, when the menses make their appearance. Suppressed discharge after delivery, with delirium. Menses too soon and profuse.

Windpipe, Cough, &c.—Cough, caused by a titillation in the bronchia, with easy expectoration; or else a dry cough. Deep, hollow cough, as if proceeding from the abdomen, with colic. Paroxysms of constriction of the larynx; suffocative fits, with protruded eyes. Paroxysms of whooping cough, with vomiting. Cough with copious expectoration.

Chest, Respiration, &c.—Difficulty of breathing, even when sitting. A good deal of oppression of the chest, with pain when drawing breath. Painful spasmodic constriction of the chest. Palpitation of the heart, with anxiety, and hurried audible breathing.

Back.—Pains in the back and small of the back, as if bruised.

Extremities.—Painful paralytic weakness in the upper and lower limbs. Paralytic and bruising pain in the arms. Icy coldness of the hands and feet. Drawing and cramp in the fingers. Difficult walking; first the right, then the left hip joint feels paralytic. Painful heaviness of the legs, as if too weary. Cramp in the calves of the legs, very violent.

SECTION 2.

The Supplementary Medicines

Of special use in a few ailments only;
With the most important symptoms for which each is curative.
See heading of Section 1, page 147. Also Preface,
and Introduction for Doses, &c.

1.—CANTHARIS.—Canth.*

Urinary Organs.—Retention of urine, with spasmodic pains in the bladder. Ineffectual urging to urinate. Difficult urination; the stream being thin and split. Dark red urine. Discharge of bloody mucus from the bladder. Bloody urine; discharged drop by

---

* NOTE.—Is particularly useful in inflammation of the kidneys, bladder, &c.; urinary ailments, &c. See foot note, page 147.

drop. Burning pain when urinating. Cutting pains in the passage before, during, and after urinating. Inflammation of the kidneys, bladder and urethra (passage). Great sensibility of the region of the bladder.

2.—CARBO VEGETABILIS.—Carb.*

General Symptoms.—Rheumatic drawing and tearing, with lameness, especially in the limbs ; with distress caused by flatulence, or with stoppage of breath, when affecting the chest. Burning pains in the limbs and bones. Throbbing in the body, here and there. Tremor and twitching of single limbs in the day-time. The limbs go to sleep. The limbs early in the morning after rising, feel lamed and bruised. Very weak, sometimes to fainting, early in the morning or when beginning to walk. Sudden prostration of strength. Liability to take cold. Ailments from abuse of mercury.

Skin.—Itch, especially dry, like rash. Fine granular eruption. Readily-bleeding fetid ulcers, with burning pains and acrid pus.

Sleep.—Very drowsy in the day time. Sleeplessness owing to restlessness of the body.

Fever.—Chilliness and coldness of the body. Night sweat. Sourish morning sweat. Disposed to sweat.

Moral Symptoms.—Restlessness and anguish. Tendency to start. Irritable and passionate.

---

* NOTE.—Is particularly useful in ailments arising from abuse of mercury ; flatulence ; hoarseness ; spasms of the stomach, &c. See foot note, page 147.

CARBO VEGETABILIS.

Head.—Heaviness of the head. Throbbing in the head, with rush of blood and heat. Headache with nausea.

Eyes.—Itching, smarting, heat, pressure and burning in the eyes. Nightly agglutination. Shortsightedness.

Ears.—Fetid pus from the ears.

Nose.—Itching of the nose. Frequent continual bleeding of the nose, especially at night and early in the morning, with pale face. Stoppage of the nose. Violent catarrh.

Face.—Pale face. Grey yellow complexion.

Teeth.—Contractive pains in the teeth. Chronic looseness of the teeth.

Mouth.—The gums are sore, suppurate and recede from the teeth. Bleeding of the gums. Dryness, or flow of water in the mouth. Offensive breath. Scurvy of the mouth.

Throat.—Smarting, scraping, and burning in the throat and palate. A good deal of mucus in the throat which is easily hawked up.

Gastric Symptoms.—Bitter or salt taste. Chronic aversion to meat. After eating, considerable distension, acidity in the mouth and sour eructations. Raising of air, or bitter eructations. Sour eructations. Nausea, early in the morning. Constant nausea. Waterbrash.

Stomach.—Contractive, or burning aching spasms, with a good deal of flatulence, and painfulness to the touch. Aching in the pit of the stomach.

Abdomen.—Stitching pains below the ribs. Tension, pressure, and stitching in the region of the liver. Distension. A good deal of flatulence. Crampy, flatulent colic. Incarcerated flatulence. Rumbling and fermentation in the abdomen. Excessive fetid flatulence.

Stool.—Constipation. Thin, pale coloured, or light coloured slimy stool. Painful piles. Discharge of blood from the anus at every stool. Stinging, itching, and burning of the anus.

Urinary Organs.—Scanty urine. Frequent anxious urging to urinate.

Menstruation, &c.—Premature and profuse menses. Itching, burning, and soreness of the parts.

Windpipe, Cough, &c.—Continual hoarseness and roughness. Dry catarrh with hoarseness and rawness of the chest. Cough with titillation in the throat, or with raw and sore feeling in the chest. Spasmodic cough; also with choking and vomiting. Cough after the least cold. Cough with expectoration of green mucus, or yellowish pus.

Chest, Respiration, &c.—Short breathing. Tightness and oppression of the chest. Burning; aching; or rawness in the chest.

Back.—Rheumatic drawing, tearing, and stitching in the muscles of the back and neck. Painful stiffness in the back and nape of the neck.

Extremities.—Drawing and tearing in the fore arms, wrists and fingers. Heat in the hands. Lameness of the wrist-joints and fingers when grasping anything. Laming, drawing pains in the lower limbs. Cramps in the legs and soles of the feet. Sweaty feet.

3.—CINA.—Cin.*

General Symptoms.—Sleeplessness. Dilated pupils of the eyes. Great emaciation. Paleness and yellow colour of the face. Picking at the nose. Canine appetite. Hard abdomen. Discharge of thread worms. Involuntary urination at night. Turbid urine. Dry spasmodic cough, with sudden starts and fainting.

4.—COFFEA CRUDA.—Coff.†

General Symptoms.—Painful sensibility. Great sensibility. Great excitability. Sleeplessness. Excessive painfulness of the affected parts. Excessive irritability of the body and mind; also of lying-in women. Great nervousness.

5.—DROSERA ROTUNDIFOLIA.—Dros.‡

Windpipe, Cough, &c.—Hoarseness. Dry, spasmodic cough with retching. Fatiguing cough with hooping, and with bluish face, suffocation, bleeding at the nose and mouth, and anxiety. Vomiting of food,

---

* NOTE.—Is particularly useful in affections produced by worms, &c. See foot note, page 147.
† NOTE.—Is particularly useful in affections of the nervous system; over-excitement; sleeplessness; effects produced by great joy, &c. See foot note, page 147.
‡ NOTE.—Is particularly useful in hooping cough; &c. See foot note, page 147.

after and during the cough. Cough with bloody purulent expectoration, and stinging in the upper part of the chest. Rough scraping feeling of dryness in the throat.

6.—HEPAR SULPHURIS CALCAREUM.—Hep.*

General Symptoms.—Ill effects of mercury. Swelling, inflammation, and ulceration of the glands. Suppuration of inflamed parts. Tremulous and weak after smoking.

Skin.—Erysipelas of external parts. Unhealthy skin. Chaps. Readily-bleeding ulcers, with stinging and gnawing, or burning and throbbing. Suppurations of every description.

Fever.—Dry heat at night. Disposed to sweat in the day time. Night sweat.

Head.—Ulcerative pain in the forehead above the eyes. Boring headache. Blotches on the head which are sore to the touch.

Eyes.—Stinging in the eyes. Inflammation of the eyes and lids; also erysipelatous, scrofulous, and rheumatic, with bruising and sore pain when touching them. Lachrymation and nightly agglutination.

Ears.—Discharge of fetid pus.

Face.—Bright-red hot face. The facial bones are painful when touched. Drawing tearing faceache, proceeding from the cheeks to the ears and temples.

---

* NOTE.—Is particularly useful in mercurial poisonings; promoting suppuration; croup; &c. See foot note, page 147.

Throat.—Sore throat as from a plug. Scraping sore throat. Stinging in the throat as from splinters, when coughing, swallowing, or drawing breath. Swelling of the tonsils.

Gastric Symptoms.—Dyspepsia, also from mercury. Eructations with burning in the throat.

Stomach.—Pressure, also after a slight meal.

Abdomen.—Contractive pains and spasms. Stitches in the left side of the abdomen.

Stool.—Slow stools as if from inaction of the bowels. Green, bloody, and slimy dysenteric stools.

Windpipe, Cough, &c.—Dry evening cough. Paroxysms of dry hoarse cough, with anxiety and retching. Seated pain at one spot of larynx, aggravated by pressure, coughing, or drawing breath.

Chest, Respiration, &c.—Anxious, hoarse, wheezing breathing, with danger of suffocation when lying down. Suffocative fits obliging one to bend the head backwards.

Back.—Drawing in the back.

Extremities.—Chaps on the hands and feet.

7.—LACHESIS.—Lach.*

General Symptoms.—Ailments of drunkards. Ailments arising from abuse of mercury. Rheumatism, with pain in the joints as if swollen, stiffness of the joints, worse at night and in the evening, and disposition

---

* NOTE.—Is particularly useful in affections of the throat; gangrenous sore throat; &c. See foot note, page 147.

to invade the heart. Emaciation. Paralysis. Dread of motion. Debility. Convulsions, spasms, and epileptic attacks.

Skin.—Itching of the whole body. Gangrenous blisters. Erysipelas. Scarlet eruptions. Suppuration of deep-seated organs. Ulcers with uneven, unclean base, or unclean fat ulcers, with fetid watery discharge. Hard tumours.

Sleep.—Though very sleepy, yet cannot fall asleep. Tossing about during sleep.

Moral Symptoms.—Restlessness. Anguish with trembling. Distrust.

Head.—Giddiness with headache; especially before the menses. Headache with nausea. Apoplexy, especially with paralysis of the left side. Heaviness in the head, followed by pain above the right eye. Throbbing headache, also worse above the left eye. Rush of blood to the head, especially after stooping. Headache, as if the head would fly to pieces when stooping. Mental alienation of drunkards..

Face.—Pale. Distorted. Heat in the face of drunkards. Swelling. Erysipelas. Lockjaw.

Mouth.—Dry mouth with sore feeling. Salivation. Burning on the tongue. Difficulty of speech.

Throat.—Gangrenous sore throat. Sore throat with difficulty of breathing and danger of suffocation. Burning; also sensation of swelling in the throat. Dryness of the throat. Pain as of excoriation in the throat. Sensation as of a tumour or lump to be swallowed. Constant desire to swallow. Constant tickling in the

LACHESIS.

throat. Ulcers in the throat. Swelling of the tonsils. Liquids return by the nose.

Gastric Symptoms.—Eructations which afford relief. Loss of appetite. Gnawing hunger. Pressure in the stomach after eating, Regurgitation of food. Nausea. Vomiting of food, or of bile and mucus in pregnant females.

Stomach.—Pressure, as from a load. Burning in the pit of the stomach.

Abdomen.—Burning. Distension, as from flatulence. Tearing in, during the menses.

Stool.—Obstinate constipation. Ineffectual urging to stool. Piles, with colic. Bleeding piles.

Urinary Organs.—Burning when urinating. Turbid urine.

Menstruation, &c.—Frequently indispensable to women at the critical age, even with profuse menses. Scanty delaying menses.

Windpipe, Cough, &c.—Hoarseness, with sensation as if something had to be hawked up. Cough with tickling in the larynx. Dry, or racking cough. Sensitiveness of the larynx to contact.

Chest, Respiration, &c.—Shortness of breath, or difficulty of breathing. Weight on the chest. Pressure on the chest, as if full of wind. Stitches in the chest. Palpitation of the heart. Asthma, chiefly after food.

Back.—Painful stiffness.

Extremities.—Trembling of the hands. Whitlow. Swelling of the legs with deep ulcers. Tearing in the legs and feet. Icy cold feet. Swollen feet.

8.—Spongia Tosta.—Spong.*

Head.—Oppressive headache, sometimes with a compressive sensation. Throbbing in the head.

Eyes.—Redness of the eyes, with burning, and lachrymation.

Gastric Symptoms.—Bitter taste, sometimes only in the throat. Violent thirst. Eructations, with cutting and tearing in the stomach. Stomach as if relaxed, with sensation as if it were open. Stool hard and delaying.

Windpipe, Cough, &c.—Hoarseness, also with cough and cold. Dry cough excited by a burning tickling at the larynx. Husky feeble voice giving out when singing or talking. Pain in the larynx when touching it, or when turning the neck. Roughness and dryness in the throat. Cough day and night, with burning in the chest, which abates after eating and drinking. Feeling of stoppage in the windpipe. Anxious difficult breathing; quick breathing. Fits of mucous rattling in the windpipe; sometimes fits of strangling and mucous rattling in the chest. Hoarse, hollow, barking, and squeaking cough. Whistling inspiration.

Back.—Large, also hard goitre with pressure, tingling, and stitching. Painful tension and stiffness of the muscles of the neck. Pressure in the small of the back.

---

* NOTE.—Is particularly useful in croup; bronchitis; convulsive coughs; &c. See foot note, page 147.

SECTION 3.

The Remedies for External Application,

REFERRED TO IN THIS WORK;
Their uses, and the forms in which they are applied.

1.—Arnica Montana.—Arn.

1. **The Lotion.**—Prepared by mixing one teaspoonful of *the Tincture with six tablespoonsful of Water, or of half the strength, if the skin to which it is to be applied, is broken.
2. * **The Opodeldoc** or **Liniment.**—Prepared especially for use, where the remedy has to be rubbed in.
3. * **The Cerate.**—Prepared as an ointment.
4. * **The Plaister.**

2.—Calendula Officinalis.—Calend.

1. **The Lotion.**—Prepared by mixing one teaspoonful of * the Tincture with two tablespoonsful of Water.
2. * **The Cerate** or ointment.
3. * **The Plaister.**

3.—Rhus Toxicodendron.—Rhus.

1. **The Lotion.**—Prepared by mixing one teaspoonful of * the Tincture with five or six tablespoonsful of Water.
2. * **The Opodeldoc** (for rubbing-in).

---

* The above may be procured, ready prepared, from any Homœopathic Chemist.

EXTERNAL REMEDIES.

Injury, &c.	Remedy.	Mode of Application.
Bedsores, ...	Arn.	Lotion (weak).
Bruises, ...	Arn.	Lotion.
Bunions, ...	Arn.	Lotion.
Burns or Scalds, ...	Arn.	Lotion (weak).
Chapped Hands or Lips, ...	Arn.	Cerate.
Chilblains, ...	Arn.	Opodeldoc.
Contusions, ...	Arn.	Lotion.
Corns, ...	Arn.	Lotion and Plaister.
Cuts, ...	Calend.	Lotion and Plaister.
Eyes, Black, ...	Arn.	Lotion.
Insects Bites or Stings, ...	Arn.	Lotion (weak).
Rheumatism, ...	Arn. Rhus.	Lotion and Opodeldoc.
Sprains or Strains, ...	Arn. Rhus.	Lotion and Opodeldoc.
Wounds, ...	Calend.	Lotion.

THOMAS B. TABB, Printer, Bath.

Trieste Publishing has a massive catalogue of classic book titles. Our aim is to provide readers with the highest quality reproductions of fiction and non-fiction literature that has stood the test of time. The many thousands of books in our collection have been sourced from libraries and private collections around the world.

The titles that Trieste Publishing has chosen to be part of the collection have been scanned to simulate the original. Our readers see the books the same way that their first readers did decades or a hundred or more years ago. Books from that period are often spoiled by imperfections that did not exist in the original. Imperfections could be in the form of blurred text, photographs, or missing pages. It is highly unlikely that this would occur with one of our books. Our extensive quality control ensures that the readers of Trieste Publishing's books will be delighted with their purchase. Our staff has thoroughly reviewed every page of all the books in the collection, repairing, or if necessary, rejecting titles that are not of the highest quality. This process ensures that the reader of one of Trieste Publishing's titles receives a volume that faithfully reproduces the original, and to the maximum degree possible, gives them the experience of owning the original work.

We pride ourselves on not only creating a pathway to an extensive reservoir of books of the finest quality, but also providing value to every one of our readers. Generally, Trieste books are purchased singly - on demand, however they may also be purchased in bulk. Readers interested in bulk purchases are invited to contact us directly to enquire about our tailored bulk rates. Email: customerservice@triestepublishing.com

You May Also Like

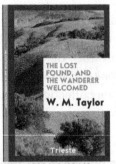

The Lost Found, and the Wanderer Welcomed

W. M. Taylor

ISBN: 9780649639663
Paperback: 188 pages
Dimensions: 6.14 x 0.40 x 9.21 inches
Language: eng

Zoe: An Athenian Tale

J. C. Colquhoun

ISBN: 9780649738618
Paperback: 144 pages
Dimensions: 6.14 x 0.31 x 9.21 inches
Language: eng

www.triestepublishing.com

You May Also Like

War Poems, 1898

California Club & Irving M. Scott

ISBN: 9780649731213
Paperback: 160 pages
Dimensions: 6.14 x 0.34 x 9.21 inches
Language: eng

The Credibility of the Christian Religion; Or, Thoughts on Modern Rationalism

Samuel Smith

ISBN: 9780649557516
Paperback: 204 pages
Dimensions: 5.83 x 0.43 x 8.27 inches
Language: eng

www.triestepublishing.com

You May Also Like

1807-1907 The One Hundredth Anniversary of the incorporation of the Town of Arlington Massachusetts

Various

ISBN: 9780649420544
Paperback: 108 pages
Dimensions: 6.14 x 0.22 x 9.21 inches
Language: eng

Biennial report of the Board of State Harbor Commissioners, for the two fiscal years commencing July 1, 1890, and ending June 30, 1892

Various

ISBN: 9780649194292
Paperback: 44 pages
Dimensions: 6.14 x 0.09 x 9.21 inches
Language: eng

www.triestepublishing.com

You May Also Like

Biennial report of the Board of State Harbor Commissioners for the two fisca years. Commeneing July 1, 1884, and Ending June 30, 1886

Various

ISBN: 9780649199693
Paperback: 48 pages
Dimensions: 6.14 x 0.10 x 9.21 inches
Language: eng

Biennial report of the Board of state commissioners, for the two fiscal years, commencing July 1, 1890, and ending June 30, 1892

Various

ISBN: 9780649196395
Paperback: 44 pages
Dimensions: 6.14 x 0.09 x 9.21 inches
Language: eng

Find more of our titles on our website. We have a selection of thousands of titles that will interest you. Please visit

www.triestepublishing.com

Lightning Source UK Ltd.
Milton Keynes UK
UKOW01f1537231017
311488UK00016B/3462/P